THE
NEW FEW

THE
NEW FEW

OR

A VERY BRITISH OLIGARCHY

FERDINAND MOUNT

**SIMON &
SCHUSTER**

London · New York · Sydney · Toronto · New Delhi

A CBS COMPANY

First published in Great Britain by Simon & Schuster, 2012
A CBS COMPANY

3 5 7 9 10 8 6 4 2

Simon & Schuster UK Ltd
1st Floor
222 Gray's Inn Road
London WC1X 8HB

www.simonandschuster.co.uk

Simon & Schuster Australia, Sydney
Simon & Schuster India, New Delhi

A CIP catalogue record for this book
is available from the British Library

ISBN: 978-1-84737-800-2

Typeset in Bembo by M Rules
Printed in the UK by CPI Group (UK) Ltd, Croydon CR0 4YY

For Tommy, Archie and Maya

CONTENTS

'Never in the field of human commerce was so much paid by so many to so few.'

ANON, 2008

'For quite fifty years past the general drift has almost certainly been towards oligarchy. The ever-increasing concentration of industrial and financial power; the diminishing importance of the individual capitalist or shareholder, and the growth of the new 'managerial' class of scientists, technicians and bureaucrats; the increasing helplessness of small countries against big ones; the decay of representative institutions . . . all these things seem to point in the same direction.'

GEORGE ORWELL, *Second Thoughts on James Burnham*, 1946

INTRODUCTION

The Few make a comeback

'Oligarchs'. It is a strange sensation to hear the word again. We had almost forgotten it existed. Oligarchs seemed to belong to the distant past, the age of the eighteenth-century Whig magnates or the doges of Venice. Oligarchy was a problem for Aristotle and Herodotus, not for us good democrats. Then, almost overnight it seemed, a handful of nimble freebooters leapt into the gap left by the collapse of the Soviet Union and scooped up for a song the country's huge reserves of oil, gas and minerals. These new 'oligarchs', as they were swiftly dubbed, amassed personal wealth on a scale not seen under the czars. They then fanned out around the world, buying football clubs, palaces and works of art with an abandon that seemed reckless to the rest of us but which scarcely dented their colossal fortunes. It has been an amazing, shocking spectacle, but one which seemed to have nothing much to do with those of us who live in what used to be called the West. Or has it? Could it be that, without knowing it, we have been hatching our own oligarchs?

For we also have had our surprise. In fact, it is the great surprise of our times, and an unwelcome one too, which is why we have taken so long to confront it. But the evidence is plain enough if we look: the Few are back on top. The twentieth century was billed as 'the century of the common man'. That century has now come and gone. But instead of democracy widening and deepening as we had hoped, power and wealth have, slowly but unmistakably, begun to migrate into the hands of a relatively small elite. That migration is now continuing into the present century and shows little sign of weakening, let alone going into reverse.

When Gordon Brown declared just before the last election that 'the Labour Party must stand up for the many, not the few', he was parroting a political cliché of our times.[1] We took it for granted that, as the years went by, the management of affairs and the enjoyment of rewards would be more widely spread. We expected to become more equal both in power and pleasure. More and more individuals and groups who had previously exercised little control over their own lives would now have a bigger say. And the worst off too would share in the rising prosperity. Of course the more agile politicians would surf this incoming tide and grab as much of the credit as they could, but the tide would be coming in whatever they did or didn't do.

But has it turned out that way? Doesn't this harping on the theme of 'the many, not the few' betray rather an embarrassed recognition that, in practice, the few have been doing very well for themselves? Far from being gradually dispersed, power seems to have been tightly gathered in the hands of a small number of dominant characters.

Now and then we do recognize, with some uneasiness, social trends that we had not expected and do not welcome. We cannot help being aware, for example, that inequality of income has been increasing in recent decades, under Labour governments as well as under Tory ones. Books such as *The Spirit Level* (2009) by Richard

Wilkinson and Kate Pickett and *Injustice* (2010) by Daniel Dorling have argued passionately that this excessive inequality lies at the root of many social evils. Both the Conservative and Liberal Democrat leaders in the Coalition accept a lot of their diagnosis. Under Tony Blair, the Labour Party was unwilling to talk much about inequality for fear of being tagged as an old-fashioned socialist party stuck in the past. But under Ed Miliband, Labour seems to be returning to its ancestral crusade for a more equal society. So there is a tacit consensus now emerging that something has gone wrong.

What confronts and confuses us is a quite unexpected change of direction. For thirty years after the Second World War – in fact probably ever since the First World War – the gap between rich and poor had been narrowing; often not by much and seldom as a result of deliberate policy, but narrowing none the less. When the sociologist W. G. Runciman published his classic *Relative Deprivation and Social Justice* in 1966, relative deprivation was actually declining. It was expected that, as economic growth continued, the poor too would enjoy their share, and more than their share of that growth. Of course people on low incomes still had very good reasons to resent being worse off than the people above them, but they also had reason to hope that this disadvantage would soften as the years went by. The slow amelioration of inequality was tacitly understood as a collective purpose, shared by all political parties.

Nobody seems to be very clear precisely why Britain has become more unequal again in the past thirty years. And the gap is still widening today. *Forbes Magazine* reports that, overall, the ratio of the total rewards of chief executive officers of FTSE 100 companies to the pay of the average UK employee rose from 45 to 1 in 1998 to 120 to 1 in 2010. According to *Missing Out*, the report of the Resolution Foundation (July 2011), over the past thirty years the share of national income going to the bottom half of earners in Britain has fallen steeply. Real wages nearly doubled overall during those thirty years, but only 8 per cent of that growth went to the bottom earners. The wages of the top 1–5 per cent of the working population have gone on zooming into the stratosphere, recession or no recession, while wages at the bottom remain virtually stagnant.

Nor, four years after the crash, is there the slightest sign of repentance. On the contrary, the men at the top have become even more insatiable. At a time when average living standards are being severely squeezed, Incomes Data Services reported at the end of October 2011[2] that the pay packages of directors of FTSE 100 companies have soared by 49 per cent in a single year, to an average figure of £2,697,644. Chief executive officers collected rather more, an average of £3,855,172. Some of their number soared far beyond that level: Mick Davis of Xstrata collected over £18 million, Michael Spencer of Icap over £13 million. Even in the Civil Service, which is after all directly under government control, bonuses continued to rise to a total of £140 million. The Ministry of Defence alone handed out bonuses worth £45 million. In that same year, the pay of the average employee rose by a paltry 2.7 per cent. The bottom tenth of workers did even worse. Their pay went up by an invisible 0.1 per cent.[3]

We did not expect this at all. And most of us are at a loss to understand exactly what has happened. If you picked your way between the tents tethered outside St Paul's Cathedral in the autumn of 2011 or listened to the protesters in other city centres, you would, I think, have been struck not only by their rage against the bankers but also by their bewilderment. Those rough-scrawled slogans and laments pinned to the cathedral railings had no coherence, nothing you could call a logical argument or a clear set of demands.

None of the conventional explanations seems to provide a

satisfactory answer. Changes to the tax system in favour of the top earners might help to explain the growing inequality in post-tax incomes. But the real shock has been the rise in the *pre*-tax incomes of the top earners. Besides, inequality in Britain went on growing during the twenty years during which Nigel Lawson's tax rates were left unchanged. As a result of those lower rates, in fact, the rich paid far *more* tax than they ever had before and provided a much higher proportion of the Treasury's total revenue. So tax changes don't look much like the main problem – and they don't look much like the main answer either.

Oddly enough, the protesters outside St Paul's agree with the high priests of capitalism that globalization is the villain. Professor Irwin Stelzer, resident guru to Rupert Murdoch, argues in his *Sunday Times* column[4] that globalization has brought a level of affluence undreamed of to millions of Chinese and Indian workers, 'but globalization has also exacerbated inequality in many Western countries, especially America'. On the one hand, managerial skills can now be marketed internationally and fetch higher prices as a result. 'The news is less good for the woman making T-shirts or trainers' in the USA. She is undercut by millions of Chinese who are ready to work for a dollar a day. Globalization hurts the workers in Britain and the USA, but it's a golden opportunity for the footloose elite.

At first sight, this argument sounds quite convincing. But if you think about it, there's a bizarre inconsistency lurking in there. If global competition levels down the wages of people who make trainers or motor cars – which it obviously does – then why doesn't it level down the wages of managers and the professionals too? There are, for example, millions of well-educated Indians who can handle a spreadsheet and could easily acquire those precious managerial skills (if they haven't already), and who are ready to travel anywhere in search of better opportunities. This sort of competition from the emerging nations ought to nudge top-level

rewards *downwards*, just as it does for workers in call centres and
car factories, other things being equal.

The suspicion grows that perhaps other things are *not* equal.
Are the markets for top talent genuinely free? Or are they constrained and distorted in various ways – by monopoly power, by
professional cartels to keep wages high, by government regulation,
by stitch-ups in the boardroom, by undetected market abuse, not
to mention by the ancient arts of carve-up, scam and outright
looting?

It seems unlikely somehow that this sharpening inequality
should have emerged as a natural economic development in so
many countries. It seems more like a symptom of something else,
some deep-lying alteration in our custom and culture, not so
much as a malign by-product of capitalism but as an undiagnosed
malfunction or series of malfunctions.

Some people would prefer to brush the whole question aside.
'Surely,' they will claim, 'it is better to tolerate some degree of
inequality if it energizes the economy. A rising tide lifts all boats.
Anyway, how can you possibly decide at what level inequality
becomes intolerable? You surely are not arguing that everyone's
income should be mathematically equal?'

This response might have sounded all right twenty or thirty
years ago. But it ignores the very different character of inequality
today. The blunt fact is that wealth is not trickling down to anywhere near the bottom. The rowing boats are stuck on the mud.
Many of the worst off are sinking into a demoralized and detached
underclass, just as the top earners are congealing into a super-class
who hardly belong to the society they flit through. What is so
dispiriting is that the gap appears to be widening all the time,
regardless of whether we are going through a boom or a slump,
and certainly regardless of which party is in power.

As a result, we begin to sense that we are living in a dislocated
society. When George Osborne says 'We are all in this together',

it sounds grotesquely implausible, which it would not have done a generation ago. Who would have expected then that there would now be a think tank called the Centre for Social Cohesion or that Tony Blair's Cabinet Office would have had a Social Exclusion Unit?

It's much the same story with the other disquieting trend that we cannot help noticing: the trend towards centralization. Power in Britain used to be spread around in a rather casual, even haphazard fashion that had grown up over the years. We rather looked down on Continental countries such as France, which had inherited a highly centralized State from Napoleon and Louis XIV. But now, to our dismay, the roles are reversed. While many other European nations, not least the French, have been busily decentralizing their arrangements, power in Britain has drained away from private individuals and local communities to central boards, and bureaucracies, and government agencies, and ministries.

Again, we lament the change without having much clue about its causes. *Why* in one area of life after another has centralization become the default solution, the irresistible option? What or who is driving this apparently inexorable trend? How come local government was so effortlessly stripped of its old powers? Is it possible that centralization and inequality are related, that the one trend enables the other, and that both are facets and consequences of oligarchy?

We have managed to identify some of the villains who were to blame for the collapse of the banks. But we have not properly pinned down how and why they did it. It seems to be the case that unconstrained and self-perpetuating oligarchies have managed to manipulate the public and private institutions that they control and scooped a hugely disproportionate share of the rewards for themselves. In the same way, MPs and Euro MPs have abused their sovereign power to collar small fortunes in expenses and to exact handsome rents from big corporations and institutions via lobbyists. These abuses are not accidental but built into the system. Indeed, the political and economic tendencies towards oligarchy appear to gain much of their strength by their intertwining with one another. But how and why has this come to pass?

It is oligarchy – the rule of the few – that appears to be the common denominator of the system. What is it that makes oligarchy possible in the first place and then sustainable over the longer term? Well, we instinctively assume that it must be the absence of constraints: legal constraints, moral constraints, constitutional restraints. Where the rules are no longer obeyed, or never existed in the first place, or have become hollow ceremonies, then the oligarchs flourish. And the reason why these constraints have gone slack, or disappeared altogether, must be because we have not kept them in good repair. We have not paid attention. We have not examined the system closely enough to identify the mechanisms (or the absence of them) that have got us where we are today.

Let us be clear exactly what we are talking about. I am not claiming that either our system of liberal democracy or the rule of law has suffered an irreversible collapse. Not for the first time in history, oligarchs flourish under the rule of law and within the framework of a democracy. It is a mistake to confuse oligarchy with dictatorship or arbitrary rule. In all the previous long-running oligarchies – the Serene Republic of Venice lasted a thousand years, the Whigs dominated Britain for most of the eighteenth century – the law protected the property of the oligarchs and also kept the civil peace which they enjoyed. At the same time, as in the Roman Republic, another long-running oligarchy, periodic elections (admittedly on a restricted franchise) gave the system a rude legitimacy. So you cannot tell simply by examining a country's formal constitutional arrangements whether that country is in reality a thoroughgoing democracy or whether it is a finely feathered (and sometimes well concealed) nest for a brood of oligarchs.

Britain in the twenty-first century is certainly not a full-blown oligarchy. What we live in would be better described as a flabby, corroded type of liberal democracy, in which the oligarchs have been enjoying a free run. It resembles a school like the fictitious Narkover invented by the humorist Beachcomber, in which life bears only a flickering resemblance to the high-minded promises of its prospectus and which is really run by and for the tough eggs of the Upper Sixth, with the tacit collusion of the masters.

It would be a comfort to be able to pin all the blame on one political party or party leader. Then we could hope that another party or a new leader could set a new direction and instantly begin to undo the damage. But the damage seems to go deeper and to reach further back. The dismal truth is that pretty much every government in the past thirty years has, wittingly or unwittingly, helped the oligarchs' cause in one way or another. It was, for example, Margaret Thatcher and the Conservatives who set Britain's bankers free in the Big Bang of 1986. It was under Bill Clinton and the Democrats that America's bankers were similarly unleashed by the repeal of the Glass–Steagall Act in 1999. The Left is certainly entitled to criticize Margaret Thatcher and Ronald Reagan where they introduced free-market policies without thinking carefully about the consequences. But that critique would be more impressive if governments of the Left had not made much the same mistakes in imitating their reforms.

The trouble is that, on the whole, politicians can only think about one thing at a time. In the 1980s and 90s, the overriding imperative was to bring Britain back from the brink of economic collapse. All that mattered was to make her industries and services competitive again, to liberate the energies of her managers and to turn the country back into a place that people wanted to live and work in. In that desperate eleventh-hour enterprise, Margaret

Thatcher was a towering figure, indefatigable and implacable.
The force of her personality was, if anything, more respected and
admired overseas, but very few people in Britain would seriously
deny the extent of her achievement. Unfortunately, in the heat
and smoke of that long and painful battle, other abiding imperatives were lost sight of: the need to maintain the shape of our
democratic institutions, the need to preserve the local dimension, the proper governance of companies and the importance of
making them fully accountable to their shareholders and to the
public interest, the need to keep markets free of harmful monopolies and to root out restrictive practices in the boardroom no less
than on the shop floor.

Half the time, I have to confess, I was as blind to these other
imperatives as most people. In fact, I was in a tiny way complicit,
a foot soldier in the long march towards oligarchy. As a junior official in the Conservative Research Department, I wrote papers for
Sir Keith Joseph urging total co-ordination and centralization of
all the local health and welfare services. Later on, in the early
1980s, when I was working for Margaret Thatcher, I was sent off
to the Department of the Environment to devise a means of cap-
ping the domestic rates. The Deputy Secretary, Terry Heiser,
warned me that, if we went down that road, local government
would never be the same again. 'But Terry,' I said, 'it's only going
to be temporary.' Of course it wasn't, and thirty years later, local
government is still a pale and neutered shadow of its former self.

Just as bad were my sins of omission. As a political journalist, I
went to the party conferences year after year and devoted hundreds of column inches to mockery of their rowdy and chaotic
proceedings. I did not fully grasp that these seaside get-togethers
were a precious remnant of how democracy used to be. They represented one of the few remaining occasions where the politicians
collided with the people. I am conscious now of how little I
bestirred myself to defend their rude integrity when both Labour

and Conservative leaders began to emasculate the conference debates and reduce them to slick PR rallies.

Only as I began to write about the British constitution in the 1990s did I begin to twig that almost all the changes that were happening to the system were dragging it in one direction, towards oligarchy and centralization. And only when I was gathering evidence as a member of the Power Commission in the early years of this century did I really grasp how deep the disillusion had sunk; how much people resented the draining away of power and how impotent they felt to contest its loss.

This is not a party-political tract, and it is certainly not a critique of the free market either. I am all in favour of the market, but I believe that what Adam Smith called 'the Invisible Hand' of free enterprise can operate to the public benefit only within a robust framework of law and practice. His masterpiece, *The Wealth of Nations* (1776), is as much a warning about the potential abuses of market power as it is a celebration of the free market. And that warning is as fresh and relevant today as when it was written 200 years ago. No one knew better than Adam Smith the dangers of monopolies and cartels: 'People of the same trade seldom meet together, even for merriment and diversion, but the conversation ends in a conspiracy against the public or in some contrivance to raise prices.' Those words should be inscribed above every minister's desk and the entrance to every luxury conference hotel. Smith devotes much of his energies to explaining the legal and social structures required to support and guide the 'invisible hand' of the market, so that it operates to the public benefit. And in his less famous companion volume, *The Theory of Moral Sentiments* (1759), he tells us that none of this would be any good without the moral sympathies that bind us together. The trouble with the so-called 'neoliberals' is that they have not been neoliberal enough. They have not read too much Adam Smith but too little. There is a moral case for reform, but there is an economic case too.

Nor is this essay a complaint about the vulgarity of the *nouveaux riches* – about their yachts the size of hotels, their wrists dripping with diamonds, their string of island hideaways and marble pent-houses, their mistresses with improbable lips and their birthday parties costing the budget of a small African nation. That is an old lament. Ancient Romans and Greeks complained about the conspicuous wealth of Crassus and Croesus and the methods used to acquire it. The poet Horace deplored the tonnes of marble wasted by the profiteers from Rome on building their holiday villas out over the Bay of Naples.

My purpose is not to launch a polemic against the personal avarice of the oligarchs but rather to identify the oligarchic tendencies that have gathered such momentum in recent years, and to try to identify the historical factors which have let it all happen. Only when we understand how we got here can we hope to work out a route to a better place.

Oligarchic control is not a natural extension of capitalism or liberal democracy. It is a preventable corrosion. It is not the case that all advanced societies are equally oligarchic, or that oligarchy is always advancing. By exercising sustained determination and ingenuity, we can begin to reverse the pernicious trends. The excessive power of the oligarchs has been broken before. It can be broken again. It is a feeble form of fatalism to suppose that capitalism cannot be reformed and regenerated so that it benefits the many rather more and the few a good deal less.

We need to remember, after all, that over the past century capitalism has gone through a strange up-and-down experience. During the first part of the period, the intellectual fashion was to pronounce capitalism a busted flush, a discredited and moribund system that would die of natural causes within the foreseeable future or otherwise have to be put down like a sick pet (the intellectuals were divided on whether euthanasia would be required). Then capitalism was pronounced, often by many of the same intellectuals, to have made a miraculous recovery. Henceforth all its operations were greeted with wonder and admiration. Almost overnight, this discredited system could do no wrong, and other ideologies such as socialism had hurriedly to make their peace with this resurrected super-system. In reality of course, the work-ings of the free market are as imperfect as any other human activity. Capitalism may have been raised from the dead, but it has not been raised incorruptible. It is time that we looked more closely, with an undeceived but not unsympathetic eye, to see what has gone wrong and began to think carefully about how we might begin to put it right.

I put the quotation from George Orwell at the head of this essay for two reasons: to remind ourselves what an unerring eye Orwell had for unwelcome realities that nobody else at the time felt like facing; and also to point out just how long it has been, more than sixty years (and as we shall see, a lot longer than that), since the oligarchic tendencies have been gathering strength. But there is another quality that we need to disinter from Orwell's work and resurrect and adopt for our own use. And that is his optimism. He is often wrongly seen as a Jeremiah in a tweed jacket. In fact, what shines through his writings is his belief that no historical process is inevitable. Even Stalin's empire, so seem-ingly omnipotent and unshakable when he was writing *Animal Farm* and *Nineteen Eighty-Four*, would pass away. In the same essay written in 1946, from which I take my epigraph, he also said: 'The Russian regime will either democratize itself or it will perish. The huge, invincible, everlasting slave empire will not be established or, if established, will not endure, because slavery is no longer a stable basis for human society.'

What is true of communism is true of oligarchy too. We make our own destiny, and we can unmake it if we really want to.

This book has, I think, a pretty straightforward plan. In Part One, we retrace the story of how capitalism began to deviate from the way it was supposed to operate, and we identify the mechanisms that opened the way for the oligarchs to grab the spoils. In 'The Oligators – A Brief Intermission', I offer a brief sketch of what an oligarchy looks like, what are the influences that tend to generate oligarchy (the 'oligators'), what are the features that enable it to survive and what are its besetting defects. In Part Two, we tackle the political realm: how our political leaders have castrated the democratic structures of their parties and under-mined the independence of local councils and other outside bodies to produce a new centralized politics. In 'Waking Up', we move on to the present: first, we look at the signs that politicians and business leaders are waking up to the dangers; we examine what sort of proposals are on the table and assess their chances of doing the trick. Then we give the Coalition a half-term report. Finally, we offer a rough route map for getting to a better place, and quite briskly too.

Part One

THE CORROSION OF CAPITALISM

The curious case
of Mr Aldinger's teeth

For a brief moment, the fate of Western capitalism appeared to depend on William F. Aldinger's teeth. It was on 30 May 2003 that the shareholders of the Hong Kong and Shanghai Bank Corporation assembled in the Barbican Theatre for their annual general meeting. HSBC was at the time the most admired bank in Britain. It probably still is, though the competition for the title is not what it was. The bank had swollen to a colossal size, swallowing among others the Midland Bank, itself one of the largest high street banks in the world. Now HSBC was to gulp down another enormous mouthful, the firm of Household International plus William F. Aldinger III, its chief executive officer. Household supplied mortgages to nearly 50 million Americans who would not otherwise have been able to obtain one – 'sub-prime mortgages' as they were politely known, or 'trailer-park mortgages', as they were more brutally dubbed.

Household did not come cheap. HSBC had agreed to pay $13 billion for the company, or £9 billion. Bill Aldinger did not come cheap either; his three-year pay deal worked out at $57 million or £35 million. His fringe benefits were equally spectacular. His salary was encrusted with as many add-on gems as Damien Hirst's skull. A private jet to ferry him to and fro from the States was a routine requirement. The jewel in the crown was HSBC's undertaking to meet the bills for the dental care of Mr Aldinger and his wife, Alberta, until the day they died.

For many shareholders this was a bridgework too far. Not only were the terms of Mr Aldinger's personal engagement absurdly sumptuous; Household itself had a decidedly dodgy reputation for pressing its needy customers too hard and charging usurious rates of interest. The company was beset by lawsuits from aggrieved customers and constantly abused on a bunch of websites dedicated to its alleged misdeeds. The whole venture was decidedly out of character for HSBC, which, for all its dazzling growth, had a sound conservative reputation. Alone among the big high street banks, it did not lend out a hazardous multiple of the money it took in on deposits. Its reputation for reliability had spread across the world, not least because of its long-term chairman, Sir John Bond, a bouncy, owlish character who had spent all his working life with the bank, the last ten years of it at the top. He had been CEO from 1993 until he took over as chairman in 1998. Sir John was famous for his parsimony – by bankers' standards, that is. He paid himself a mere £2.1m million a year in salary and bonuses, and collected the same amount again from a long-term incentive plan. Far from demanding a private jet, he had been known to travel economy class, at least on short-haul flights. He was not in the Aldinger class.

Why, then, did he persist in laying out these huge amounts for a dubious company and a CEO, both of whom had been repeatedly accused of 'predatory lending'? Neil Collins, city editor of the *Daily Telegraph*, wrote the day after the AGM that 'Household is the sort of acquisition that has danger written all over it'.[5] If you specialize in lending money to borrowers whom other banks won't touch, Collins argued, 'you have to charge them more to com-

THE CURIOUS CASE OF MR ALDINGER'S TEETH 19

pensate for the ones who don't pay, and such is the desperation of some borrowers that the temptation for usury is ever-present.' As a result of succumbing to such temptations, Household's name was mud. And of course HSBC could hope to make the company more profitable only by squeezing its customers harder still, at incalculable cost to HSBC's own reputation.

Yet Sir John insisted to indignant questioners that Bill Aldinger, like the company he ran, was worth every penny. His services could not have been obtained for less. If they replaced him, they would have to pay the same or more. So ungrasping had Bill been that he had not even asked for a contract. A handshake was good enough for him. As for Household, it was a first-rate company, which lived up to its motto 'helping everyday people every day'. As for predatory lending, well, the New York State definition of it was 8 per cent above the rate on long bonds, and this would catch most credit card companies in the UK.

As Bond carried on, imperturbable, unflustered, I looked along the row of distinguished directors up on the Barbican stage. Aldinger was sitting at the end, equally imperturbable. He was mild and pale with a long face, a Milquetoast of a man. In an Ealing Studios film about a man who got away with £35 million he would have been played by Sir Alec Guinness, or in the remake by Tom Hanks. He kept his mouth firmly shut throughout the meeting, offering the shareholders no clue as to the scale of the dentists' bills they were letting themselves in for.

While I was watching Mr Aldinger's unmoving lips, the debate had now switched from his teeth to the pay rates of the office workers on the forty-first floor of HSBC's tower at Canary Wharf, a magnificent structure visible from the middle of Essex to the North Downs. Abdul (he offered no other name) rose to complain that the contractors who employed him to clean Sir John's office gave him a mop and a bucket and £5 an hour, with no pension and a lousy sick-pay scheme. Sir John, for the first time looking a bit flustered, said that the contractors paid the going rate (just as he had argued five minutes earlier that they were paying Mr Aldinger the going rate, only the going rate happened to be a smidgeon higher).

Abdul was loudly applauded by his fellow toilers who had come with him. After he had sat down, the shareholder action groups – the Pensions Investment Research Consultants (PIRC) and the National Association of Pension Funds – went on grumbling about this and that. But none of it made the slightest difference. The remuneration packages of all the directors, including Bill's golden hello and the care of Bill and Alberta's teeth, were approved with only a scattering of dissentients. The acquisition of Household had already been approved by 99.3 per cent of the votes at an extraordinary general meeting. Like almost all such AGMs, the whole occasion was a charade, an empty ritual which gave the shareholders the semblance of a hearing and put the management through the semblance of a grilling.

Two years on, Sir John was still cooing with delight at getting hold of Household. The *Financial World* described it as 'one of Bond's greatest achievements'. In an interview headed 'Premium Bond',[6] Sir John claimed that 'external observers suggest that we could have paid £6 billion [to] £11 billion more than we paid for it. It has done everything we expected of it.' Eighteen months later, on 7 February 2007, the new CEO of HSBC, Michael Geoghegan, had to announce the first profits warning in the history of the company. Debt provisions were over $10 billion, almost entirely because of catastrophic bad debts in Household. What had happened was that cash-strapped customers had taken out second mortgages to enable them to repay their first mortgages and they were now failing to make payments on these second mortgages as well. Yet despite having to issue this profits warning and the unmistakable shadow of worse to come, Geoghegan declared defiantly, 'This is a dream portfolio.'

Looking back, we can see that this HSBC profits warning was the first brick in the Great Wall of capitalism to crumble. The first distant rumbling of the rapids was audible to anyone who cared to listen. Within days of the HSBC warning, shares in other sub-prime mortgage specialists began to collapse one after the other – New Century Financial, Fremont General, Novastar Financial. Big banks such as Barclays and UBS shyly admitted that they too were exposed to the sub-prime market. UBS closed its hedge-fund division. Bear Stearns was engulfed in speculation. It emerged, to general consternation, that nobody seemed to know, not even the banks themselves, exactly how far they were exposed through parcels of sub-prime loan that had been 'sliced and diced', transformed into securities and sold on to other traders. Then in September 2007, the Northern Rock disaster began.

By the time the credit crunch had reached its worst across the Western world, there was no more disguising the fact that HSBC's acquisition of Household International had been a hideous mis-take. Bond's successor as chairman, Stephen Green, who had been CEO when the purchase of Household went through, also hap-pens to be a priest in the Church of England (he is now Lord Green and a minister in the Coalition government). He could do no other than tell the truth: 'It is an acquisition we wish we hadn't done with the benefit of hindsight, and there are lessons to be learned.'

In March 2009, HSBC abandoned its sub-prime lending busi-ness, and Household was run down. The whole investment was written off and the company was effectively worthless. The damage was far worse than the $13 billion that HSBC had paid for the business. HSBC had to set aside no less than $53 billion in three years for bad loans, most of them relating to Household. Fund managers who had always been sceptical of the deal now described it as a 'catastrophic investment' and 'an absolute disaster'. It is important to remember just how many people had from the start thought that the venture was crazy. There was no need for 'the benefit of hindsight'. Shareholders and commentators alike could see at the outset that the whole idea was irrationally conceived and likely to benefit scarcely anybody, not the shareholders, not HSBC's existing customers nor its existing workforce – with one crucial exception. Senior management could expect to draw even larger salaries and claim even more extensive perks, now that the empire they controlled was significantly larger. Prince among this small group who would benefit from the deal was of course their new colleague, William F. Aldinger III, not to mention his wife and his dentist.

Any reasonably sane person would, I think, have come away as I did from the Barbican Theatre that day at the end of May 2003 thinking that there was something seriously wrong with the workings of capitalism at the beginning of the twenty-first century. Sir John Bond was, at a rough computation, being paid not ten or fifty times but 400 times what Abdul the cleaner was being paid, and he was being applauded for taking an enormous gamble with the firm's money that seemed, to most rational observers, rather unlikely to succeed. Ultimately, the firm's money – its capital base at any rate – consisted of the savings of a vast number of ordinary citizens, most of whom would have thought it crazy to fork out so many billions for the privilege of taking on the mortgages of people who could not afford to pay them off. Trooping out of the bowels of the Barbican, even those who believed devoutly in the free market as the least bad system of supplying human wants would have experienced a little queasiness, like confirmed meat-eaters after their first visit to an abattoir.

Back at the Barbican for the annual general meeting eight years later on 27 May 2011, shareholders were if anything angrier than ever. They revolted against everything: the manner of the appointment of the new chairman, Doug Flint; the pay of the new chief executive, Stuart Gulliver, who earned a total of

£6.2 million; and the new remuneration plan. Flint, who himself took home £4.11 million per annum, had to admit that the acquisition of Household had been 'a very black mark on our history', and that HSBC had delivered 'disappointing and inadequate' returns over the past five years; even the FTSE index had improved by 25 per cent, while HSBC shares had risen by a pathetic 3.5 per cent. In fact, if you go back to the day of the Barbican meeting in May 2003, HSBC shares had not risen at all in the past eight years but actually declined, from 721 on 30 May 2003 to 627 on 4 July 2011. Easy enough to blame this abysmal performance on the Bank Crash, but not so easy when it is the conduct of your very own mega bank that helped to trigger the crash. And yet here was Gulliver's pay, just as substantial as the wodge that Sir John Bond had taken home. The gap between the remuneration in the boardroom and the wages on the shop floor had become, in the words of one small shareholder present, 'obscene'. Nothing could stop the gravy train, not even the biggest disaster in the history of the bank.

You might charitably consider the possibility that the Household catastrophe was a one-off accident, the consequence of a rush of blood to the head. Many other British companies, not just banks, had come to grief trying to gain a foothold in the US market; it seems to be a challenge that is hard to resist for CEOs with oversized egos.

Yet the evidence from the great bank crashes of 2008 is too overwhelming to dismiss the HSBC debacle as a freak. For exactly the same hubris, the same unwinnable bet brought down Lloyds and brought down the Royal Bank of Scotland.

Nobody in their right mind would have acquired HBOS, which was a festering morass of bad debts, least of all in the middle of the biggest financial crisis since the Great Depression. Yet that was what Eric Daniels, the supposedly cautious conservative CEO of Lloyds, did, seemingly without a second thought.

It was offered as an excuse that Gordon Brown had suggested the
idea to Daniels's chairman, Sir Victor Blank, at a party. But no
grown-up executive would bet the future of a bank as large and
venerable as Lloyds on the strength of a passing whim of a Prime
Minister. Daniels lamented afterwards that they had not had time
to do due diligence on the state of HBOS. But every observer
could see that HBOS was a stinking midden. Who could possibly
benefit from such a merger? Not the staff, many of whom would
lose their jobs as the number of branches was cut. Not the customers, to judge by past experience: as banks have grown larger,
their service to the customer has become increasingly peremptory
and impersonal, especially to small business lenders. To the shareholders then? Forget it. Any payback from swallowing such an
indigestible beast as HBOS would be years away, if indeed there
ever was one. No, as with HSBC and Household, the only beneficiaries on the horizon would be the senior management, who
could start paying themselves even larger bonuses, and start doing
so immediately, simply because they now presided over an even
larger company.

This rebarbative conclusion applies with even greater force to
the case of Sir (now Mr) Fred Goodwin and the Royal Bank of
Scotland, to which I now turn with a mixture of horror and fas-
cination.

Fred's tenner

A few minutes after the train had left Edinburgh, I gave the bar attendant a £20 note for a cappuccino and got a tenner in my change. The sumptuous engraving of the earth-brown bank-note caught my eye: 'The Royal Bank of Scotland promise to pay the bearer on demand TEN POUNDS STERLING AT THEIR HEAD OFFICE HERE IN EDINBURGH BY ORDER OF THE BOARD 19th September 2006.' This stirring promise was signed by the Group Chief Executive, whose sprawling signature sliced across the Royal Bank's coat of arms with its thistle at the bottom and above it the bank's motto 'FIRM'. For all its flam-boyance, the signature was still easy enough to decipher. It read: 'Fred Goodwin'.

By the time I pocketed the tenner, four years after it had been printed, almost every word on the banknote was a howling lie. The Royal Bank of Scotland had effectively gone bust and could no longer promise to pay anyone anything unaided. It continued to exist at all only because it was considered 'too big to fail', and the government had stepped in and taken a majority shareholding, which eventually came to constitute 70 per cent of the equity, in return for pumping in billions to keep the business alive. Between

them, RBS and the other ancient Scottish bank, the Bank of
Scotland, which had already merged with the Halifax and was
soon to be merged with Lloyds Bank, had received no less than
£37 billion of public money. The RBS share price had collapsed
from a peak of £18 to a nadir of 11p. And Sir Fred Goodwin, the
famous Fred the Shred, once voted 'European Banker of the
Year', had resigned in utter ignominy. The company's motto now
looked like a hideous joke. The Bank had turned out to be about
as firm as porridge. All that remained, four years on, was Fred's
faded signature on a crumpled note. That and, I suppose, the
thistle on the coat of arms.

Goodwin might have departed in ignominy, but he certainly
did not depart in poverty. During his eight years as head of RBS,
he paid himself around £30 million in salary and bonuses. And he
left with a pension pot of £16 million or more, estimated to
deliver him about £700,000 a year for the rest of his life.

Was his downfall, and the bank's, to some extent a matter of
bad luck? Was the collapse of RBS at least in part a knock-on
consequence of the worldwide credit crunch, for which Fred
Goodwin can at worst shoulder only a fraction of the blame? Did
he really deserve the title that stuck to him of 'the world's worst
banker'?

The answer is No, No, and emphatically Yes. Goodwin's
increasingly reckless conduct of the mega bank cannot be excused
simply because other people, both in the City and the media,
were taken in by his abrasive manner and cheeky self-promotion
and were impressed by his eagerness to seek out bigger and bigger
deals at whatever price. The bank he inherited was in pretty
sound shape. Even during his first couple of years as Chief
Executive Officer, the bank was more or less fully funded; its
lending was pretty much covered by the loans it took in from its
depositors. The massive expansion of its loan book, the headlong
acquisition of business after business, culminating in the takeover

of the Dutch bank ABN-Amro at a comically inflated price, coupled with RBS's growing dependence on borrowing from other banks as well as its exposure to virtually limitless losses on derivatives and other complex financial products turned it from one of the world's safer banks into an accident waiting to happen. To have transformed RBS in so short a time from a leading if unadventurous provincial bank into one of the largest banks in the world was a measure not of Goodwin's genius but of his hubris. After his downfall, it was pointed out that he lacked any training in banking or any formal banking qualifications – a deficiency he shared with another sharp-elbowed thruster, Andy Hornby, who over more or less the same period hugely expanded what had once been the staid old Halifax Building Society, took over Scotland's other ancient bank and brought the resulting HBOS Group to its knees in almost exactly the same way Goodwin destroyed RBS. What both men really lacked were the essential qualities of any banker: prudence, thoughtfulness and a sense of proportion.

Everything about Goodwin was monstrously overblown: the enormous new company HQ at Grogarburn outside Edinburgh, a small town the size and shape of the US Pentagon and costing £350 million; his Dassault Falcon 900 Jet; his scattering of £200 million on promoting RBS at celebrity events, while at the same time he was winning plaudits from City observers by his ruthless attitude towards costs and his readiness to shred the employees of the companies RBS acquired. During his reign, power within the bank became increasingly centralized. At the same time, the rewards paid to those at the top of it progressed by leaps and bounds. Goodwin became the *roi soleil* of Grogarburn and, like other sun kings before him, surrounded himself with toadies and flatterers who bowed before the brilliance of Fred the Shred. He was in fact the model of a modern oligarch.

Now of course ambitious young thrusters have always gone

into banking expecting much of the cash that passes over the counter to stick to their paws. And Goodwin was not the first bank chief in Scotland to gain a reputation as a predator.

On that same earth-brown tenner there is a fine engraving of a shrewd-looking gentleman in a full-bottomed wig. This is Lord Ilay (1682–1761), originally known as Archibald Campbell and later as the third Duke of Argyll. Ilay was the first chairman of the Royal Bank and it was his main aim in that role to do down his rival, the somewhat older Bank of Scotland, and secure for RBS a monopoly of issuing banknotes. He was a cunning, lecherous fellow who played a role that still remains murky in the negotiations leading up to the union of England and Scotland. Ilay was pretty cynical about politics, as about most things. He wrote to his brother-in-law Lord Bute:

> Politics is a continual petty war and game, and as at all other games, we will sometimes win and sometimes lose, and he that plays best and has the best stock has the best chance ... It is enough that we can maintain an interest with some of both sides without giving up anything we must and ought to maintain, and if I can save myself or my friend by being thought a Mahometan by a Turk, I'll never decline it.

In other words, if he believed in anything, it was in the necessity of double-dealing, hedging your bets and watching your back at all times.

It was because of rather than despite these unromantic qualities that Ilay was such an agile and successful financier. He borrowed from his fellow Scot, the rather more mercurial John Law, the idea that a nation could build a sound commercial future on paper money. That idea has had its ups and downs over the centuries. Law himself was disgraced and had to flee France after the Mississippi Bubble of 1720, when the Banque Royale, of which he was the chief director, was brought to its knees by issuing too much paper. But paper money has remained the foundation of modern credit. And it is the huge expansion of credit that has fuelled modern capitalism. The Royal Bank of Scotland under Ilay was the first bank anywhere to offer its customers overdrafts. Ilay can in fact be accounted the father of modern banking, not just in Scotland. He was also a classical scholar, mathematician and botanist; his patronage was an energizing source of the Scottish Enlightenment. Yes, he could certainly be tagged as a Whig Oligarch and not a particularly nice person. Yet at every turn in his long and tumultuous career you sense his keen mind weighing the odds, looking out for the least worst option. While keeping a sharp eye on his own interests, he was always anxious that the people of Scotland generally should prosper from his policies. He would have been horrified that such fecklessness should have simultaneously brought down Scotland's two oldest and grandest banks.

What a contrast with the modern oligarch whose signature sits next to Ilay's portrait. Brash, boastful, heedless of the damage he might do, looking always for the next deal without seriously calculating the interests of the shareholders of RBS, let alone of its employees and customers. What a contrast too with the clearing banks (as the high street banks used to be called) at any time up to the 1990s. It was not simply that the clearing banks were cautious and conservative, indeed often reviled for being too much so. They were also continent and economical. Even their chairmen and managing directors took home pay packets of modest size, and not absurdly out of proportion to the wages they paid their employees, perhaps twenty times as large, not 400 times. Young thrusters who wanted to make a pile would not think of going into Barclays or Lloyds; they would go into one of the merchant banks in the City, although even these exercised some restraint over pay and liked to shovel a good deal of their profits away into their hidden reserves, unlike say, Goldman Sachs today, which pays out nearly half its earnings in salaries and bonuses.

If you look back over the rise and fall of Sir Fred Goodwin, you can only rub your eyes and ask yourself: how did it come to this? How did such a foolish, arrogant hothead gain control of a staid old bank and lead it to disaster while he piled up his own personal fortune? Whatever happened to Edinburgh's reputation as a city of canny and cautious men of business? How had modern banking come to throw away so many of its old checks and balances? A prudential tradition which had lasted more or less since Ilay's day (with the usual rude interruptions of booms and bubbles) seemed not so much to have gone astray as been deliberately abandoned. How and why had all this come about?

RBS, like Lloyds, is still a shattered cripple, limping along on the taxpayer's arm, still discovering fresh bad debts on its books three years later. Yet HSBC remains one of Britain's greatest banks, and it has come through the credit crunch and the recession with far fewer dents in its reputation or its finances than its few remaining rivals. But it was at HSBC that the trouble started. And it is perhaps in a great company run by honourable and intelligent men like Bond and Green that one may gather the clearest clues to the systemic failings in the way big business operates today. For we cannot accuse HSBC of being run by crooks or idiots. If such an excellent bank can be led so horrendously astray, there must be pernicious elements embedded in present custom and practice, elements so prevalent that people both inside and outside the banks and other big businesses have come to take them for granted. What is it that has gone wrong?

The twilight of the shareholder

After all, capitalism is supposed to be a quite simple system. Someone sets out to launch an enterprise. He persuades some other people to join with him in putting up the cash to buy the tools, rent the premises and hire the staff. These *investors* are each allotted shares in the business in proportion to the amount of money they put in. They become *shareholders,* and the money they have put in forms the *capital* of the business. The shareholders then appoint *directors* (who may or may not include the original launchers of the business) to manage the business from day to day. But the shareholders retain the power to hire and fire the directors, and to decide the firm's strategy: whether to expand the business by raising more capital, or to sell off part or all of it, or in extreme cases to close it down. They also decide how much money to take out of the company for themselves each year in *dividends*. If the company needs to raise more capital, the shareholders have priority rights to invest, so that they can maintain their percentage share of the total capital. The shareholders between them own the company; the directors manage it on their behalf. That's the theory.

And at the beginnings of modern capitalism, that was pretty

much how it worked. The shareholders were often allied by blood, or they might be members of the same class or trade guild. They were a *society* or *company* of venturers, whether they were sending out trappers and furriers to the icy wastes of Hudson's Bay, or prospectors for gold to the Americas or traders in cloth and spices to India, or whether they were hiring men to dig for coal on their estates or build a mill on their river. The investors were few in number, and they often commanded the enterprise themselves. When they sent out agents, they kept as close a watch on them as distance and communications would allow. In many such enterprises, the State or the King and his relatives were allotted a hefty share of the action, which helped to ensure legal protection at home and naval and military protection overseas. This royal share allocation might be said to constitute a sort of tax, but it was one well worth paying, for without it the enterprise might be damaged or forcibly suppressed by jealous rivals.

Gradually, as the size of the enterprises grew, so did the number of shareholders and their physical distance from the operations. Instead of being intimate collaborations, the larger firms became public companies, or *sociétés anonymes*, to use the evocative French term. The introduction of *limited liability* for investors, in the UK by the Limited Liability Act of 1855 and soon after in most other advanced countries, further reinforced and facilitated this distancing. When a business failed, the shareholder now forfeited only the money he had put into it. No longer was he liable to meet his share of all the firm's losses. The dangers of being wiped out, like Miss Matty in Elizabeth Gaskell's novel *Cranford*, were much diminished. A prudent investor who scattered his or her eggs between enough different baskets did not have so much to fear if any single one of them was smashed. Only in rare survivals such as Lloyd's of London did the partner or 'Name' stand to lose a penny more than he had put in.

So now there was an incentive to distribute your savings as widely as possible, at the cost of losing such influence over the management as you might have had if you put them all into a single firm. This wider distribution greatly diminished risk, but at the same time it also diminished control. The Limited Liability laws did little more than give legal expression to the new reality. It was no longer practically possible for creditors of a bankrupt firm to pursue all the thousands of shareholders, many of whom might live abroad.

This trend began to become visible during the second half of the nineteenth century in Britain and the United States, but theories have a way of sticking in people's minds long after the reality on the ground has altered, and it was not until after the First World War that some bright sparks woke up to the fact that capitalism in practice was no longer quite what it was supposed to be.

Early sightings of the new reality were offered by the great critic of conspicuous consumption, Thorstein Veblen.[7] But the classic description of the new world was *The Modern Corporation and Private Property* by Adolf Berle and Gardiner Means, which came out in New York in 1932 in the midst of the Great Depression.

Adolf Berle was one of those public servants who possessed both acute judgment and the self-confidence to back it up with action. As a young American diplomat after the Great War, he had gone to Versailles as part of the team to negotiate the peace agreement, then resigned in disgust at the terms. For the rest of his life, he was professor of corporation law at Columbia, but he was also a member of Roosevelt's 'Brains Trust' which designed the New Deal, and he lived long enough to be part of Kennedy's task force, which came up with the Alliance for Progress, a plan that transformed US relations with Latin America. He was a hard-headed idealist who did not shrink from going to Roosevelt with a list of Communist spies inside the US government, headed by Alger Hiss. (Roosevelt waved him away with 'Oh forget it, Adolf.')

Berle the lawyer collaborated with his Harvard friend, the economist Gardiner Means. Together, they transformed our understanding of the way capitalism actually works. Their book seems to me just as relevant today, regardless whether we are going through a boom or a bust. None of the revisions and additions subsequently offered by scholars, including by Berle and Means themselves, really shakes their thesis. It is the collaboration between the lawyer and the economist that unlocked the problem.

For the functioning of modern property law 'has destroyed the unity that we commonly call property'. Thousands of shareholders scattered all over the world can have little control over the business of which they are the nominal owners. 'At the same time the shareholder bears no responsibility with respect to the enterprise or its physical property. It has often been said that the owner of a horse is responsible. If the horse lives he must feed it. If the horse dies, he must bury it. No such responsibility attaches to a share or stock.'

Who has that responsibility in the real world? Well, if you want to sue a company because it has sold you damaged goods, or because it has discharged noxious chemicals on your land, or because it has sold you a drug which turned out to be harmful, or because it has caused you injury as an employee by compelling you to operate unsafe machinery, who do you sue? Not all those scattered shareholders who had no part in the management of the company and are in any case unreachable. No, the only people who can be held responsible are the Board of Directors and their agents. In terms of practical law, they *are* the company.

For 'the property owner who invests in a modern corporation so far surrenders his wealth to those in control of the corporation that he has exchanged the position of independent owner for one in which he may become merely recipient of the wages of capital.' He lives off his dividends, not off the sweat of his brow. He becomes an idle, functionless *rentier*, a man who rents out his capital, the sort of fellow who, in Stanley Baldwin's trenchant phrase, considers that he has done a good day's work after flicking his cigar ash over his roses to keep off the greenfly. Berle and Means believe that the shareholders have 'accordingly surrendered the right that the corporation should be operated in their sole interest'.

Of course, in cases of many private companies and several public ones, there is still a majority shareholder or group of shareholders who continue to exercise total control over the running of the business. They may run the company themselves; they will certainly choose the board of directors and perhaps several of the senior executives as well. Such effective control can be exerted with a shareholding well short of 50 per cent, so long as there is no large active opposing group of shareholders. Where a company has been built up by a single individual over the years, his authority may enable him to continue to be in charge, even if his own family shareholdings are diluted as the company has grown until they are no higher than, say, 10 per cent; Rupert Murdoch and Richard Branson are prime examples. Effectively such dominant individuals *are* the company, and the company may well be broken up on their death if their heirs are not up to the task. But what Berle and Means showed conclusively was that, even in the early 1930s, these headline-catching counter-examples were very much the exception among large firms. Of the 200 largest quoted firms in the US at that time, virtually none of them had any shareholder on their register commanding more than 3 or 4 per cent of the total equity.

Keynes, writing a few years later, thought that this shift of power would lead to the gradual extinction of the shareholder altogether. If interest rates were kept low (as they were throughout the 1930s), then there would cease to be a shortage of capital and so less and less need for shareholders to stump up. In his classic *General Theory of Employment, Interest and Money* (1936), the founding document of what has come to be called Keynesianism, he prophesied: 'I see, therefore, the rentier aspect of capitalism as a transitional phase which will disappear when it has done its work ... the euthanasia of the rentier, of the functionless investor, will be nothing sudden, merely a gradual continuance of what we have seen in Great Britain, and will need no revolution.'[8]

The wealth of innumerable individuals had been concentrated into huge combines, the mega corporation, and subjected to a single directing power, the Board. 'The power attendant upon such concentration has brought forth princes of industry,' whose position was yet to be determined, according to Berle and Means, but was obviously destined to be a dominant one. 'Princes of industry' or, as Tom Wolfe dubbed them no less memorably in *The Bonfire of the Vanities* (1987), 'the masters of the universe'.

It is tempting at this point to blame individuals for the failings of the system. There must be villains, rapacious big businessmen, greedy monopoly capitalists. But if we look back over history, it may seem more plausible that the shift of power from the theoretical owners to the actual managers is always likely to happen as soon as businesses grow beyond a certain size. There is a genuine inbuilt problem here.

You can, after all, see the whole process at work in the very first great corporation in modern European history, the Dutch East Indies Company, or VOC (for Vereenigde Nederlandsche Geoctroyeerde Oost-Indische Compagnie). As Niall Ferguson describes in *The Ascent of Money* (2008), when it was first set up in 1602, the VOC was a trailblazer in a number of respects. Subscription was open to all residents of the United Provinces, to artisans and servants as well as to merchants and aristocrats. In Amsterdam alone, there were 1,143 subscribers, half of them subscribing 1,000 guilders or less. The VOC was also created by government, in the shape of the Dutch States-General, which considered that the half-dozen fledgling companies trading out of Dutch ports needed more firepower – both financially and literally, since the VOC was to be supported by warships and troops. In due course, it became the trading arm of the Dutch empire in the East. Even more striking is how quickly a market developed in VOC shares. Trading in the shares was so brisk in the open-air markets of Amsterdam that soon a splendid covered *Beurs* had to be built on the Rokin – the world's first purpose-built stock exchange.

Within five years, no less than a third of the company's stock had been transferred from the original owners. Discontented shareholders who were fed up with the lack of the promised dividends and the impossibility of exercising any control over the directors and the captains of their faraway trading fleets could sell their shares to more hopeful punters. Or they could complain. There was even a term for the discontented shareholder – the *Doleanten*. Bad-tempered pamphlets appeared, criticizing 'the self-serving governance of certain directors' of the VOC, who were ensuring that 'all remained darkness': 'The account book, we can only surmise, must have been rubbed with bacon and fed to the dogs.'[9] Thus, right at the beginnings of modern capitalism we hear anguished complaints from the shareholders of their own impotence and the lack of transparency in the management of the business.

The *Doleanten* had their way. When the VOC charter was renewed in 1622, they were granted the right to appoint Nine Men from among their number, whom the Seventeen Lords who ran the company were obliged to consult on 'great and important matters'. These nine shareholder directors not only had to give their approval to company strategy; they were also entitled to scrutinize the accounts, to appoint auditors and to nominate

future candidates for directorships – a model recipe for what we
now call 'corporate governance'. In the event, what really molli-
fied the *Doleanten* was the steady flow of dividends which began
as soon as the Dutch navy tightened its hold over Java, Ceylon and
other parts of South East Asia.

The hard-faced men who did well out of the VOC became
merchant princes, often from quite modest beginnings. Their
sudden wealth was an amazing transformation for a nation of
sturdy Protestant artisans and farmers. It was, as Simon Schama so
brilliantly describes, 'an embarrassment of riches'. These middle-
class merchants did the best they could not to let it go to their
heads. Outward display continued to be frowned upon. Only
within the privacy of their homes could they delight in jewelled
cabinets and glowing Rembrandts and Vermeers, and in their
brick courtyards plant tulips they had bought for prices which
were for some to prove ruinous.

But could such self-restraint last for ever? How would the new
princes of industry behave in the twentieth and twenty-first century? Would not the sheer scale of modern capitalism lead those
in charge to succumb to the temptations of affluence? Berle and
Means were sure of one thing: there was no reason to assume

> ... that those in control of a modern corporation will also
> choose to operate it in the interests of the owners... If we are
> to assume that the desire for personal profit is the prime force
> motivating control, we must conclude that the interests of con-
> trol are different from and radically opposed to those of
> ownership; that the owners most emphatically will not be
> served by a profit-seeking controlling group.[10]

The actual controllers of the company would cream off the profits
into their own pockets, direct profitable business into other companies controlled by themselves, as well as award themselves

magnificent salaries and other perquisites of office. If the new masters of the universe were out primarily to feather their own nests – as the theory of the free market taught us they would be – then they would not give the shareholders any more of a look-in than they had to.

For example, in drawing up the charter of its incorporation, the promoters, soon to be the managers of the new company, will see to it that 'the management will have as complete latitude and as little liability as possible, as large a power to arrange and rearrange participation in its own interests as can be secured; and that the prospective shareholder will have as little power and as few enforceable rights as can conveniently be arranged'.[11] In practice, most prospective shareholders will never read the document. 'In the course of his practice of the law, one of the writers [i.e. Berle] has never come across a shareholder who had read the corporation charter, let alone the underlying corporation act.'[12] Not much change there, I suspect.

Ever since corporations really came into style, from the mid-nineteenth century on, their managers have sought, and usually obtained, every usable legal loophole that would enable them to run the company just as they pleased. Again and again, by such devices as the dilution of those pre-emption rights which were intended to enable the original shareholders to keep their due share of the action whenever the company wanted fresh capital, the directors have persuaded the courts (in Britain and elsewhere, no less than in the United States) to allow them 'to do pretty much as they will with the existing shareholders'.[13] Even devices intended to protect the rights of shareholders may have the opposite effect, such as the provision for proxy voting at company AGMs and other shareholder meetings: 'Legally the proxy is an agent for the shareholder; and necessarily under a duty of fidelity to him. Factually he is a dummy for management, and is expected to do as he is told.'[14]

In our own day, directors and managers have taken advantage of
these inherited latitudes and added on a few more of their own. In
finance, for example, they vastly extend their opportunities for
profit – and for catastrophe – by expanding their activities in the
field of options and other derivatives. These are essentially
straightforward bets on the future, familiar from medieval times,
but they had been relatively a cottage industry, little more than a
sideline and a way of laying off the bets they had taken in the form
of ordinary investments. Now they transformed some banking
firms into a huge casino which threatened to dwarf the original
bank – and all without any need to seek the approval of shareholders. In the case of Barings, a single maverick clerk in this
department was able to destroy the bank.

Again, the business of buying and selling debt had always been
a modest part of any bank's activities. Now, by bundling assorted
debts together and selling them on in parcels of securities – 'slicing and dicing', as it was called – huge new assets and liabilities
were acquired, vastly expanding the balance sheet, again without
needing any sort of nod from the shareholders. This vastly swollen
balance sheet continued to rest on a tiny cushion of capital contributed by the bemused and impotent shareholders; and the
bank's credit in the markets still ultimately relied on the deposits
of their high street customers. Behind those deposits stood a government guarantee. After the 1933 crash in the United States, the
federal government's scheme offered a sizeable assurance of repayment; in Britain, the government guaranteed only a miserable
fraction of the total deposits, a figure which was hastily upped to
£50,000 per deposit after the crash of 2007–8, and in December
2010 was raised again to £85,000.

The point is that neither the shareholders nor the customers,
on whom the whole enterprise still ultimately relied, had more
than the glimmerings of a say in how the managers behaved.
True, when the bank or building society wanted to diversify by

buying a building society or bank or insurance company or stockbroker, then fresh capital might need to be sought from the shareholders, especially if the authorities had raised concerns about the thinness of the firm's capital base. But such capital issues could usually be nodded through by those willing proxies, and even if the issue should turn out to be a flop with the investing public, there was no shortage of willing underwriters to subscribe, in return for the usual generous fees (these gradually rose from 2 per cent to 4 per cent of the money to be raised, as ordinary shareholders became wary of punting more of their savings).

As the big bank took over other financial institutions, its size rather than its profitability gradually became the measure of its reputation and of the prestige of the CEO. Thus 'the deal' became the prime ambition of the ambitious chief executive. He came to think of the bank as his personal project, not as a repository of value with a duty of care to his shareholders and customers. The modern bank was a predator on the prowl. Sir Fred Goodwin declared that he wanted RBS to be regarded as the biggest predator of them all.

The most compelling part of Berle and Means's masterpiece is where they spell out just how many of the shareholder's original rights had, even by the early 1930s, been eroded or rendered hollow and worthless by legal judgments. For the courts almost invariably favoured the arguments from practical necessity put forward by the directors and their agile attorneys. The statutes of most American states favoured the freedom of the directors to take any short cut, if it could plausibly be argued that the short cut was in the interests of the business. Yes, the common law did offer the shareholder some rudimentary protection. But 'the indefiniteness of the application and the extreme expense and difficulty of litigation still leave the stockholder virtually helpless.'[15] Only the most stubborn obsessive would take the risk of going to court.

If, even with all these advantages, the managers still feel that
the laws of their particular state or nation are too rigid and
inhibiting, they can always register the company somewhere
else – in the state of Delaware, for example, then as now 'the
loosest of jurisdictions'. Which is why Conrad Black chose to
incorporate his companies in Delaware and was so startled to
find himself standing in the dock there and being tried by a
judge who took a decidedly un-Delaware-ish view of Black's
conduct.

In a passage that seems as surprising today as it must have in
1932, Berle and Means even make a comparison between the
modern corporation and a communist regime. 'The corporation
director who would subordinate the interests of the individual
stockholder to those of the group more nearly resembles the communist in mode of thought than he does the protagonist of private
property.'[16]

Of course the shareholder has exchanged all these disadvantages
for one desirable advantage. He has exchanged control and
responsibility for the delights of liquidity. Unlike a farmer or even
an old-fashioned factory owner, he can realize his wealth at a
moment's notice and he does so without a backward glance. He
no longer sleeps next door to his property. Nor does he cherish it.
All he has are tokens, pieces of paper (now not even that, but
merely entries in the electronic archive). He is utterly remote
from the operation. Its ups and downs, its triumphs and disasters
are of no concern to him until and unless they affect the share
price and the dividend. This total separation from the workforce
prompts an inescapable question that Berle and Means are not
slow to ask. If we believe that profit-seeking is what drives businessmen on, 'Are no profits to go to those who exercise control
and in whose hands the efficient operation of the enterprise ultimately rests?'[17] In short, if you want results, there must be
bonuses.

I have rehearsed Berle and Means's arguments at such length, partly because they put them so nicely, but also to show how, back in 1932, the problems of modern capitalism were already in full view for those who cared to look. Most people were reluctant then to examine the realities with unprejudiced eyes, and they are scarcely less reluctant today, even after another gigantic crash has shown how badly things can spin out of control, if the controllers – that is, the directors and CEOs – lose their judgment and self-control. For this is surely the abiding and intrinsic flaw of the system, or lack of system. We pretend that the shareholders still possess powers that they effectively lost long ago, and we imagine that the behaviour of the corporation is disciplined by an array of checks and balances that are often no more than decorative today. Thus when the search for personal profit injects perverse incentives into the minds of the managers, there is nothing and nobody to stop them from pursuing a course of conduct that is against the interests of the company and all those who work for it and have money locked up in it.

The rise of the giant corporation dazzled Berle and Means, as it was to dazzle many who came after them. The future, they thought, would see the economic organism, now typified by the corporation, not only on an equal plane with the State, but possibly even superseding it as the dominant form of social organization. Politicians began to seem dusty and impotent figures beside these new supermen who were able with a flick of the finger to hire and fire the entire working population of a town, to build new towns and to desolate old ones.

We had, it seemed, experienced a 'managerial revolution', to quote the title of a hugely influential book published in 1941 by James Burnham, a former Trotskyite who was in later life to become a pillar of the American conservative movement. The book was subtitled 'What is happening in the world', and it argued that over a relatively short period, which Burnham dated

from the First World War, a new society had emerged and a new
social group, the managers, was now engaged on a drive for social
dominance, intending to exercise all the power and prestige that
belonged to any ruling class. Berle and Means had been right
about the separation of ownership from effective control, and the
managers had taken power as a result. Burnham believed that
roughly the same thing had happened in Nazi Germany and
Soviet Russia as had happened in Roosevelt's America. Whether
it was the State and the government that claimed ownership of the
means of production, or whether it was private shareholders, in
reality it was the managers and bureaucrats who ran the show.

George Orwell became fascinated by Burnham's book. While
half-agreeing with its analysis (which finds echoes in his two
dystopian fables *Animal Farm* and *Nineteen Eighty-Four*), he
accused Burnham of equating social-democratic states with Nazi
and Communist states. This rather overstates the thesis. Through
all his changes of view (he began life as a Catholic and ended it as
one too), Burnham was always a democrat in his benign crusty
way. All he was saying was that if you wanted to know who called
the shots in any modern society, regardless of the political system,
it was the managers – which is not the same as saying that all
modern states are identical.

The Managerial Revolution is, however, ruinously flawed.
Burnham had only recently escaped from his years of Trotskyite
agitation, culminating in fierce exchanges with the exiled Trotsky
himself, fuming down in Mexico. Though he had abandoned not
only Trotsky but Marx and Marxism, Burnham could not shake
himself free from their basic conviction that capitalism was
doomed. It was clear, he still thought, that 'the capitalist organization of society has entered its final years[18] . . . It will disappear
in a couple of decades at most and perhaps in a couple of years.'[19]
This was largely because 'Experience has already shown that
there is not the slightest prospect of ridding capitalism of mass

unemployment.'[20] Accordingly, the State would take over. The social dominance of the all-conquering managers would be based upon State ownership of major instruments of production.[21] 'There will be no direct property rights in the major instruments of production vested in individuals.' There would be no more capitalists. No individual would be able to make money by investing private capital in economic enterprise. 'Capital, so far as it would be proper to use the term will be supplied entirely, or almost entirely through the State.'[22] Capitalism as we had known it would be 'smashed' – a verb to which Burnham, like his Marxist mentors, is addicted.

Burnham was hopelessly wrong about all this. And he was wrong about something else too. His Marxist past had trained him to concentrate his attention upon manufacturing industry, especially the then staple heavier industries – coal, steel, automobiles and railways. It was, he thought, the managers of these industries and other such industries yet unborn who were to become the demigods of the new age. What he called 'finance-executives', or indeed the executives of the service industries, scarcely got a look-in. Their activities seemed to him parasitic on the scientists, engineers and assembly-line managers who actually produced the goods. Thus he defined his 'managerial class' too narrowly, and he located it in the wrong place. He failed to foresee that in the new dispensation it was those finance executives – board directors, chief executive officers and their bankers – who would collar the biggest share of the spoils, while the engineers and scientists who worked for them often continued to receive relatively modest salaries. This misunderstanding was rather influential, because it blinded Burnham's readers to the real whereabouts of power.

After the Second World War, this belief in the manager as master of the universe became the new orthodoxy, not least because it seemed that it was the managers, both in government and the private sector, who had won the war, certainly not the capitalists. This belief was aided by the wisecracks of John Kenneth Galbraith, the world's most popular economist (not a title for which the competition was hot). Galbraith was a brilliant rhetorician if not a brilliant economist. One of his greatest skills was to poke fun at what he called 'the conventional wisdom' – in the process broadcasting an equally conventional wisdom of his own.

In polemics such as *American Capitalism* (1952), *The New Industrial State* (1967) and most famously *The Affluent Society* (1958), Galbraith did more than anyone else to popularize the view that the large corporation was the new master of the world. Big Business was the Cosa Nostra of the modern economy, the managerial class were its remorseless Capos, themselves unconsciously controlled by the System, or Systems. Galbraith grouped large-scale manufacturing firms under the title of 'the planning system'. Opposed to them in his scheme were the smaller-scale, predominantly service firms, which he grouped together as 'the market system'. The planning system, according to Galbraith, served the interests not of the public but of the executives, managers, scientists, engineers and marketing men who together made up its 'technostructure'. This technostructure was primarily concerned not with making a profit for the firm but with maximizing its own status, security and remuneration. The way they did it was to take the growth of the firm as their primary aim. The planning system first decided what it would produce, then controlled the costs of its raw materials and components by forcing long-term contract on its weaker suppliers in the market system and in poorer countries overseas. After amiably settling the demands of its own trade unions, these giant corporations then went on to set their prices at a congenial level and set about persuading the public to buy their goods by the deceitful but irresistible techniques of advertising, or in the case of goods to be sold to the government, such as defence equipment, by bribing the relevant members of Congress and the bureaucracy. All quite simple really.

These masters of the universe then got down to the real business which was dividing up their own rewards. Here the sky was the limit and the shareholders merely a troublesome afterthought. As Galbraith famously put it: 'The salary of the chief executive of the large corporation is not a market reward for achievement. It is frequently in the nature of a warm personal gesture by the individual to himself.'

The essential flaw was the lack of any external check on the pay of top executives. By the end of the twentieth century, even the shareholders began to wake up to the fact that in some cases the self-remunerators were in effect looting the company. Indignant groups of shareholders began to insist that special remuneration committees be appointed to settle the pay of senior executives. In the UK, these demands were given impetus by a series of official reports on the governance of corporations – Cadbury 1992, Greenbury 1995, Hampel 1998.

These remuneration committees were intended to be impartial bodies, composed of non-executive directors who had no personal interest in the outcome. This was a naïve hope. For the non-execs were to be nominated by the existing executive directors who, not surprisingly, chose people very much like themselves. An executive director of one firm might well sit alongside one of his non-execs on the board of another firm where the non-exec was an executive. This mutual admiration society – and mutual remuneration network – could scarcely be expected to take an austere view of their colleagues' personal needs, and in most cases they did not.

Nor did they purse their lips at the size of the fringe benefits expected by CEOs to sweeten their labours. Pension pots worth millions of pounds were routine. So were clauses stipulating vast pay-offs for loss of office, if the CEO were to depart before his allotted time. This was to compensate for the crippling insecurity of the CEO's position in the new business world. But of course the generous basic salary and bonuses already offered handsome compensation for any shortness of tenure – and in fact some research tended to show that the CEO's average length of tenure had not altered much over the years. On top of that, stock options of heroic proportions were available to the CEO who succeeded in ramping up his company's share price to the required level, regardless of whether his actions were in the long-term interests of the firm.

These basic benefits were decorated by a profusion of perks of a kind that could scarcely be described as intrinsic to the workings of the business: memberships of golf clubs and health clubs, debentures for Wimbledon, boxes for Ascot or the Arsenal, school fees, rent-free country houses, and so on. The lifelong free dental work for Bill and Alberta Aldinger might catch the eye, but it was certainly not a unique or extreme demand. In fact, we do not have to presume that the Aldingers themselves would have insisted on this item. Increasingly, the frills were dreamed up by third parties, by the lawyers drawing up the contract of employment or by the headhunters who found the new recruit. These head-hunters were themselves paid vast sums for providing a list of suitable candidates, including a substantial percentage of the successful candidate's salary for the first few years – a further incentive to boost the level of that salary as high as possible.

This picture of the giant corporation whose power ranged over many countries was highly persuasive to many people in the 1950s and 60s. It was not only left-wingers like Tony Benn who believed that the 'multinationals' as they were now known 'have got far greater power to decide what is to happen in any country than its parliament has'.[23] Such was the power of these giants to shift their capital and their technologies over the surface of the

globe that Benn said that, meeting their top men as Britain's
Secretary of State for Energy, he 'felt like a parish councillor
meeting the Emperor'. As Anthony Sampson put it, 'The global
company overwhelming the small state has become a new ogre.'
Yet so indispensable were these companies for the generation of
prosperity that 'if there is one thing more alarming to a small
country than the presence of multinationals, it is their absence.'
Those poorer nations that had failed to attract investment from the
multinationals or had deliberately erected barriers to their entry
were likely to become poorer still. The multinational was a force
so omnipotent that it was foolish as well as futile to resist it.

The original insight of Berle and Means had been that in the
modern world the managers could and would ignore or override
the interests of their shareholders. That insight had now swollen
into a larger and even more alarming claim: that the managers had
now become so all-powerful that they could afford to ignore or
override the interests of governments and parliaments as well.
They were the masters not just of the peevish and functionless
shareholders, the *Doleanten* of the twentieth century; they were
the masters of all they surveyed.

Galbraith, like Burnham, like Keynes, got a lot of things wrong.
It was not true that the shareholder was doomed to disappear. Nor
was it true that the multinational company was invulnerable, irresistible and enduring. The laws of the market ultimately applied to
the pike as well as to the minnows. In our time, we have repeatedly seen great companies crash or be broken up or dwindle into
insignificance – GEC, ICI, Hanson, and half a dozen airlines that
once dominated the skies, not to mention all those mega banks.
The FTSE Index of the 100 leading shares has a constantly chang-
ing cast list.

Where the prophets were right was not so much on the economics as on the human psychology. What they saw with
merciless clarity was that, little by little, the managers of great

companies would feel free to run those companies largely in their own interests rather than in the interests of the shareholders, the customers or the workforce. Certainly the shareholders, the customers and the workforce had to be kept happy. But the ultimate determinant in any major decision – take-overs, mergers, disposals, expansion into new markets – was going to be: what's in it for us? Naturally, if the company is doing well by the normally accepted criteria, then its top managers will be justified in increasing their own rewards. But what has shocked the public are those numerous instances when the managers have abused their power to take more out of the company when its performance has been at best mediocre. At the worst, this is little better than looting. Even on the most charitable interpretation, it is an unmistakable demonstration of the fact that the interests of the managers are no longer aligned with those of the company.

The depersonalizing of savings

For a short period in the mid–1980s, I worked as a part-time adviser to a famous and long established merchant bank. Its premises in Bishopsgate were deeply impressive: there was a panelled hall with a butler of grave and imperturbable demeanour to greet you; marble washrooms of daunting splendour; and a fine partners' room where the partners sat opposite each other at huge mahogany desks smoking fat cigars although it was only nine o'clock in the morning. The scene can have changed little since their fathers and grandfathers sat smoking at each other before the Second or indeed the First World War. It was a scene of deeply reassuring affluence and stability.

I had known several of the directors since school or university and the welcome I received could not have been more friendly. The greatest possible efforts were made to initiate me into the mysteries of merchant banking. Yet I cannot claim that I ever penetrated to the heart of it. Large parts of the business continued to elude me. At some moments, I would survey the placid smoke-filled scene and find it incomprehensible exactly what it was that they did all day. Nor was I alone in this occasional bewilderment. The chief executive of the bank, who was also later a Governor of the Bank of England, confided to me after I had been there a few months: 'I don't have anything to do with these derivatives because I don't like to get mixed up in anything I don't understand.'

I stayed only a year because I came to the conclusion that I was not doing the bank any good and the bank was not doing me any good either, apart from overpaying me for my non-existent services. But in retrospect my bewilderment looks a slightly more laudable reaction. For it turned out that both the stability and the contentment of the place were illusory, and so to a considerable extent was its prosperity.

Within a year of my departure, the chairman Rupert Hambro, who had hired me, left the firm which bore his name together with his two younger brothers and set up a new boutique finance house which did extremely well. The corporate camaraderie which had so impressed me turned out to conceal a maelstrom of feuds and resentments. At the same time, it also emerged that the profits from most of the bank's activities had dwindled to very little, once the large salary bill had been paid. The underwriting of new issues, the corporate finance department, the inter-bank lending, everything that constituted old-fashioned merchant banking in fact – none of these was making enough money to secure the bank's long-term future. The only exception was the virtually separate retail arm, Hambro Insurance, which continued to gather in armfuls of premiums from the public, and the asset management side, which launched an array of unit trusts and other funds to private investors. But the banking side was flat, verging on moribund. A few years later, what was left of the bank was sold to a much bigger French bank, and the great house on Bishopsgate no longer stood proud and independent among the foremost names in the City.

This was a sharp lesson in the underlying fragility of all commercial enterprises, perhaps of all human enterprises. Almost nothing lasts for ever, and most things don't last for nearly as long as you expect. It is a hard lesson to accept until you have experienced it yourself. Our brains do not seem to be programmed to look out for the cracks in the foundations. The behemoths of the age always look as if they are here to stay.

But what my brief sojourn also taught me was that in the new City of the 1980s it was the people's savings that were the great fresh source of wealth. By persuading individual investors, large and small, to put their eggs in its alluring purpose-woven baskets, a bank could have access to a stream of income which would keep on flowing, pretty much regardless of the state of the stock market. As well as the established pension funds and life insurance, unit trusts and investment trusts, ingenious variants and subdivisions were devised: funds that spread their investments over a particular industry, such as mining or energy, or over a particular region, such as South America or the Far East, or which simply followed the FTSE indexes or its sub-indexes, the so-called tracker funds; there were funds of funds and even funds of funds of funds, which invested in a range of funds, each of which was itself a bundle of selected stocks and bonds. But in every case, come rain or shine, the fund manager could charge an annual fee, and perhaps an initial fee too, which might tot up to as much as 5 per cent of the value of the funds under management. There might be incentives built in for success, so that the fee increased if the fund's value rose beyond a certain point, but never, oh never a penalty for failure.

This was all most agreeable for bankers, and for some hard-pressed banks it was a source of salvation. In fact, it was so agreeable that many bright sparks quit banking in the strict sense and went straight into the new science of 'asset management' – claiming to look after other people's money better than they could themselves.

Almost nothing in finance is ever entirely new. And none of this was either. In the 1920s, in the stock market frenzy that led up to the Great Crash, there was a craze for investment trusts. This was an ingenious response to the perceived shortage of stock to feed to eager investors, especially small investors. There was only a limited quantity of capital out there in the real world, financing railroads and factories and chain stores. The simple answer was to multiply that quantity by promoting exciting new companies which would do no business of their own except to invest in other companies. In Britain there had been such investment trusts for a number of years. The City of London Trust had been launched in 1891, the Foreign and Colonial Investment Trust had its origins as far back as 1868, but they were sober and staid vehicles for canny savers, especially Scotsmen.

Now, inflated by American pizzazz and salesmanship, the investment trust took what was not yet described as a quantum leap. Often the new trust would have no office or furniture of its own; the sponsoring bank or broker would run it out of its own headquarters (as many such trusts are run to this day). Such was the respect for the financial genius of these promoters that the shares of the new trust would be snapped up by investors at far more than the total value of its underlying investments in real existing companies providing goods and services. By contrast, in less frantic times, the shares of investment trusts often stand at a discount to the total value of their underlying investments, because of the difficulty of unbundling them for sale.

The shares in the new trust would soar to dizzier heights, leaving the underlying value of its component stocks far behind. This premium seemed so delicious that the promoters saw the opportunity of doubling it by launching even more ingenious trusts whose principal or only assets might be the shares they held in the first trusts. By such means, middle-ranking bankers and brokers, such as Goldman Sachs, rapidly became giants of Wall Street, as they erected platform upon platform of these new financial constructions.

All this ended in tears, for the bankers and their customers alike, in 1929, or rather in the years 1929–32, for the crash took quite a time to bottom out. It was not until the 1960s and 70s that in Britain the movement for unit trusts in particular experienced a real resurgence, which has lasted more or less up to the present day. It was accelerated by the introduction of various tax-exempt savings schemes sponsored by the government of the day, such as TESSAs and ISAs. The Money sections of the newspapers, themselves a recent innovation, were filled with advertisements for every type of unit trust and in between ran long rivers of editorial copy offering advice on which fund to choose. Each year, as the deadline for putting your money into TESSAs or ISAs approached, the Money sections ballooned and the punters responded with their hard-earned billions.

From the point of view of the individual investor, this method of placing your savings appears to offer two advantages. You get a good spread of risk. Each fund may invest in twenty stocks or more, something which only a rich man could effectively do on his own account. This is a genuine advantage. The other supposed advantage is that you have an expert picking your stocks for you. He can tell you which stocks to go for, which to avoid, and guide you if you wish to venture into unfamiliar territory such as biotechnology or the Far East. As we shall see, this advantage is not so certain. Fund managers are creatures of fashion like the rest of us. They may all herd into one stock together at the wrong time and herd out again at the wrong moment too. The IT bubble of 2001 is but one of dozens of examples in history in which the professionals have been just as carried away as the amateurs. Worse still, the fund managers have an inbuilt incentive to shout 'Buy' in the hope of boosting the funds under management; recommendations to sell are less often heard.

What cannot be denied, though, is the staggering success of the fund managers' pitch for business. No change in the financial structure has been more striking than the decline of the individual private shareholder in the past half century. In 1963, 54 per cent of shares were held by private individuals. By 1981, that figure had dropped to 28 per cent. By 2011 the percentage was below 10 per cent. The campaign for wider share ownership has been a dismal failure, if you are talking about direct share ownership by private individuals.

In the years before these figures began to be systematically collected in the 1960s, the overwhelming majority of shares were in private hands. Now the fund managers rule the roost and award themselves the most glorious rewards for doing so. The Stock Exchange has become an oligarchy, in which a relatively small number of managers scoop a disproportionate share of company earnings for doing what private shareholders used to do for themselves with the aid of their brokers.

Savings are now almost entirely held collectively. In 1963, the unit trusts and insurance companies between them owned only about one fifth of shares in Britain. By 1998 they owned two thirds. In addition, many of the shares that are still privately owned are held in nominee accounts by banks, stockbrokers and City law firms. These companies will exercise on behalf of their clients many of the shareholders' functions, such as voting on rights issues and remuneration reports, so that, as far as governance of the investee companies goes, the private shareholders too may not play even a vestigial role in management.

So the great bulk of savings in the UK have been effectively *depersonalized*. The shareholder's functions are exercised by the fund managers and nominee account managers, not by the ultimate beneficial owners.

This then is the second great change in the relationship between the shareholder and the company he has invested in. The first, as we saw earlier, was to reduce him to near-total impotence because of his remoteness from the running of the company and because of the vast scatter of his fellow shareholders, who could not therefore be expected to combine to exercise any real oversight. In that first devil's bargain, he paid for the delicious freedom to buy and sell his shares without a backward glance by losing effective control over the day-to-day management of the company.

Now, in his second devil's bargain, he gains a comforting spread of risk by spreading his investments, but he loses any personal stake in the individual companies where his money is invested. His name is no longer on the shareholder's certificate. He is not a shareholder in United Widgets or Whizzo Detergents. Instead, he holds units in the Infallible Unit Trust or shares in the Rocksolid Investment Trust or a policy with the Sunset Pension Fund.

Within the general 'managerial revolution' across the whole economy, there is a second inner managerial revolution within finance. Now it is the money managers, not the ultimate owners of the money, who call the shots and who, as a consequence, collar a glittering share of the rewards. The Middleman is king.

The division of the spoils

So how does the new system work? Where exactly do your savings go after you have made out the cheque to your chosen money manager? This is not a subject much discussed in the Money sections. After all, the existence of these columns depends on advertising, which comes predominantly from those same money managers who hope to persuade the public to place even more of its savings in their direction. It would be discouraging if it were suggested that too much honey sticks to greedy paws. But occasionally a creditable effort is made to calculate the precise division of the spoils. What then, to borrow the evocative phrase minted by Charlie Munger – the partner of Warren Buffett, the most legendary investor of our age – is 'the croupier's take'?

Jonathan Ford, in a *Financial Times* article,[24] sets out nicely the moments in the process at which the croupier's rake sweeps across the table and deposits his share of the action down his personal chute. Let us say that the real return (after taking account of rising prices) on your stock market investments averages out over the years at 5 or 6 per cent. That doesn't sound too bad, but that is only the beginning.

The growing craze for share options to reward top executives means that, according to Standard & Poor's figures, in 2002 one fifth of reported profits was set aside for these indispensable incentives. Bang, as Ford points out, goes one per cent of the shareholder's profit. He suggests that we should then dock another half a percentage point to cover the fees paid to investment banks by companies for mergers, acquisitions and other services rendered. Then allow one per cent for commissions to brokers and for the 'spread' between the bid and offer price of shares. On top of all this, a fund manager will on average expect one per cent for his trouble. So the return has pretty well halved, and that is before the poor retail investor has paid his stamp duty and his taxes.

But the croupier, as Ford points out, can and does increase his take still further, simply by spinning the wheel more often. The more frequently that fund managers buy and sell their shares, the larger the croupier's take. In every sort of market over the past few decades the increase in turnover or 'churn' has been remarkable. In 1965, the turnover of British equities, for example, was worth 10 per cent of Gross Domestic Product. In 2007, turnover had risen to almost 300 per cent. If a pension fund turns over the equivalent of all the investor's holdings each year – which is quite typical – then over a 25-year period the costs of all this to-ing and fro-ing will reduce the original value of the pension fund by more than a quarter. In other words, this is a highly lucrative tax on savings. I cannot see any way in which it could be justified as optimizing the allocation of capital.

In a similar calculation, a *Daily Telegraph* investigation reported that no less than £7.3 billion was being skimmed off our savings every year by City bankers, brokers and asset managers.[25] According to David Norman, a former chief executive of Credit Suisse Asset Management, an investor putting £50,000 into a fund providing typical returns over twenty-five years would lose a total of £108,000 over the period because of unnecessary and extortionate charges. There is the initial charge on the investment which might be as much as 4 per cent, then an annual management fee of around 1.5 per cent. Then of course there is the 'churn' – the constant buying and selling of the stocks in the portfolio, which may cost the investor up to 1.8 per cent in further commissions. Nor is there much evidence that such 'active' fund management is likely to beat the market in the long or even the medium term – or outstrip the performance of the far cheaper alternative of a tracker fund which simply uses a computer to mimic the movements of the market.

The senior managers of these funds take huge personal scoops out of the funds entrusted to their care. Michael McLintock, head of M&G, the Prudential's investment management arm, received a bonus of £1.7 million in cash and shares in 2009 and also had £2.5 million worth of shares released to him under a three-year performance scheme. McLintock was among those fund managers who received a letter from Lord Myners, the City minister, asking him to explain how they set about keeping some sort of control over the pay of bankers and other senior executives in the companies they invested in. McLintock replied blandly that his group was 'playing our part through our active dialogue with boards and remuneration committees'.[26] Which doesn't sound exactly dynamic, but then what can you expect from a conversation between people who basically share the same views about the levels of pay to which they are entitled?

We are getting close to the heart of the matter. In brute terms, we have one set of oligarchs – the fund managers – whose task it is to approve the size of salaries, bonuses and pension pots for another set of oligarchs – the CEOs, board members and senior managers of the companies they invest in. Alas, the interests of the two sets are all too neatly aligned. In many cases, they may be the same people, with the representatives of the big fund managers taking seats on the boards of those companies. Neither side has any reason to insist on pay restraint. What matters is that the share price should be boosted by whatever means (often regardless of the long-term health of the company), for it is on the share price that will depend the bonuses for both sets of managers.

The effects of this unconstrained drive for higher pay and other rewards has been spectacular. It is hard to think of any comparable period in our history when the top earners have streaked so far ahead of ordinary mortals in so short a space of time. Between 2000 and 2008, the FTSE All-Share Index fell by 30 per cent. But cash payments to executives increased by 80 per cent. The figures are no less startling for the single crash year of 2008: the stock market fell by 30 per cent and the salaries of top executives rose by 10 per cent. The average annual pay received by the bosses of major American companies reached an amazing $9.1 million. The highest-paid boss of a multinational operation in Britain was Bart Becht, CEO of Reckitt Benckiser, which older readers will remember as the manufacturer of the old-style detergent Reckitt's Blue Bag, but which now makes a few other things as well. Becht received roughly £37 million in 2008, the equivalent of the pay received by 1,374 average workers at his Slough HQ.[27] Sir Terry Leahy of Tesco was paid nearly 900 times as much as the average Tesco employee. Sir Martin Sorrell, head of the advertising firm WPP, got 631 times the wage of his average employee, Paul Adams of BAT 391 times.

The great New York banker J. P. Morgan (1837–1913) once said that no one at the top of a company should earn more than twenty times those at the bottom. I doubt whether that was true at Morgan's own bank at the end of the nineteenth century. It certainly is not true now. Recent research suggests that the average pay ratio of CEO to employee has risen from 47 to 128 over the past ten years. This of course takes no account of all the perks that gild the executive's package and are not available to his underlings.

In one remarkable case, that of François Barrault, the head of BT's Global Services offshoot, the perks outweighed the basic salary. Before he was fired on account of the company's appalling performance, Barrault was picking up handsome payments for housing, school fees, company car, insurance, club membership, home security, financial advice and health care.

By contrast, over the past thirty years, lower-paid workers, the bottom 10 per cent, have seen their share of every £100 generated by the economy fall from £16 to £12, while the amount paid to the elite, the top 1 per cent, has increased from £2 to £5, if we include their bonuses, as we should because these are now an integral part of the expected pay package.[28] Matters are if anything worse for those at the bottom of the heap in the US, where real pay rates scarcely rose at all in the 1980s and 90s. Families managed to maintain or improve their standard of living only by dint of more family members going out to work, working longer hours and taking shorter holidays.

Efforts to restrain the executive pay stampede have made only modest headway. Great hopes were placed on a campaign for shareholders to use their new right to vote against the company's remuneration report. But the average vote against these reports reached a peak in 2004 and then began to fall back again. PIRC, the campaigners for better corporate governance, and the pension fund Railpen still have hope. Since the voting on remuneration was introduced, the element of a director's pay that is dependent on long-term performance certainly has increased. And the length of directors' contracts has been sharply reduced, in most cases to one year rather than three, four or five as used to be common. This reduces the size of the 'golden parachute' if they are sacked. Every now and then, the 'say on pay' does make an impact. After its downfall, the Royal Bank of Scotland suffered a 90 per cent vote against its remuneration report because of the intolerably large pension pot awarded to Fred Goodwin.

But these are rare and extreme cases. And as often as not, even a substantial vote against a remuneration report will be blithely disregarded. The top executives at the recruitment firm Robert Walters kept their bonuses, which had doubled the money they took home, despite the shareholders voting against the rises by 25–22 million, for the votes are purely advisory. It is a tiny but revealing irony that the remuneration report was signed off by Lady Judge, who is chairman of the Pension Protection Fund.[29] At the 2011 AGM of the bookmaker's William Hill, 38 per cent of shareholders voted against the 56 per cent increase in pay for the company's chief executive, Ralph Topping, taking his total remuneration to £1.65 million. Since Topping became CEO in 2008, the shares have sunk to 218.7p from 280p. Five weeks later, in a statement that failed even to mention the shareholders' revolt or the mediocre performance, the chairman of William Hill, Gareth Davis, announced that Topping would also be given £1.2 million worth of company shares to deter him from leaving the company – an event which sounds on the face of it unlikely, since Topping has spent all his life with William Hill, starting as a 'Saturday boy' at a Glasgow betting shop.[30] The argument that a CEO must be paid megabucks to prevent him from being poached by a competitor looks a little shaky. The High Pay Commission could find only one such case in any FTSE 100 company in the past five years, and no case at all of a CEO being lured away by an overseas competitor.[31] It is hard to avoid the conclusion that these oligarchs live in some kind of parallel moral universe.

Almost worse in many people's eyes than Goodwin's pay-off was his inability to understand what he had done wrong and his refusal to make any kind of restitution or even any unforced statement of contrition. Here he was soon to be rivalled by the chutzpah that the chief executive of BP, Tony Hayward, displayed after the oil spill in the Gulf of Mexico and the size of the package

he walked away with after he was forced out: a year's pay of more
than £1 million and a pension pot valued at £11 million, which
was reckoned to deliver him an annual pension of £584,000
when he turned sixty. It was Hayward's predecessor, the egregious
Lord Browne, who was fingered as responsible for the corner-
cutting on safety. What was so deeply shocking about Hayward's
conduct was his repellent mixture of nonchalance and self-pity in
coping with a catastrophe in which eleven men died and an entire
coastline was devastated. He kept complaining of being vilified
and demonized, dismissing the spill as 'tiny' in comparison with
the amount of water in the Gulf and saying 'I want my life back',
before being spotted on his yacht in the Solent while the clean-up
in the Gulf was still in progress. His chairman, Carl-Henric
Svanberg, became almost equally notorious for saying that BP
always looked after 'the small people'. He too was spotted on his
yacht, in his case off Thailand. Such conduct convinces us that
company chief executives are beginning to imitate not only the
conspicuous consumption of the aristocrats of the *ancien régime* but
also their arrogance and contempt for ordinary people. We are
beginning to find the answer to the question that Berle and Means
asked all those years ago: how will the new merchant princes
behave? And the answer is not a pleasant one.

All this has happened relatively recently. In retrospect, what is
remarkable is how long it took for mere managers to realize that
they now had the whip hand and could with impunity grab a
huge slice of the action. For many decades, the appetites of the
managers, in both the public and the private sectors, were constrained by stern institutional and political inhibitions. In a
devastating article in the *New Yorker*,[32] Malcolm Gladwell points
out that between roughly 1930 and 1960 the rewards enjoyed by
top managers in the US actually fell. In 1935, American lawyers
made on average four times the country's per capita income – a
modest enough multiple – but by 1958 that figure was down to

2.4. The President of DuPont, Crawford Greenewalt, told Congress in 1958 that he was taking home half what his predecessor had taken home thirty years earlier. People at the top of their professions then simply did not expect to be paid vast multiples of the earnings of their colleagues on average and lower salaries. This was as true of sporting heroes as it was of lawyers, bankers and managers. Star pro baseball players, like star football players in the UK, were paid peanuts.

At the dawn of modern capitalism, the era in which J. P. Morgan flourished, there had been some conspicuous tycoons who paid themselves enormous salaries and lived on a lavish scale. Elbert H. Gary, the President of US Steel, was estimated to be paid a salary of $100,000 in 1903, at a time when the average industrial annual wage was no more than $700. But Gary was also a pioneer in offering his employees the opportunity to buy stock at below-market prices and rewarding long-term workers with bonuses. In any case, he was exceptional. Most top company executives earned far less. George Thomas Washington, in a rare study of this obscure subject (obscure because then and now companies have been incurably secretive about how much they paid their top people), concluded that, until the 1920s, 'the corporate executive simply had no place in the upper income levels'.[33]

In the Roaring Twenties, executive pay did begin to take off in a serious way, but this trend was severely shaken, if not brought to a shuddering halt, by the Great Crash of 1929 and the recriminations that followed it. Between 1932 and 1934, the *New York Times* published a series of articles castigating executive compensation schemes, calling for executive salaries to be lowered, for a government inquiry and even for taxes on excessive pay. The US Senate badgered the Federal Trade Commission to launch an inquiry into executive pay. The resulting report, published in February 1934, was an eye-opener and probably did a lot to dampen executive pay levels for years to come. Of course, the oligarchs fought back in time-honoured style. Lammot du Pont told the annual stockholders meeting of General Motors in 1938 that 'in meeting their obligation to secure the best brains possible to manage the property, the directors of General Motors had to establish executive salaries in competition with other employers of executive talent, as well as in competition with what high-class executives could earn in business with themselves.' Just what CEOs today tell their indignant shareholders. Pretty much too what Sir Martin Sorrell of WPP told the newspapers in October 2011. His own basic salary of £1 million was 'very low', he said, and his total income, which had risen by 83 per cent to £4.2 million, was fully justified, because 'the only planet I am living on is looking at our company in terms of the competition – that's the planet.'[34] In fact, I can only echo what Katherine M. Savarese says in her valuable paper in 2010, on the history of arguments about executive pay in the US, 'I have been continually struck by the amazing, if somewhat eerie, similarities of the sentiments expressed by reporters and CEOs in the early twentieth century and what is being said by those same groups today.'[35]

Income inequality in America shows a remarkable U-shaped curve, beginning with extremely high levels in 1928, dropping for most of the rest of the twentieth century and only in recent years increasing again to 1920s levels. Professor Emmanuel Saez of Berkeley records that inequality of income in the US is now at an all-time high.[36] The evidence suggests that this U-shaped curve applies to the UK too, especially to the financial sector. The High Pay Commission records that:

... from 1909 to 1933 the financial sector was a high-wage industry. During the 1930s a dramatic shift occurred and the financial sector lost much of its wage premium relative to the rest of the economy. This dramatic drop was followed by a more moderate decline from 1950 to 1980. Indeed by the 1980s wages in the financial sector were similar, on average, to wages in the rest of the economy. However, during the stock market 'big bang' in the 1980s there was a rapid shift and the financial sector became once again a high-skill, high-wage industry. It is notable that relative wages in finance had returned to the levels of the 1930s by 2006.[37]

Over the course of the twentieth century the pay of bankers and brokers has soared far above the rest of us, then come back down to our level, then soared back up out of sight again. There is no good *economic* reason why it should not come back down once more. And there are excellent moral reasons why it needs to.

These violent movements to and fro over the years are not strictly determined by supply and demand. They blossom out of the prevailing business culture. All sorts of factors may influence the amount set aside for the 'executive comp' – it is a piquant oddity that executives should need to be 'compensated' for getting out of bed in the morning while the rest of us simply toil for wages. The level and structure of taxation, the laws and regulations governing fees, commissions and other income that the company hopes to receive (or the lack of any such laws and regulations), the restraining hand of dominant shareholders in the company, if there are any – all these may play a part. But not the least important factors are the prestige and respect enjoyed by the executive class. When their prestige is at rock bottom, as it was after the Great Crash of 1929, their pay slumps. When they are widely perceived, not least by themselves, as masters of the universe, their pay soars.

The real point is that, whatever CEOs may say, competition alone is not the implacable determinant of pay levels and hence of inequality. Social expectations may rein in the pace of top people's pay increases, or they may gee it up to a frenzied gallop. Such expectations will vary hugely between one period and another, and between one country and another. It was not until the 1960s that Player Power in both business and sport really began to take off. Today, half the income of a successful merchant bank such as Goldman Sachs or a successful football team such as Chelsea may be consumed by the players' wages. As Gladwell puts it, Capital has crumbled in the face of a determined collective assault by Talent – even when Talent is producing mediocre or even dismal results.

In the public sector too, the rewards earned by management in the early postwar decades were kept in check, largely by those harassed and underrated defenders of the public interest, ministers of the Crown. Ministers directly controlled the pay of the chiefs of the Coal Board and the railways and dozens of other public or publicly owned bodies; and while the salary scales of doctors and dentists, headmasters and senior civil servants and university vice chancellors were recommended by outside bodies, it was ministers who had the final say and who would have to defend their decisions to MPs and to the media. If you look back at the diaries and memoirs of the period, you will be struck by how much time and effort ministers spent in disposing of these ticklish matters in a way that did not affront public opinion.

One of the first consequences of privatization was to relieve ministers of these thankless tasks and set managers free to determine their own pay. How aghast we were to see unremarkable managers of public utilities transformed overnight into superstars who needed to be paid three times as much as before. The *locus classicus* was the case of Cedric Brown of British Gas – something about the name suggested irredeemable plod. The whimpers of Sid and other shareholders and stakeholders could be safely disregarded. With one bound, the manager was free at last to fulfil the delicious destiny mapped out by Berle and Means half a century earlier.

The ballooning of executive pay in the private sector has been copied, admittedly from a much lower starting point, in public institutions, even in those where there are no commercial risks, no commercial competitors or analogues and no serious measure of success or failure, let alone of profit and loss. In 2005–6, the Director-General of the BBC, Mark Thompson, received a salary of £609,000, up from £459,000 the year before. This was in a period when the BBC was economizing by shedding 3,000 staff. The governors of the BBC said that the increase was part of a two-year process to bring the pay of top executives up to 'market levels', heedless of the fact that the commercial sector of broadcasting was in deep financial trouble at the time, not least because it had been paying everyone too much. The governors kept their word. The following year, Mr Thompson was paid £788,000. By this time, his deputies and department heads had all risen into the £300,000–400,000 bracket – many of them lifelong BBC employees who would have been reluctant to leave the Corporation. By 2008–9, Thompson was receiving £834,000. No fewer than forty-seven BBC executives were earning more than the Prime Minister's salary of £192,250.

Nor is the BBC unique. Then chief executive of the Post Office, Adam Crozier received a 26 per cent pay rise in 2006, taking his total remuneration to £1.29 million. In that same year, the employees of the Post Office received an average pay rise of 2.9 per cent. The Post Office pointed out that £469,000 of Crozier's earnings came as a performance bonus. But this is not exactly convincing as a justification, for this was the year when the Post Office finally ended twice-daily deliveries and began its long-term programme of closing thousands of branch post offices. Since then, the standard of service has plunged to an all-time low, being plagued by a series of national and local strikes.

The heads of NHS quangos too are in the habit of receiving double-digit pay rises, while nurses and clerical staff are lucky to receive a third of that. Most NHS chiefs too have overtaken the Prime Minister's salary and are likely to charge further ahead if the non-execs on their boards continue to take this generous view of their deserts. Ron Kerr, for example, the chief executive of Guy's and St Thomas' NHS Foundation Trust, earned £270,000 in 2008–9, after receiving a 12 per cent pay rise in a single year. Even the regulator set up to scrutinize NHS Foundation Trusts, Monitor as it is called, recently awarded all its board members an 8 per cent rise, taking them up to £237,500 per annum. Other State regulators are beneficiaries of the same trend. Ed Richards, the head of Ofcom, receives over £400,000 a year. The chief executive of the UK Hydrographic Office had a rise of 16 per cent to take his pay up to £252,000 in 2008–9. Three board members at the National Treatment Agency for Substance Misuse received pay rises of 17 per cent, which reflected bonuses earned the previous year. Isn't there something a bit sad about importing the bonus culture into such a redemptive business as getting people off drugs?

University vice chancellors have increasingly been remunerated on a scale which bears little or no relation to the money earned by their wretched lecturers. Professor Sir Howard Newby, the Vice Chancellor of Liverpool, was paid £386,000 in 2008–9, an increase of 20 per cent on the year before; the Provost of University College, London, Professor Malcolm Grant, saw his pay top the £400,000 mark after a rise of 15 per cent. Somewhere above £300,000 seemed to have become the going rate, after a series of massive leaps from the old, much more modest levels. With the heads of universities as with other top jobs in the public sector, it was simply taken for granted that the rewards needed to approach those on offer in the commercial sector. No serious effort was made to demonstrate why the risks run and the skills demanded were in any way comparable. It is clear that none of these public sector managers would have achieved anything like

THE DIVISION OF THE SPOILS 71

the same levels of pay if their remuneration were still subject to parliamentary approval; that is, if ministers had to fear a roasting in the Chamber or in a select committee.

We have already seen how capitalism has always been vulnerable to various types of corrosion. Outright looting and the distortions of monopoly are nothing new. But what I think is new is the *pervasiveness* of capitalism, especially in its preferred form of the limited liability joint stock company, nowadays the plc. In the early days of the Dutch East Indies Company or the Royal Bank of Scotland, and in the centuries that followed, the economy was made up of half-a-dozen types of organization: there were single owners of factories and mines and farms and landed estates, there were partnerships in professional undertakings – lawyers, GPs, publishers, banks, stockbrokers, and so on – there were family firms, there were mutual and co-operative enterprises, and non-profit-making public trusts and associations, and many variants of these, both large and small. The joint stock companies were certainly powerful, especially from the mid-nineteenth century on, when they began to enjoy legally limited liability. But they were not so universal or so dominant then as they are today. In fact, it is only very recently that what is now called 'the PLC model' became so ubiquitous, taking over building societies and other mutual financial institutions, remodelling the old partnerships of professional men, and invading public and/or charitable bodies such as schools and hospitals.

Many charities have grown enormous trading arms, the managers of which enjoy mega salaries. Look at the extraordinary saga of the Colonial Development Corporation, founded by the Attlee government as a philanthropic enterprise to assist farmers in the poorest countries of the Empire. After being privatized by Tony Blair, it is today a massive private equity fund which seeks out the most profitable investment opportunities across the world, not usually in agriculture at all and usually in the richer rather than the poorer countries of the Commonwealth, and which naturally dishes out large rewards to the top managers who have engineered this transformation.

Here we encounter for the first time what I would call the *alchemist oligarch,* the sharp operator who perceives a massive business opportunity where the rest of us see only a public service. He is the alchemist who converts non-profit-making base metal into untold gold. Nowhere is the triumph of this agile entrepreneur more conspicuous than in the field of sport. The Fédération Internationale de Football Association (FIFA), the International Olympic Committee (IOC), the Fédération Internationale de l'Automobile (FIA) – all these organizations, set up for public benefit before the First World War, led a largely blameless if unadventurous life for decades in Zurich or Lausanne or Paris, until their potential for exploitation became too juicy to be missed.

What began as public service is now big business. Millions of dollars are now paid, above board, to those who secure and administer championships and televise them and, under the counter, in even larger bribes to those who decide the venues. Leaving aside the accusations of corruption against him, Sepp Blatter, the interminable head of FIFA, is paid a million dollars a year for starters. The bribes paid to secure recent World Cups are reckoned to be many times that. Nor does the Olympic code of sportsmanship extend to the decision-making process on venues for the Games. Evidence was found to show that no fewer than twenty of the 110 IOC members had received large bribes to vote for Salt Lake City for the 2002 Winter Olympics. The IOC Korean vice president was jailed in 2004 for embezzling more than $3 million from sports organizations he controlled and for accepting $700,000 in bribes. He is said to have secured the Summer Olympics for South Korea in 1988. According to a BBC *Panorama* programme,[38] these days there are professional agents who promise to secure the votes of Committee members, at a steepling price. For nobody could possibly argue that the problem of corruption has been seriously addressed. As I write, four members of FIFA's executive are suspended pending the results of an inquiry by FIFA's ethics committee, with two more members under suspicion. João Havelange, the 95-year-old honorary president of FIFA, submitted his resignation from the IOC in December 2010, having previously been accused by BBC *Panorama* of accepting a million-dollar bribe. Blatter himself, who is also a member of the IOC *ex officio* as head of FIFA, condemns the IOC for a lack of transparency. 'It is, I would say, a club. In the 115 members of the IOC only 45 are directly linked to sport. The other 70 are individually appointed members'[39] – that is, they are the beneficiaries of patronage at national level which elevates them to membership of the international *nomenklatura* of sport, with all its free air fares and five-star hotels, trinkets and junkets, and outright cash bribes.

But the most striking examples of alchemist oligarchy need involve no illegality. There was nothing illegal in the battle that Max Mosley and Bernie Ecclestone fought and won to remove the rights to Formula One Grand Prix racing, especially the television rights, from the dozy non-profit-making FIA and begin making millions for themselves. Bernie Ecclestone is currently estimated to be worth about £1.5 billion.

So when he donated £1million to the Labour Party in January 1997, he was only shelling out small change. And it was of course purely coincidental that later that year he should have secured a meeting with Tony Blair to plead that Formula One should be excluded from the new ban on tobacco advertising, which was such an important source of its revenue. Mr Blair was, as he told us in his own defence, 'a pretty straight kind of guy', and there could be no question of bribery. But he was overruling both his own Health Minister and the European Union directive which instigated the ban.

The whole affair was extraordinarily reminiscent of the way the great Soviet oligarchs have gained and secured their billions: by privileged access to the top and by the subversion of established structures designed to protect the public welfare. The conversion of public assets into market goods is an extremely difficult business to manage, and in the West as in Russia the alchemist oligarch usually runs rings round the bureaucrat (even when there is no bribery involved). This intertwining of economic muscle and political power is one of the unmistakable features of oligarchy, and it is painfully visible in Britain now. In the postwar years, the conventions erred in the other direction. Politicians and senior civil servants were extremely leery of contact with big business-men, except on carefully constructed occasions. I remember nervous civil servants actually refusing to attend seminars at which businessmen might be present. That was absurdly stuffy and cut Whitehall off from the real world. But have we now gone too far the other way?

In the spring of 2009, both David Cameron for the Opposition and the government announced that in future the top executives of quangos would have their salaries frozen or cut, or at the very least enjoy no larger percentage pay rises than the rest of their staff. But the damage is already done. The circulating elites – 'the stakeholders' as they like to call themselves in the quangos – have successfully conspired to elevate themselves above the common herd. There is no chance of compressing the differentials back to the old levels of the 1960s.

In any case, freezes and even actual cuts are likely to prove temporary. The pressure will return to push top people's pay up to 'market levels', aided by the insidious mantra of 'working to the top quartile'. You do not have to be a mathematical genius to see that if every fresh pay settlement is fitted into the top 25 per cent of the existing range of settlements, then that range will be steadily tugged upwards, so that all the players in the game benefit. This is telling evidence that the upward pressure is not merely a transient deviation from sensible behaviour. It is both systemic and conspiratorial.

Whether in public or private bodies, the awards are made by colleagues on the board, who may be non-executive but who regularly sit around the same table in this and other boards and belong to the same revolving elite. These elites are welfare capitalism's equivalent of the *nomenklatura* in Soviet Russia. Once you are on the inside, you stay inside. One board membership deserves another, one nice pay rise sets the 'market level' for the next one. The loss of a full-time executive post is speedily compensated, not just by the previously agreed pay-off, but by the offer of another comparable job or at any rate by a portfolio of non-executive directorships. Only in very rare cases – Fred Goodwin may be one – does failure make the CEO responsible a pariah. Andy Hornby, who had led HBOS into follies as extreme as Goodwin (some say his loan book was even worse), was speedily consoled with the top job at Boots, though he did not last long there.

In this world, a director who regularly votes for the lowest plausible pay rise for his comrades is unlikely to prosper. He is the equivalent of the man who never stands his round, or the journalist on expenses who never signs the restaurant bill for his colleagues' lunch. Ebenezer Scrooge would never make a non-exec.

The overall outcome of this whole ratcheting-up process should come as no surprise. Professor John Hills, in his report *An Anatomy of Economic Inequality in the UK*,[40] found that the average household wealth of the top 10 per cent was over 100 times higher than the wealth of the poorest 10 per cent, £853,000 as against £8,000. Income inequalities in 2007–8 were at the highest level for half a century. Of course, changes in taxation could reshape the distribution of income and, at the very least, slow down this drift towards renewed inequality. But it is doubtful how much impact any such changes would have when the tendencies in pay-setting at both ends of the scale might have been designed to widen the gulf: at the bottom, pay levels in the service industries are sharply restrained by competition from immigrants and, in manufacturing, by the threat of relocation overseas; while, at the top, pay levels are egged on by the genial conspirators of the remuneration committee. Never before in our postwar history have we had a system which was so strongly geared to deepen inequality.

The three illusions

Any impartial observer would, I think, be vaguely aware of the corrosions of the economic system that I have been listing, or at least would have a shrewd suspicion that something was wrong and that the corrosion had been building up for some considerable time, probably decades. There have been too many sickening financial crashes, exploded bubbles and jarring crunches over the past half-century to assume blandly that, by and large, the system has been working well enough. Yet there has been little appetite for reform, indeed little inclination to identify the shortcomings. Either we have been pretending that we have not noticed anything amiss, or we genuinely have failed to notice. Why?

There seem to me to be three broad reasons for our misguided insouciance. They bleed into each other, but each is sufficiently distinct to be treated on its own. I'll call these illusions, or excuses, and they are these: 'The market is always right', 'Big is beautiful' and 'Complexity equals progress'. Let us take them in turn.

The market is always right. In the 1960s – that decade which in retrospect seems in economic terms so placid and benign – there had emerged the Efficient Market Hypothesis. This hypothesis was developed by Professor Eugene Fama at the University of

Chicago School of Business. The germ of it had first been published by a French mathematician, Louis Bachelier, in his dissertation as far back as 1900. Bachelier's Theory of Speculations built on the observation that even professional investors were in the long run unable to outperform the market. This suggested that the prices of traded assets already reflected all the known information about their value, and that the price would change as soon as any relevant fresh information became available. As a general rule, therefore, the value of a stock was already 'in the price', or very soon would be, as soon as investors got to know of the latest news – the appointment of a dynamic new chief executive, a good or bad profits forecast in the pipeline, the discovery of a new oilfield or gold seam. All the actors in the business of investment were assumed to be rational and alert. Even if individual players made mistakes, their mistakes would balance out to give a true valuation.

The Efficient Market Hypothesis, or EMH, became popular among economists and professional market-makers and analysts. The small investor might find it a bit discouraging, since it tended to dampen his hopes of beating the market. The EMH was helped along by the prestige of some of its foremost supporters such as the great Paul Samuelson, Nobel laureate and author of *Economics,* the fat brown-and-grey textbook that first-year university students in my day were expected to treat as their bible and prayer book rolled into one.[41] Samuelson was temperamentally the sort of man who expected things to roll along as smoothly in the future as they had in the past. As late as 1989, one of his textbooks continued to proclaim that 'The Soviet economy is proof that, contrary to what many sceptics had earlier believed, a socialist command economy can function and even thrive.'

To someone who has never heard of EMH before, the theory sounds a little weird. There is a whiff of Dr Pangloss in Voltaire's *Candide* about it: 'Everything is for the best in the best of all possible worlds.' What about all those Stock Exchange bubbles and crashes that we read about in the newspapers? Surely it won't do to brush these aside as merely 'necessary corrections'. After all, some of these collapses have a nasty way of turning into prolonged slumps. On the eve of the Great Crash of 1929, the *New York Times* index of industrial stocks closed at 224. Nearly three years later, in July 1932, it stood at only 58, barely a quarter of its high. This violent and prolonged collapse could scarcely be explained as the outcome of rational investors acting on their rational expectations, since the crash on the Stock Exchange helped to cause the Great Depression, rather than the other way round.

Some might conclude rather that the EMH is a feather bed for featherheaded optimists. Nothing can go wrong because we are all sensible people buying and selling on strictly scientific principles. In particular, what the EMH encourages is the belief that the latest financial wheeze is always a boon to humanity. This illusion was first visible in the 1920s when two innovations in the financial system contributed, especially in the United States, to the speed and ferocity of the Crash.

The first innovation, as we have seen, was the enhanced craze for investment trusts. The other great innovation of the 1920s was also not strictly new, but had hitherto been practised on a modest scale. This was the practice of the broker's loan. You did not even have to stump up the cash to invest in these exciting new opportunities. Your broker merely advanced you the money at an agreeably low rate of interest. As the stock soared, the whole transaction more than paid for itself.

Galbraith points out in his masterwork, *The Great Crash of 1929* (1954), that this avalanche of speculative money was ultimately based on existing businesses which were perfectly sound, not on fanciful or fraudulent projects 'For a Wheel of Perpetual Motion' or 'For an Undertaking which shall in due time be revealed', to quote only two of the most alluring prospectuses in the South Sea Bubble of 1729. The bubble of 1929 was entirely generated by and within the financial world, although its terrible consequences spread far beyond, into every state in the Union and into most of the industrialized world. The same was to be true of our own Great Crash of 2007–8.

The optimism was, if anything, even more unshakable in the run-up to our own Crash. In the 1920s there had been a counter-current of scepticism led by the *New York Times* and the specialist financial press, such as *The Commercial and Financial Gazette* and *Poor's Weekly Business and Investment Letter*, which warned against 'the great common-stock delusion'. In our own time, the voices of the few Cassandras were drowned by the super-optimists in the business world. The sceptics, it was said, simply failed to understand that we had entered a new golden age, 'the Great Moderation', in which the normal economic tides scarcely moved and 'there would be no more boom and bust', to quote Britain's Chancellor, who was just about to take over as Prime Minister.

Yet far from living through a Great Moderation, if we look back over the past twenty years we see a series of spectacular crashes within Anglo-Saxon capitalism: the stock market crash of 1987, the failure of the US savings and loan institutions in the late 1980s and early 90s, the bursting of the Dotcom Bubble in 2000 and the Credit Crunch of 2007–8.

Big is Beautiful. Over the past half-century, there has been a huge expansion of the financial sector. Jonathan Ford[42] reports that in the 1960s banking, broking and insurance accounted for a mere 10 per cent of corporate profits in most developed economies. By 2005, this had swelled to nearly 35 per cent in the US and roughly the same in Britain, the two countries that host in the shape of New York and London the world's largest financial centres. During the heyday of 'turbocapitalism', as it was called without much irony, the sheer size of our financial sector was regarded as a cause for self-congratulation. The bond traders in *The Bonfire of the Vanities* boasted of their 'big swinging dicks'. This was a perfect example of synecdoche, the part for the whole, since they regarded themselves as alpha males whose natural role was as masters of the universe. In the same way, nations that possessed engorged financial sectors – predominantly Britain and the United States – regarded themselves as thereby possessed of a unique dynamism. They represented advanced industrial society, and could look down on nations that might be doing well enough in other ways but possessed only a modest financial sector. Now that the heavy old industries such as steel and shipbuilding were largely carried on in what had been dubbed the Third World, being 'underdeveloped' seemed mostly to mean having fewer bankers. Advanced nations had big banks, and the size of those banks was one of the driving causes of their being advanced.

Only now, after repeated financial crashes have culminated in the Big One, the collapse or near-collapse of the largest banks in the world, are a few questioning voices raised. Do we really need such a huge financial sector? For whose benefit do these leviathans principally operate? Can an efficient market get along with fewer of them or with smaller leviathans? In any case, how does our experience of their rampages square with the Efficient Market Hypothesis?

The first sniper to put his head above the parapet was Adair Turner, the incoming head of the Financial Services Authority (FSA). In an interview in *Prospect* magazine and at a Mansion House banquet on 22 September 2009, Lord Turner bluntly asserted that one cause of the trouble was that the financial sector was simply too big: 'Not all financial innovation is valuable, not all trading plays a useful role and a bigger financial system is not necessarily a better one.' In fact, an overlarge financial sector could be positively damaging: 'There are good reasons for believing that the financial industry, more than any other sector of industry, has the ability to generate unnecessary demand for its own services – that more trading and more financial innovation can under some circumstances create harmful volatility against which customers have to hedge, creating more demand for trading liquidity and innovative products; that parts of the financial services industry have a unique ability to attract to themselves unnecessarily high returns and create instability which harms the rest of society.'

This indictment received a mostly frosty and occasionally indignant response from the City. In some quarters, Lord Turner was treated as a cardinal who had denied the existence of God while presiding at Mass. The senior strategist of BGC Capital Partners declared himself 'appalled, disgusted, ashamed and hugely embarrassed that I should have lived to see the head of the UK regulatory regime making such damning and damaging remarks'. A lawyer in Clifford Chance, the grand City solicitors, predicted a race to see who would sack Lord Turner first. Newspaper editorials declared that no person was qualified either to say just how large the financial sector ought to be or to separate necessary from unnecessary demand. It had been an article of faith for so long that the size of Britain's financial sector was a cause for national pride that to question it seemed a mixture of treason and blasphemy.

But Turner's remarks were not simply a knee-jerk response to the calamities of the previous two years. They were certainly not a partisan polemic from an instinctive opponent of the capitalist system. Turner was not alone in believing that something had gone badly wrong with that system as it was practised, especially in Britain and the US, and we needed to stand back and reflect what that something might be and how it might be put right.

Complexity equals progress. This headlong growth of the financial sector has been driven by a wave of financial innovation not seen since the 1920s. The liberation of financial institutions from government regulation has unleashed an unparalleled amount of fertility and ingenuity. The Big Bang in Britain, in the US the Tax Reform Act of 1986 and the repeal of the Glass–Steagall Act in 1998, and the triumph of 'light-touch' regulation in both countries encouraged bankers, brokers, insurers and mortgage providers to throw off their pinstriped waistcoats and unbutton their minds. The walls had come down. Any type of firm could undertake any type of business and do that business in pretty much any way it fancied. The guardians of the system argued that these innovations in finance represented amazing breakthroughs in human commerce. Parcelling up debts into securities that could be sold on to a wider public, for example, was a brilliant method of spreading risk and so accelerating growth.

As recently as 2005, Alan Greenspan, the seemingly immortal chairman of the Federal Reserve Bank who then enjoyed Olympian status, was still confidently proclaiming that 'As is generally acknowledged, the development of credit derivatives has contributed to the stability of the banking system by allowing banks, especially the largest systemically important banks, to measure and manage their credit risk more effectively.' Every part of that sentence turned out to be untrue, as did the verdict of the *IMF Global Financial Stability Report* for 2006:

> There is growing recognition that the dispersion of credit risk by banks to a broader and more diverse group of investors, rather than warehousing such risks on their balance sheets, has helped make the banking and the overall financial system more resilient. The improved resilience may be seen in fewer bank failures and more consistent credit provision. Consequently the commercial banks may be less vulnerable today to credit or economic shocks.

This remarkably fatuous pronouncement was issued just as the bricks in the wall began to crumble, and it came not from some

fly-by-night sharepusher but from the body responsible for
ensuring the stability of the world financial system.

Three types of innovation deserve to be singled out. Note that
all these innovations add significantly to the complexity of the
operation. They also add to the power and wealth of the oligarchs
who introduce and operate them.

The first is the transformation of the mortgage market. In the
old days – still within active memory – this was a simple business.
Customers left their savings with the (frequently local) building
society, and the building society advanced money to other customers (or sometimes the same customers) for the purchase of a
house or flat. Such a simple business was also simple to regulate.
And its growth was automatically regulated by the growth of the
deposits. If no new money was coming in, then the building
society could offer no new mortgages. Not surprisingly, a mortgage was hard to come by. It was almost a privilege, certainly not
a right. You had to have saved a good fraction of the price of the
house you had your eye on. You had to produce proof of a steady
income. And even then you had to endure the frosty glare of the
manager of the local building society before he would admit you
to the certifiably respectable ranks of his customers. All this rapidly changed as the law was reformed in both the UK and the US
to allow banks and other lenders to invade the area once
dominated by the non-profit building societies in Britain and the
savings and loan institutions in the US, although banks always did
some mortgage business in both countries. At the same time, the
building societies were allowed to de-mutualize themselves and
turn themselves into profit-hungry banks, and almost all of them
did so. In America, the savings and loan institutions had to bestir
themselves to compete with the big banks. In the frenzied
competition for business that ensued, several new tricks were
turned.

Instead of being an audacious rarity, 90 per cent or even 100 per cent mortgages became standard. Some of the more go-ahead building societies like Northern Rock in the UK began to hand out 125 per cent mortgages, which enabled young couples to furnish their homes as well as buy them and take a foreign holiday to recover. Many of these enticing deals were 'self-certifying' or, as they were cruelly nicknamed, 'liar loans'. Your mortgage provider would rely on your unsupported word when he assessed your reliability. Not unnaturally, a new class of customer began to apply, the sort of people who would not have been granted so much as an interview by the old-style building society manager. Such go-ahead finance houses were proud of extending home ownership to those who would previously have been debarred from a mortgage, because they were self-employed or their earnings were erratic.

But how were these new easier mortgages to be financed? The depositors whose savings had provided the cash hitherto were insufficient to finance this influx of new business. The banks and building societies, Northern Rock again to the fore, began to borrow from each other on a huge scale – 'wholesale lending' as opposed to the retail lending provided by ordinary depositors. Soon loan books were bulging with these inter-bank loans. It was profitable business, even though the practice might offend against the stuffy old bankers' adage: 'Never borrow short and lend long.' The trouble was that these short-term loans were constantly falling due and needing to be replaced. Sooner or later, this wholesale market would become exhausted and credit would dry up almost overnight, with catastrophic consequences for those who were caught short. The whole business became a great deal more complicated and a great deal more perilous.

At the same time, as the balance sheets of all financial institutions swelled to spectacular proportions, fresh and ever more ingenious methods were sought to dampen the risk, by 'hedging' or 'laying off' their bets, as racecourse punters would put it. In the

financial world, the products by which risks were insured against
were known by the generic term 'derivative'. Among poets and
painters 'derivative' was a term of abuse, but for a period in the
financial world, it was a magic elixir that enabled huge fortunes to
be built by whizzkids who never took possession of a single actual
share certificate and enabled the banks to make money on a scale
not equalled by traditional banking activities – 'these rather agreeable profits', as the head of Barings Bank described the money
that Nick Leeson was making for them on the derivatives market
out in Singapore. For a time, this sub-world of options, swaps and
futures seemed the most desirable realm of finance to be in. The
hedge-fund manager became the Croesus of his day, adored,
feared or hated, according to taste.

The third great source of new money, after the mortgage and
the derivative, was the securitization of debt, or 'slicing and
dicing' as it was vulgarly known. Like most of these so-called
innovations, it was not entirely new. In the Victorian era, one
man's debts were freely bought and sold at suitable discounts, and
even then solid fortunes could be made in the business. But never
before had this parcelling up and selling on to third, fourth and
fifth parties reached such an epic scale. Soon it was difficult to be
clear what risks you might be taking on when you bought these
alluring new securities. This uncertainty multiplied when credit
seized up, even if the underlying debts might be reasonably sound
risks. This 'distancing' of lending helped to make any mass financial panic worse, as the lenders veered from blithe optimism to
unreasoning despair as to the chances of getting repaid. It might
well be that when all the debts incurred before the Crunch are
unwound, some lenders including the government may be pleas-
antly surprised (while others, in commercial property for example,
will have lost the lot). But the damage has been done, in the
shape of the worst recession since the 1930s and millions of lost
jobs.

The moral hazards involved in these deliberately complex financial inventions were slow to emerge. But when they were finally dragged out into the light of day, they turned out to be horrendous. To put it as simply as possible, the more complicated the minestrone of debt being sold on from party to party, the harder it became for the innocent new investor (who might just as well be a large bank as an individual person) to make a reasonable estimate of the risk involved. You could not be sure exactly what it was that you were buying, because the ultimate debtors were so far back down the chain.

What now became clear was that the prevailing murk offered an irresistible temptation: to design a product which offered a huge advantage to the knowing insider (whether buyer or seller) over the bemused other party. And to nobody's surprise, this temptation was succumbed to, most notoriously in the case of Goldman Sachs and the New York hedge fund of Paulson and Co. John Paulson was rightly convinced that the sub-prime mortgage market was going to collapse soon, and he had placed so many enormous bets on this happening that he had run out of sub-prime products to bet against, or 'short'. So he asked the wizards at Goldman Sachs to design a purpose-built package of this toxic mortgage debt. They made to measure a product entitled Abacus 2007-AC1. Paulson duly shorted this toxic bond, and when the sub-prime market duly collapsed he made a profit of something approaching a billion dollars. The parties on the losing end of the deal made an equivalent loss, in the case of our old friend RBS an estimated $840 million.[43]

Whether Goldman had committed a fraud or not was a question for the lawyers and regulators to determine. Goldman's own lawyers argued that Paulson had simply guessed right and RBS and the other losers had guessed wrong; that was in the nature of any such transaction and was entirely legitimate. But would RBS have invested in Abacus 2007-AC1 if they had known that it came into being solely as a vehicle for the agile Mr Paulson to short? Surely the bank had a duty of care and transparency to all its clients. What is clear is that the whole opaque and complex transaction was characteristic of a gilded age of oligarchs in which the ordinary punter was always liable to be stuffed.

For with the introduction of the new complexities fresh questions needed to be asked, and were not asked. How could it be that the introduction of new uncertainties actually assisted the efficient use of capital? The fact that the risks involved in these instruments were so hard to quantify could scarcely encourage confident planning for the future. The critics of the Stock Exchange had always likened it to a casino. Now it seemed to be a casino in which anyone could find himself betting the entire firm without knowing it and losing the lot in a single session. The old City scandals had involved larger-than-life public characters like Bob Maxwell and Horatio Bottomley, who were both MPs. But when Barings Bank went bust in 1995, it was brought low by an obscure derivatives broker, Nick Leeson, on Singapore's International Monetary Exchange. Leeson forged entries to cover his tracks as he redoubled his disastrous trades. But the fact that he was shown to have deceived his superiors and was sent to jail as a result does not mitigate the unnerving reality: a lowly dealer had destroyed the oldest surviving merchant bank in London. By contrast, when Barings had nearly gone under a century earlier, in the Panic of 1890, and was rescued by a consortium led by the Bank of England, it had been because of the board's general policy error, of overexposing themselves to South American debt.

That the Leeson Affair was not an isolated, freak incident was shown by the fraud committed at the far bigger French bank, Société Générale, in 2007. Like Leeson, a junior futures trader, Jérôme Kerviel, had got in deep and tried to rescue his positions by a series of fraudulent trades that cost the bank no less than €4.9 billion. This mammoth loss, far larger than that caused by Leeson's efforts, placed Société Générale, then the third largest bank in the eurozone, in a fragile position which was made infinitely worse by the collapse of AIG during the bank crash. As a result of its dealings with AIG, Société Générale needed a bail-out of $11 billion from the American taxpayer.

Nor, it seems, have the banks learnt by their disasters to take a firmer grip on their in-house dealers. In September 2011, UBS became aware that one of its traders, Kweku Adoboli, had racked up a loss of $2.3 billion for the bank. The UBS group had subsumed, among many other banks, S. G. Warburg, the famous merchant bank of London. I shudder to think what the legendarily prudent Siegmund Warburg would have thought of such unregenerate laxity.

Professor John Kay points out in his essay *Narrow Banking* (2009)[44] that not only had the largest source of systemic risk in the crisis of 2007–9 been within individual financial institutions; the people responsible for the activities, I mean the non-fraudulent ones, that brought the bank to the edge of collapse might be a tiny group within the firm – barely 100 traders in RBS out of the bank's 170,000 employees, at AIG 120 people in the financial products division in London who caused the collapse of America's largest insurer. The beating of the wings of these gaudy butterflies had unleashed a tornado across the world.

Thus turbocapitalism seemed to increase rather than lessen the fragility of large institutions, and contrary to the IMF's cheerful prognosis, to make them more rather than less vulnerable, both to individual fraud in the dealing room and to collective policy error in the boardroom. The enlargement of the financial sector, the staggering new complexities of its operations, the huge salaries and bonuses paid to its staff – none of these things had reinforced the solidity of the banks. The new reality seemed to mock that ancient phrase denoting security, 'money in the bank'.

For it also emerged that there was, as a matter of fact, less and less money actually *in* the bank. The proportion of its assets that a bank was required to hold in its reserves had diminished steadily over the second half of the twentieth century. For example, cash reserves in the UK held by banks in 1968 represented 20 per cent of its deposits. By 1998, the figure was 3.1 per cent. Capital ratios – the amount of shareholders capital and other reserves in relation to the amount it has out on loan – have also declined from around 20 per cent in the early days of modern capitalism to 10 per cent under the Basel Accords, which purport to set a common standard for banks in all countries. Only in antique survivals from the old days, such as the bankers C. Hoare of Fleet Street, do you find a high priority attached to the level of reserves. An even better example is that of Wetherby's, the stakeholder for the Jockey Club, which over 200 years has accumulated so much cash that it has in effect become a bank. After two centuries, the Bank of England politely pointed out that since they were taking money in on deposit, they ought to have a banker's licence. And so Wetherby's Bank was born. But it is a bank of a very old-fashioned sort. Unlike the high street banks, it lends out a good deal less than the money it takes in on deposit – only 42 per cent according to the latest report – the rest being carefully invested. And when they lend, they lend against solid security.[45] Unfortunately, the delightful reassurance of having that sort of banker is reserved for 'high net worth individuals', people who have a million or two to deposit. The rest of us must make do with the perilous helter-skelter of Lloyds or Barclays.

Yet, if we are asked what are the qualities we hope for in a bank with which we are to have dealings, we would place solidity and stability high on the list. We want our bank to be 'bankable', and if we are risking our money with it, we want the bet to be as near a 'banker' as is possible in human affairs. Most of us do not like to think of 'our' bank as a fox whose jaws are dripping with blood. We would prefer it to be more like a squirrel hoarding away nuts for the winter, preferably in places where the mice cannot get at them. It is small comfort that the sceptics were proved right when Goodwin vastly overpaid for ABN-Amro and brought both banks crashing down, so that the government was forced to take a majority holding in RBS and supply it with lifesaving transfusions of cash.

There was in short a bizarre mismatch between our staid expectations of banks and the glamorous daredevil self-image of bankers themselves. We would have approved of Walter Bagehot's famous definition of banking as 'a watchful but not a laborious trade'. Bagehot mused in his wonderful essay *Lombard Street* (1873) that 'A banker, even in large business, can be pretty sure that all his transactions are sound and yet have much spare mind. A certain part of his time, and a considerable part of his thoughts, he can readily devote to other pursuits. And a London banker today can have the most intellectual society in the world if he chooses it.'[46] What a contrast with this generation's obsessive workaholics. Bankers today like to boast of their fourteen-hour days, their thousands of air miles, their relentless appetite for deal-making, their broken weekends and their broken marriages.

It is these three illusions that have between them brought about such a perversion of the traditional theory and practice of finance. If the market is always right, if big is always beautiful and if every financial and commercial innovation is regarded as *ipso facto* a good thing, then neither the financial authorities nor the government will possess the self-confidence to intervene in the old ways: to regulate market dealings, to break up monopolies, forbid mergers that damage competition, ban risky practices, monitor the stability of financial institutions – all the things that Adam Smith believed the authorities were there to do.

How then do we begin to minimize the risks of reckless oligarchs wrecking the whole economy? How do we begin to put things right?

Escape routes

The first step, I think, is to clear our heads and recognize one quite simple fact: the way that we have treated financial institutions is exceptional. We have assumed that whatever practices they adopted must be legitimate because they seemed to be making so much money from them. We have taken it on trust that, whenever and wherever they asked to be freed from regulation, their wishes must be met.

In dealing with other economic activities, we are not nearly so indulgent. We do not assume that because both the buyer and the seller of other goods and services are content there can be no further questions to be asked. It is, for example, to the advantage of both the building firm and the householder if the painter or roofer can shin up a ladder, instead of scaffolding having to be erected at great cost and inconvenience. When I last had my house painted, the scaffolding alone cost over £3,000, a hefty proportion of the total bill. But European law now insists on scaffolding, and I cannot really complain. I have seen several building workers fall off ladders. I have not yet seen anyone fall off scaffolding.

Similarly, we do not assume that because both the drug dealer and his customer are happy, all is well; ditto with the consumer of child pornography and the provider. The merchant of pesticides and fertilizers may be doing nicely; so may the farmer who deci-mates wildlife and allows rivers of nitrates to leach into the local watercourses. But the rest of us may not be so content. These 'externalities', as the economists call them, may injure all sorts of people not directly connected with the operation, which is why such activities may be regulated, either compulsorily by the state or voluntarily by self-regulation. We do not assume that the prin-cipals in these exchanges are always the best judges of the public good, or even of their own good.

So it has been a curious but stubborn illusion that the money dealers are almost always the best judges of the public interest no less than of the interests of their customers and themselves. We need to be more sceptical, to make a harder-headed assessment of the risks involved in financial practices and to be less ready to take the benefits of them on trust. This need for vigilance is all the more urgent because the harm that a delinquent bank can cause reaches far beyond the bank's own staff and shareholders.

Personally, I am by temperament a deregulator and a believer in the free market. But the question is not whether one has a preju-dice in favour of 'light-touch' regulation or one instinctively believes that the State ought to take a tighter grip. We need to look dispassionately at what is actually happening and, where risks have not been properly catered for, to see what might be done to minimize them.

The really striking thing is that many of the problems of runaway markets today are not unprecedented. Bank crashes and runs on banks have been happening as long as there have been banks, which is pretty much as long as recorded civilization (back to the Babylonians at least). In finance, as in all other businesses, the occasional failure may well be the necessary downside of dynamism. In fact, banks are probably more intrinsically prone to failure than any other type of business, and always have been.

Walter Bagehot wrote in 1873 that 'In exact proportion to the power of our banking system is its delicacy, I should hardly say too much if I said its danger.' According to Bagehot:

> There is no country at present, and there never was any country before, in which the ratio of cash reserves to the bank deposits was so small as it is now in England. So far from our being able to rely on the proportional magnitude of our cash in hand, the amount of that cash is so exceedingly small that a bystander almost trembles when he compares its minuteness with the immensity of the credit which rests upon it.

Nor would it do to comfort ourselves with the thought that British bankers had learnt from long experience how to manage this fragile situation with discretion. Not ten years earlier, in 1866, there had come the great crash of the firm of Overend Gurney, which had stood next to the Bank of England and was better known throughout the world than any other purely English bank. Now Overend Gurney and its partners were ruined – 'and their losses were made in a manner so reckless and so foolish that one would think a child who had lent money in the City of London would have lent it better'.

So fragility and folly are nothing new. Nor are the remedies that governments and central bankers have devised to minimize both the frequency and the impact of bank crashes and the collateral damage they inflict.

In looking for escape routes, the best place to start looking is the past, often the fairly remote past. Almost all the remedies that been have discussed or begun to be implemented since the Great Crash of 2007–8 have had a long and often effective history. We have been here before, and we have responded in much the same way before. Those responses often worked pretty well for many years, until we forgot the reasons why we responded in that way, and then repealed the responses or let them rust into disuse. So it is well worth re-examining these old devices and shining them up to see whether something on the same lines might do the trick again today.

The four lines of action most under discussion or reconstruction since the Crash are all at least fifty years old; some of them date back to the nineteenth century. This would suggest that the tendencies which they were designed to control are recurring and endemic. These are the chronic infections of capitalism, which is why the remedies are as familiar as the symptoms.

Please note also that in each case the proposed remedy is anti-oligarchic in its effects. It sets out to curb the oligarch's reach by reducing the size of his empire and his unfettered powers, and it seeks to spread economic activity among a greater number of players.

Nowhere is this clearer than in legislation to regulate **monopolies and mergers**. Where a large company is seeking to dominate its market to such an extent as to suppress competition and exploit the customer, the State has for a long time felt justified in stepping in to break up the monopoly or forbid the merger. In the US, they call it 'trust-busting', and it dates back to the Sherman Act of 1890, promoted by Senator John Sherman, 'the Ohio Icicle' – younger brother to General Sherman, who marched through Georgia and burnt Atlanta in the Civil War. British governments were rather slower to interfere with monopolies and mergers. The first formal statute on the books was the Monopolies and Restrictive Practices Act brought in by the Attlee government in 1948. This was followed by the Tories' Restrictive Trade Practices Act of 1956, and by the creation of the Monopolies and Mergers Commission in 1965. In the decades that followed, the commission has sometimes been regarded as a bit of a patsy and unduly vulnerable to political interference on behalf of moguls such as Rupert Murdoch. But it has never entirely lost its bite nor its deterrent effect on companies considering a take-over or merger that might fall foul of it.

Of equal antiquity is the insistence by the government or the central bank that banks should maintain prudent **capital reserves** against a rainy day. In the US, the National Banking Acts date back to just before the Civil War (which they helped to finance). To obtain a charter allowing him to trade, a would-be banker had to deposit a prescribed amount of bonds with the state or federal authorities. In Britain, always a less legalistic nation, the Bank of England has maintained a voluntary system of 'reserve ratios'; in return for the informality of the system, the Bank had until recently the right to exercise detailed supervision over the banks to make sure that they were solvent and had prudent levels of reserves.

In recent years, anxiety about the slipping ratios of capital reserves across the EU has led to a series of negotiations in Basel, which have produced a string of agreements to stiffen the ratios, known as Basel I, II, and III, no doubt with more to come. Similar agreements to ensure the solvency of insurance companies, known as Solvency I and II, are also in force across the EU. Of course banks often try to evade the full impact of these restrictions by piling up complex assets and liabilities that do not appear on their balance sheets. It is these off-balance-sheet risks that have led to so much trouble. We cannot be sure that even the more sophisticated provisions of Basel III will prevent all future malfeasance.

All the same, these restrictions are likely to prevent financial companies expanding their balance sheets to such giddy extents. This is clearly shown by the fact that, whenever the new codes are issued, shares of the banks or insurance companies plummet sharply.

The next remedy against overmighty oligarchs arises out of this question of what level of reserves can be considered prudent. The choice between 'rules-based' and 'inspection-based' regulation may sound rather dry and theoretical. It does, in fact seem to be crucial. In the Thatcher–Blair years, the fashionable, 'adult' answer was to lay down a set of clear rules and leave the banks to get on with it. Alas, for your average oligarch, rules are for wriggling round. After the crash, the fashion now is to return to the old detailed supervision by the authorities, to what used to be known as **the Governor's Eyebrows**; we are going back to something like the old days when the Bank of England supervised the banks, and when the disapproval of the Governor was sufficient to compel a reckless bank to clean up its act.

The last of the four familiar types of remedy against recklessness is **separation of activities.** The most famous example of this is the American Glass–Steagall Act of 1933, which separated commercial banks from investment banks, or in old British parlance, the high street banks from the merchant banks. Senator Carter Glass, a former US Treasury Secretary, and Congressman Henry B. Steagall subscribed to the general belief that a leading cause of the Great Crash of 1929 had been that commercial banks had been taking too many risks with their depositors' money. Speculation had been piled on top of speculation, all resting on the implicit security of ordinary people's savings. The only safe way to protect those savings was to set up a firewall between the sedate bankers on Main Street and the hectic speculators on Wall Street. You could be one kind of bank or the other, but not both at the same time.

The Glass–Steagall Act endured until 1999, without noticeably impeding the rise of American capitalism to world dominance, as its enemies claimed it would. Similarly, the McFadden Act of 1927, which prohibited banks from operating in more than one US state, did not appear to much inhibit the growth of the great

American banks. Later on, in 1956, Congress passed the Bank
Holding Companies Act, which set up a partial firewall between
banking and insurance. These restrictions, like Glass–Steagall,
were repealed in 1999 (the McFadden Act had bitten the dust in
1994).

In Britain, similar restrictions and separations were also in force.
Typically they were imposed more by City practice and Bank of
England guidance than by statute law, but the results were much
the same. High street banks and merchant banks, building societies
and life assurance companies, stockbrokers and stockjobbers all
tilled their own acres and did not stray much on to their neigh-
bours' ground. All these separations were swept away by the Big
Bang of 1986. In future, any licensed financial company could
offer any type of service and do any type of business, subject only
to the provisions of that year's Financial Services Act. It was a new
liberated financial universe.

And in its turn the new universe exploded. All the dangers that
the stick-in-the-muds had warned of came to pass, on a terrifying
scale. The perils of unrestricted mingling of very different types of
business, with their different risks and responsibilities, turned out
to be as real as ever.

So is it time for an updated Glass–Steagall Act, along with a
return to the Governor's Eyebrows and a reinvigorated scrutiny of
monopolies and mergers plus stiffened requirements for capital
reserves? Should we go back to the future?

I cannot do better than borrow the argument and proposals
outlined by John Kay in his essay *Narrow Banking*. Professor Kay
urges the establishment of distinct 'narrow banks'. The first thing
to note about these banks is that they would be smaller: 'The
claim that innovation in modern financial markets makes it essential to have large conglomerate banks is precisely the opposite of
the truth – these innovations make it possible *not* to have large
conglomerate banks.' All the complex business of spreading and

pooling risks and of managing the mismatch of maturities – the different dates at which debts fall due for repayment – all this can now be managed by computers through the market, instead of requiring a single large company to sort it all out.

These narrow banks would be the only banks licensed to take in deposits from the public. Those deposits would be guaranteed by the government, as they are now. In return for this privilege, the narrow bank would be strictly regulated. Its licence would spell out the level and type of lending that it could undertake. The regulator, a body more like Ofwat or Ofcom than the present Financial Services Authority, would step in whenever it felt that a narrow bank's activities were breaching the rules. These retail deposits would be completely covered by safe liquid assets, primarily if not wholly government securities. The narrow banks could lend to businesses, especially small and medium-sized businesses, as the old high street banks used to specialize in doing. They could also engage in mortgage lending, again on a properly secured basis, just as the old building societies used to do; their mortgage lending would be primarily financed by deposits from savers, rather than by short-term lending from other banks. In other words, in return for its licence and the government guarantee to its depositors, the narrow bank would behave much like the old high street bank used to behave.

In fact, rather than the unappealing title of 'Narrow Bank', we might christen them 'High Street Banks'. The early contenders would probably be fenced-off subsidiaries of existing banks or financial holding companies. Some would be subsidiaries of non-financial consumer businesses, such as Tesco or Sainsbury's. Others would be stand-alone institutions of varying sizes. Big banks are already thinking of reviving the titles of some of the old banks they have swallowed up over the years, such as Williams and Glyns, National Provincial and so on, or of giving independence to subsidiaries who have kept their old titles, such as Coutts.

Some public authorities might follow the lead of Essex County Council and start their own high street banks as a haven for local savers and a resource for local businesses. The common feature is that your money would be safe in any one of them. Even if the holding company went bust, the ring-fenced high street bank would be safe.

Since the success of such a business would depend directly on the number of savers and customers that it attracted, genuine competition would be the order of the day. I myself would be far happier to see my savings lodged in such a place than left to the mercy of Sir Fred Goodwin's predations, and the bonds that it would issue would be no less attractive.

All this is not a sentimental retro proposal. Kay points out that limited banks of this nature continue to exist and prosper in large parts of Asia and the Middle East. The emergence of the mega conglomerate bank in the US and Western Europe was a case of elephantiasis, not a natural healthy development. Narrow banking would have many of the characteristics of a utility such as the electricity and water industries, where the principal objective is to keep the current flowing and serve the customer and where there is a regulator to prevent extortionate charging and inadequate standards of service.

Objectors to any renewal of Glass–Steagall complain that it would be impossible these days to separate legitimate lending from excessively risky lending. The Governor of the Bank of England, Mervyn King, cannot see why. He has been doing precisely that for much of his life. Until the late 1970s, Britain had a banking cartel that pretty much operated according to Glass–Steagall lines. The same applied to France and Germany until rather later. What we then called the clearing banks ran the show and provided a sound if haughty service. Customers were treated as supplicants rather than kings. Nor were the clearers eager to innovate, certainly not to provide the customer with speedier or friendlier service. But then our own new-style superbanks weren't either. On the contrary. For their own convenience, they removed most of their services from geographical proximity to the customer; they removed useful information from their customers' bank statements; they abolished the role of the local bank manager; they charged punitive rates of interest on their credit cards; and, perhaps worst of all, in a world of instantaneous electronic transmission they made no discernible effort to speed up the pace of settlements. All my life I have been hearing that dismal phrase 'within five working days'; that is, effectively, a whole week. Now the culture of banking has indeed become sales-driven, but primarily for the benefit of the bank, which is cross-selling its products, rather than for the benefit of the customer, who is being cross-sold to.

By separating high street banks from merchant banks – another old term which is also worth reviving – we would be forcing the high street banks to concentrate first on service to the customer rather than on making money for themselves. Meanwhile, the merchant banks would be left to soar, sink or swim in the market without more than the minimum regulation to ensure that they were managed by 'fit and proper persons' to engage in the business at all. They would no longer have the secure cushion of all those depositors with their guaranteed deposits. As a result, they might borrow and lend more cautiously. It would be entirely their own responsibility – and their own funeral.

Or to put it the other way round, other financial institutions might be more cautious about lending to them. In an ingenious wrinkle to his proposals, Kay suggests that retail depositors (and, in their shoes, the government guarantors of those deposits) should be given priority over any other creditors in the event of a liquidation. If that had been the case, all those other banks that lent money to Northern Rock would have had little or no security if Northern Rock went bust. They would therefore have been much more reluctant to finance Northern Rock's breakneck expansion. Ergo, no breakneck expansion, and no broken neck.

The system would be purged of the central moral hazard: that of high-stakes gamblers using the savings of ordinary mortals as the collateral for their mega-punts. High street banks would be returned to their old modest but vital function, that of keeping the juices of commerce flowing.

From within the banking world, the objection to any official division between one sort of bank and another is that the breakdown of the old division accelerated economic growth to the benefit of everyone. In his apology for the behaviour of some banks, John Varley, then CEO of Barclays, argued that

> ... those calling for an age of simpler, old-fashioned, more tightly regulated banking were probably not around in the days of Bretton Woods or Glass–Steagall. Because if they were, they would remember a time when less than 50 per cent of the adult population in the developed world had a bank account, when credit was strictly rationed, when a mortgage cartel controlled home loans and when, with credit supply directed by governments, industry complained constantly of being starved of funds.[47]

This argument fails to convince me. If it is true that a decent rate of economic growth depends on unrestricted credit, then under our new division of powers plenty of extra credit would be available from the unregulated merchant banks. As for mortgage availability, the greatest expansion of home ownership took place under the old restrictive regime. It is in recent years that house building has dwindled, partly because of planning restrictions; all that the super-cheap mortgages have achieved is to inflate the price of homes out of reach of first-time buyers, even with low interest rates.

What John Kay is also asking is in effect: what are banks *for*? And if their purpose is to serve their customers, how are they to do it? These are questions which we would immediately ask if we were talking about grocery supermarkets or clothes shops, and the managers of Tesco or Marks & Spencer would have their answers ready. In asking such questions, we do not denigrate the principle of competition or the goal of making a profit in a free market. Banks have always been regulated in modern industrial society since their beginnings in late seventeenth-century Holland and England. The question is rather: how are they to be regulated, and for what purpose?

A stewards' inquiry?

Yet we are still left with one great unsolved problem, which also happens to be the problem we started with. We still have not fixed the Great Disconnect which we first saw emerge in the affairs of the Dutch East Indies Company 400 years ago: the disconnect between the shareholders and the company which they legally own.

In modern times, we have seen this become a Double Disconnect. First, those scattered thousands of shareholders were uncoupled from effective management of the company. Then, in the 1960s or thereabouts, shareholders started choosing to spread their risks by investing in unit trusts and other collective funds, rather than directly in companies that produced goods and services. In making this choice, they further removed themselves from any pretence of control. Today company managers speak only to fund managers: this is the completion of the Managerial Revolution.

Here we have no ancient remedy to draw on, for we have never faced this dilemma before. What, if anything, can we do?

When in unknown territory, we might as well consult any available map, no matter however clumsy and imperfect it may look. Ever since the 1990s, the financial authorities have been issuing and then refining and reissuing Codes of Corporate Governance. The latest version is the UK Stewardship Code, published in July 2010. The Code does not provide an answer to the Great Disconnect. But it does make it clear that the question needs to be asked, and it sets off down the right road, a timid pilgrim perhaps but not an unworthy one.

Fund managers, the Code says, have a duty to engage with the companies they invest in, and they must tell their own investors exactly what they are doing. What should this 'engaging' amount to? For a start, the fund managers obviously have a duty to use all the votes they have at company AGMs and at extraordinary general meetings called to approve some major new departure, such as a rights issue of new shares or the acquisition of another company. They also have a duty to tell the company when they are unhappy with its performance or direction or leadership. And they should band together with other fund managers when they feel they need to compel the company to listen to their complaints. All these activities and the principles that guide them then need to be reported back to their own investors on their websites. The whole two-way process ought to be open and transparent, not a matter of a discreet word in the chairman's ear. There must be a clear and public assumption of stewardship.

So far, pretty good. Most institutional investors will, I fancy, find it quite easy to comply with both the letter and the spirit of the Code. The practice both of engaging and of reporting on the engagement is likely to become richer, more detailed and more productive over the years. We can expect compliance to become nearly universal, as it is with codes operating in many other business and professional communities. The conversation between institutional investors and the companies they invest in should become increasingly lively. But if it would help the progress towards universal and wholehearted compliance if we enacted the Code into law, well, we should not shrink from that step either.

Of course there may be managers who will opt to flee the Code, either by taking their company offshore to some less demanding regime or by taking it private, much as do managers today who find the obligations of running a plc too onerous. If this seemed likely to happen on a significant scale, the government could choose to offer preferential tax treatment to 'stewardship companies'. These tax breaks could be withdrawn if a stewardship company was found to be drawing, one way or another, on the resources of a non-stewardship company, rather as some people refuse to patronize cafés selling non-Fair Trade coffee.

None of this does much, though, for the other leg of the disconnect: between the individual shareholders and the managers of the funds to which they entrust their savings. The Stewardship Code has nothing much to say about that. As far as the Code is concerned, the role of the individual shareholders is to remain pretty passive. They simply have to trust to the vigilance and energy of their fund managers to look after their interests.

Unfortunately, as we have seen, the interests of the fund managers are often aligned more with the short-term interests of the investee company managers than with the long-term interests of the poor old personal shareholder. The brute fact is that the fund manager is not playing with his own money. His personal rewards depend rather on the short-term performance of the investee company's shares: on that will depend the quarterly ranking of the fund he manages, and on that ranking will depend both his own bonus and the fund's prospects of attracting more investors. The bonus prospects of the investee company manager depend on that same short-term share price. The two managers are in the same game. Questions that may occupy the minds of the individual shareholder may not concern either of them in the slightest: questions such as the obscene salaries paid to top management or the wretched wage levels at the bottom, or the long-term stability of the company, or its record on ethical or ecological issues, or even the level of the dividend. The voice of the personal shareholder may not be heard on these issues at all; he has no individual stake in the company; he cannot turn up at the AGM and make trouble. Only those few small shareholders who insist on holding the company's shares in their own name can do that. And the only reward for their persistence is usually to be patronized by the chairman and voted down by the big battalions of proxy votes.

But all is not lost. The idea of stewardship is now lodged in the public realm. A start has been made. There is something to bite on.

As so often, the computer can help us out. Already, stockbrokers make it possible for those clients in whose name they hold nominee accounts to vote their shares online by proxy. If you do not like the remuneration report at Amalgamated Widgets (now also available online), you can cast your tiny parcel of votes against it. It is not beyond the wit of IT to extend the principle to collective funds: if you own one per cent of the GetRichQuick Fund's shares, then one per cent of GRQ's holding in Amalgamated Widgets could be cast against that same remuneration report. Either the holding could be disaggregated, so that GRQ would be voting, let's say, 57–43 against the report: or it could operate by an internal majority vote, so that the whole GRQ holding would be voted against. Such a thought may sound far-fetched even today; but the IT revolution has overcome many more complicated challenges than this.

But these are not the only possibilities. As soon as your fund manager's voting record and his guiding policy are available to shareholders, then direct, candid feedback becomes possible.

Your personal feedback may be reinforced by feedback from other quarters. Pressure groups with a particular interest in certain issues – the low-paid, carbon footprint, mega bonuses – may offer critiques of either bunch of managers. They may recommend you to switch out of GetRichQuick Funds into NicerWorld Funds. Some shareholders, who have better things to do than monitor companies all day long, might be enabled to switch their proxies to one of these ginger groups, who could then come to command an extensive body of support, as PIRC and the National Association of Pension Funds do today. Armed with a fistful of such proxies, the Bonus Control Association, let's say, would become a nagging presence at every AGM.

Such mass movements and ginger groups have traditionally been regarded with disdain by big business as ineffectual and short-lived. The record is beginning to show otherwise. The burgeoning of the organic shelves in every supermarket and the success of the Fair Trade campaign have been rapid and irresistible. There is no reason to suppose that, with the aid of new technology, individuals should not be able to band together to make their voices heard in serious questions of company management too.

This may sound alarming to the old-fashioned top-down manager. I do not think he has really much to fear. Most people have as much common sense in their role as investors as they do in other areas of life. I am struck by how many of those small shareholders who do bother to attend the AGMs of big companies come not to carp but to express their gratitude for the sound and steady managements of the company and for the regular dividends they receive.

Nothing could do more for the sadly diminished popularity of business and businessmen than a growing sense of democratization in their affairs. I do not believe that any such democratization would be likely to impede the taking of bold and difficult decisions. People invest in companies primarily because they want them to succeed and make a profit. But they do not see why that overriding aim should stop the company from behaving decently and in accordance with the normal values of the society it operates in. There should not be one code for business hours and another for private life.

The oligators – a brief intermission

What do we mean by 'oligarchy'? What does an oligarchic regime look like to outsiders? What does it feel like to the people who live under it? What are the defining characteristics of the oligarchs themselves? How do they make it to the top and how do they manage to stay there? How long does the average oligarchy endure? And when it comes to an end, is it with a bang or a whimper?

Most political terms are notoriously slippery. When we talk about 'an apple' or 'a squirrel', we are pretty clear what we are talking about and we can reliably point to a specimen if there's one available. Talking about 'a liberal' or 'a conservative', or about 'democracy', is a much trickier business. American liberals are different from British liberals, who are different again from liberals on the Continent. Some people who describe themselves as conservatives are denounced as phoneys by other conservatives. A parliamentary democracy is utterly different from a people's democracy of the sort that formerly prevailed in most of Central and Eastern Europe.

'Oligarchy', though, seems to be a surprisingly straightforward idea. We are more or less agreed what the word means both in theory and practice, and we can usually recognize one when we see it. What's more, the word has always denoted the same sort of phenomenon ever since the philosophers Plato and Aristotle and the historians Herodotus and Thucydides first used the term 'oligarchia' (*oligos*, 'few' + *archia*, 'rule'). The few ruled the many, and the few who ruled were the rich. An oligarchy was always also a plutocracy (*ploutos*, 'rich' + *kratos*, 'power'). Plutocracy was a rather less common word that also came into Greek conversation at much the same time, the end of the fifth century BC. To live in an oligarchy was to live in a state, in classical times a city-state, where both political life and economic life were dominated by a small number of very rich individuals and families. Much the same was true of other famous oligarchies later on – the Venice of the doges, the Whig oligarchy of Queen Anne and the early Georges, quite a few Latin American states during the twentieth century.

But as we saw in the introduction, 'oligarchy' does not necessarily describe the outward form of government. Oligarchs may prosper under constitutional monarchies or under moderate autocrats. In eighteenth-century England, for example, the ultimate veto over taxation and public expenditure rested with a house of elected commoners (as it had, off and on, for several centuries before). But the Glorious Revolution of 1688 did not prevent the great Whig magnates who had come in with the new regime from gaining control of large blocks of their local MPs. Bribery and the open ballot meant that the dukes and earls could rest easy, knowing that 'my men in the Parliaments' would not inhibit their profitable enclosure of common land or the piling up of juicy sinecures for their friends and relations.

Similarly, the Serene Republic of Venice developed an unbelievably complicated system for preventing the great families from dominating the city, but somehow the Cornaros and the Loredans, the Contarinis and the Mocenigos went on becoming

doges and building their spectacular palaces and adding to their
trading empires. The oligarchs may be cuckoos in the nest, their
status not officially recognized but none the less powerful for that.
So the term is not quite as straightforward as it looks. Yet like a
cuckoo in a nest of smaller birds, we know one when we see one.

Life in any one of these oligarchies had certain common characteristics, which appeared to apply regardless of where or when
it flourished. Oligarchies tended to be a rather *stable* form of government. Individual oligarchs and their families might quarrel or
be disgraced or lose their wealth and power or simply die out; but
there were usually ambitious rivals thrusting to take their place.
The Venetian oligarchs ruled for a thousand years. The Whigs
lasted for most of the eighteenth century; some of the Latin
American oligarchies, despite or because of their deplorable
record on human rights, had plenty of staying power.

Oligarchies also tended to be *corrupt*. Favours and bribes were
the lubricants which oiled the wheels of the system and got things
done. The Whig oligarchy was known by its critics as 'Old
Corruption', and Sir Robert Walpole, the dominant statesman of
the era, was not only the longest-serving first minister in British
history, but also the most corrupt.

Oligarchies tended too to be unpleasantly *arrogant*. Their leading figures were either cruel or indifferent to the poor. The
awareness of their power went to their heads and gave them a
sense of self-importance and invulnerability, amounting to hubris.
This hubris would in the end lead to nemesis, as their cumulative
callousness provoked some sort of popular uprising or revolution.
These qualities – callousness, corruption, arrogance – are clearly
described in Aristotle's *Politics* and have been equally visible in
modern times. We would expect therefore decent observers like
Aristotle to denounce without qualification this unappealing and
unfair form of government. After all, Aristotle does not disguise
his personal preference for a state which is dominated by a large

and hardworking middle class – something much closer to our own idea of a parliamentary democracy.

But in his cool and unprejudiced way, Aristotle also tells us that, although oligarchies are inferior to middle-class democracies, they too can endure, as long as their rulers treat the poor humanely and do not quarrel amongst themselves. And in prosperous oligarchies, even if they have authoritarian inclinations, wealth may 'trickle down', as we would say now, so that even the poorest citizens may well feel better off under an oligarchy than under some other form of government that claims to respect their rights better and listen to their views more. In modern times, some supporters of Reagan and Thatcher, such as Ambassador Jeane Kirkpatrick and Professor Alan Walters, would extend this tolerance to oligarchies in Latin America for this very reason. When Peter Mandelson, the creator of New Labour, says that 'we are intensely relaxed about people getting filthy rich' – and himself consorts with the filthy rich (including a couple of Russian oligarchs) on their yachts – he is making the classic defence of oligarchy. By letting the filthy rich entrepreneurs have their head, the rest of us will be better off too, including those who are at present worst off.

Oligarchies may arise in all sorts of different circumstances. The oligarchs in Russia were born out of political chaos following the breakdown of a regime that had regarded itself – and was regarded by the rest of the world – as all-powerful. Its power seemed so pervasive that a special adjective had been minted to describe such modern regimes: totalitarian. These totalitarian regimes were expected to last for anything up to a thousand years, and so it came as a shock to their supporters and opponents alike when they dissolved overnight, and the agile New Men leapt into the empty space left behind.

Our own British oligarchy is not like that at all. On the contrary, it has arisen because our society seems to us so *congested*. Only by concentrating and streamlining power, it seemed, could

we hope for it to work as we would like it to. What was needed
was simplification, and part of that simplification consisted in
establishing defined lines of control and therefore clear and
unquestioned leadership. In the old days, before the Second
World War and even for a few years in the postwar period, power
in Britain was quite widely dispersed. I am not going to argue at
this point where and when power was exercised better or worse as
a result. The point is that more people had the final say on how
this or that matter was to be resolved. Supervision or control
from Head Office or from Whitehall was sketchy and intermit-
tent, and sometimes remarkable by its absence. In local
government, for example, there was scarcely a head office at all.
Local authorities had untrammelled power to set the level of their
own taxes – the business and domestic rates – and while their
powers were defined and limited by Acts of Parliament, within
those limits how they exercised their powers was up to them.
Constitutional theorists like A.V. Dicey would sternly remind
them that ultimate power lay with Parliament, which could abolish local government altogether in a single Act if it fancied. But
the key word was 'ultimate'. Once their legal framework had
been established, local councils, like many other British institutions, public and private, were mostly left to their own devices.

Not any more. Since the Second World War, that kind of day-
to-day freedom has been whittled away by an ever-intensifying
network of financial controls and regulations. This is equally true
of public institutions such as hospitals, schools, universities and
police forces as it is of private commercial organizations, such as
banks, bookshops, insurance companies, broadcasting and building societies.

To the managers at the centre, these thickening networks of
control appeared increasingly normal, in fact indispensable if they
were to manage properly. The controls became their own justification, since they transformed the haphazard scatter of branches

and members into a single body that could live and breathe only if it operated on consistent and thoroughly enforced guidelines. Gigantism led to centralization, and centralization led to something else.

As they gather unto themselves more and more extensive functions of leadership, the managers at the centre come to think of themselves as a single organ set apart from and responsible for the rest of the body. They become Management. These 'corporates', as they are happy to call themselves, develop quite naturally their own shared interests and strategies. They become a self-conscious class in the old Marxist sense, one which learns to look out for itself and whose members, while engaging in strenuous competition for the top slots, do also look out for each other. Long ago, sociologists such as Pareto and Mosca realized that the distinguishing feature of such elites is that they *circulate*. Years later, Anthony Sampson incorporated the same insight in *The Anatomy of Britain*. Once admitted to membership of the elite, these characters crop up again and again at the head of every type of organization, public and private. We have seen how the interlocking elites in the boardroom contrive to fix each other's remuneration at magnificent levels, regardless of the performance of the firm in question. By exerting an effective monopoly of power, they capture value both in terms of money and prestige. Indeed, the two types of benefit enjoy a pleasant reciprocal arrangement: the prestige entitles them to the cash, and the cash enhances and confirms the prestige.

Meanwhile, the institutions of liberal capitalist democracy continue in their traditional forms: the Houses of Parliament with their select committees and periodic elections, the Cabinet with its committees, annual general meetings with shareholders' votes held on important decisions and on the election of directors, public inquiries and courts of appeal, local authorities with their elections, trusts and boards of governors for public institutions.

None of these institutions is wholly defunct. *In extremis*, any one of them may rouse itself to put a stop to runaway oligarchs, even to dismiss or disgrace them. But in normal circumstances they do not often exercise the continuous scrutiny and control which they are allotted in theory. For effective purposes, it is the oligarchs who are in control.

This may seem an extreme statement of the position. And in any case, is it always such a bad thing? Surely representative democracy does include and must include a good deal of latitude for the top executives to take decisions promptly and on the basis of their broader view of the situation, rather than leave those decisions to ignorant provincial apparatchiks, on the one hand, or, on the other, to be second-guessed by their theoretical political overlords who do not really understand the situation. Once chosen, the managers must be given space to get on with the job. That at any rate is the theory behind what Lord Hailsham once called 'elective dictatorship', or (putting the same thing the other way round) 'executive democracy', which was how Jack Straw formulated it.

In the past, some famous analysts of oligarchy have argued that this tendency is inevitable in a large and sophisticated modern society. The twentieth-century German sociologist Robert Michels asserted that all forms of organization tend to develop into oligarchies: every organization needs leaders to give direction and drive efficiency; those leaders will defend their own interests and harden into a class; their followers will develop an unthinking loyalty to them. This was Michels's Iron Law of Oligarchy. It was supposed to apply just as much to democratic and socialist parties as to conservative and monarchist ones, as much to trade unions as to large corporations. Acting in accordance with his own theory, Michels abandoned his anarcho-syndicalist sympathies and, as a professor at the University of Perugia, became a publicist for Mussolini.

His predecessor, Vilfredo Pareto, a more formidable and influential thinker, argued that power and wealth inevitably were sucked up by an elite and that democracy was an illusion. He too had a soft spot for Mussolini, but, unlike Michels, had the excuse of dying too soon (in 1923) to see fascism in full action. Such theories have about them a sort of Vulgar Darwinism: only the fittest survived, and they cashed in, quite legitimately, at the expense of their weaker brethren. Nature was as red in tooth and claw in human society as it was in the animal kingdom.

I mention these dismal theories only to reject them. They are crude caricatures, and it is as ridiculous to swallow the idea that oligarchy is irresistible as it is to blind ourselves to the recurring dangers that it presents. I do not deny that there is a grain of truth in Michels's theory. The chosen few who are charged with the running of any organization will always be tempted to try to perpetuate their own rule and look after their own interests. But Michels oversimplifies reality. Some societies are much more oligarchic than others. Some governing committees are open to newcomers from different classes or ethnic groups; some are not. Some are greedy and rapacious; others are relatively self-denying. Britain in the eighteenth century was a great deal more oligarchic than it was to become after the Great Reform Bill of 1832; and a great deal more oligarchic before 1914 than after 1945.

Of course, the aristocracy still dominated high politics throughout Victoria's reign, though not exclusively so, and the bankers and brewers and mill owners used their weight in Parliament to defend their interests. But there were plenty of other interests in play, and big businessmen were not disproportionately privileged or indeed universally admired. They were already grumbling about high taxes and low public esteem. After the Second World War, quite a few oligarchs felt so little loved and so heavily taxed that they took themselves and their businesses offshore. Even today, when British governments have striven for thirty years to provide a friendly climate for businessmen, the families which own the three principal newspaper groups have all taken refuge overseas from British taxes.

Even in our own times, none of the symptoms of oligarchy is evenly spread across the world. The gap between rich and poor, for example, is nowhere near as wide in Scandinavia and Japan, nor is the gap widening at the same pace. In many countries, local and regional government is as strong as it ever was, if not stronger. It is certainly not declining in the USA where the powers of the States are rooted in the Constitution. In France, decentralization has made great strides. Being a *maire* not only matters locally, it is an avenue to national prominence. Germany has never lost that tradition of provincial government which derives from its historical origin as a combination of assorted duchies.

Nor is it the case that globalization somehow demands the rule of the few. It is simply not true that the more the world is interconnected, the greater the need for oligarchy. For one thing, it is still not entirely clear that today's globalization is unique and unprecedented. In the great era of free trade that was brought to a brutal end by the First World War, British goods and British capital flowed across the world with a reach and rapidity that dazzled people as much as 'the global market' mesmerizes us today. Yet local and provincial life continued through the era with much of its old vigour. It was the era of state control initiated by war that began the long slide into oligarchy, not globalization per se.

Nor is economic progress dependent either on sky-high bonuses for top earners or on steepling pyramids of debt. Both in the great American expansion of the postwar years and in the rapid recovery on the Continent at much the same time, banks pursued conservative lending policies (and were often pilloried for doing so), and, as we have seen, top executives were paid only modest multiples of the average worker's salary.

Besides, throughout the so-called 'global banking crisis' of 2007 to the present, banks in the Middle East, in most of Asia and in Australia remained untouched, and their local economies continued to achieve high rates of growth, despite (or because of) sticking to cautious lending practices.

What has gone wrong is not the outcome of some unstoppable world-historical process. The drift to oligarchy arises from our own lazy assumptions, our willingness to be impressed by the claims of the powerful to have all the answers, our lack of confidence in our ability to design our social and economic and political arrangements to suit ourselves. In particular, what we failed to take notice of were the influences that enable the oligarchs to flourish. Bureaucracy is certainly one, but there are quite a few others.

Let us call these influences the 'oligators'. I apologize for this rather clumsy pun. Its purpose is to help us keep in mind the deceptive qualities in play here. An oligator may look like something else, something quite harmless, just as an alligator may look like a log moving quietly along with the current, its sharp teeth and ferocious long jaw completely hidden.

An oligator may present itself as an opening towards democracy, for example, as a historic opportunity to empower the powerless. Revolutions often have this alluring appearance. The danger is that, as we all ought to know by now, the necessary loosening up shakes power and property from their old anchorages and gives the nimble interloper a window of opportunity to grab as much as he can and, like a successful pirate on the high seas, take his prizes in tow. This is more or less what happened in England in 1689, in France in 1789, and in Russia in 1989. A genuine, if imperfect democracy was established, but under cover of this welcome innovation, wealth and power were concentrated in a new ruling class of oligarchs.

We tend to think of such a disappointing outcome as an

accident, the result of weak or evil men being in charge during the momentous transition. We do not care to contemplate the possibility that the outcome may rather be a natural consequence of the country's chaotic condition. It may be that only an exceptionally tough and clear-headed leadership could have prevented such an outcome.

Settlements after great wars often, though not always, have this character too. After all the death and destruction, we hope for a new dawn. But looking around us in the aftermath, we often find, as Stanley Baldwin did looking around the House of Commons after the First World War, that we are surrounded by 'a lot of hardfaced men who look as if they had done very well out of the war'.

War itself is a great oligator, perhaps the greatest oligator of them all. For war offers the best excuse imaginable to bring every aspect of life under the control of the men at the top. It is not simply industry and the public services that have to be centrally directed, 'because there is a war on'. Our bodies and often our minds are conscripted into the war effort too. It is in wartime that we are taught to believe that national control is intrinsically more efficient, that 'the man in Whitehall knows best' – a proposition that would have sounded bewildering, not to say fatuous, before the advent of total war. And after the war is over, although rationing of food and other commodities may eventually be abolished, and although some publicly owned industries may eventually be denationalized, the notion persists over decades that it is government which is best equipped to introduce and direct new systems and that centralized administration remains fairer and more economical. Spectacular examples to the contrary, such as the humiliating failure of the £12 billion NHS computer system, tend to be ascribed to the shortcomings of individuals rather than any systemic inferiority. The rhetoric of modern all-out war is that 'we are all in this together' – a slogan revived during the current economic crisis. War, it is said, enables ordinary men and women to make a real contribution in a way that is seldom available to them in peacetime. So it does, but it also enables the lives of those ordinary men and women to be brought under an unprecedented degree of control by their political and economic masters.

Similarly, great technical developments often have the same double-edged quality. Revolutions in communications are usually presented as empowering the ordinary person. The mass media have always advertised themselves as champions of the little man and boasted of their mission to speak up for the voiceless against the Establishment. Yet ever since Northcliffe's *Daily Mail* set the pattern at the end of the nineteenth century, popular newspapers have also enabled thrusting businessmen to amass huge fortunes and accumulate head-spinning power and influence. Press barons are chronically vulnerable to delusions of grandeur. Northcliffe and Beaverbrook sought to make and unmake governments and to force ministers to adopt their own pet causes, such as Empire Free Trade; Rothermere demanded that his son be instantly elevated to the Cabinet. Today Rupert Murdoch expects to be wooed by each new leader of both the Conservative and Labour parties. In return for the support of his newspapers at the general election, he also expects to be unhindered in his hoovering up of newspapers and TV companies. When you see David Cameron and Tony Blair flying to pay homage at NewsCorp's annual fiesta, you see oligarchy in full bloom. What a contrast with Baldwin's contemptuous dismissal of Beaverbrook and Rothermere as aiming for 'power without responsibility – the prerogative of the harlot through the ages'.

I am certainly not arguing that the consequences of the mass media are unequivocally bad. In an age when the power of Parliament is fading so fast, newspapers still offer a feisty running critique of the government. Nor are the billions of the media oligarchs necessarily ill-spent. Bill Gates's work in Africa is exemplary. But there is no denying the mass media are an oligarchic force, one which concentrates wealth and attention upon the metropolis, and controls and narrows public opinion into approved channels.

For journalism has its own professional deformations, which journalists themselves are no more likely to be aware of than other professions are aware of theirs. Journalists are by nature critical of others rather than self-critical and unlikely to be sensitive to the biases which come instinctively to the mass media: to personalize, to oversimplify, to focus on central events. In any given country, politics is reduced to the ups and downs of one or two leaders or would-be leaders. The humdrum and complex doings of parliaments and congresses, let alone those of state assemblies and local councils, receive less and less attention in the newspapers and on TV news programmes. This unbalanced concentration reaches absurd extremes in Fleet Street's coverage of American politics, which focuses almost exclusively upon the President, ignoring the Congress, the Supreme Court and the individual states, which between them exercise quite as much power as the man in the White House, in fact rather more. This tendency has always been central to the operations of the tabloids. It is only more recently that the personalizing habit has taken hold of the supposedly more serious newspapers.

To take one example out of thousands that present themselves every morning, *The Times* of 10 October 2011 carried a report on French political doings under the headline 'Bruni delivers a pregnant pause to Socialist triumph', with a picture of Madame Sarkozy looking winsome and heavily *enceinte*. The real news was buried in paragraph five: the French Socialist party had held a primary open to all voters, in which no fewer than two million people had voted. This remarkable counterpunch against oligarchy was thought to be of little interest to *The Times* readers compared with Madame Sarkozy's impending birth.

This personality cult, unlike such cults in dictatorships, is generated by the media themselves rather than by the leader's propaganda bureau. And its effect is to induce a public expectation that the leader should take charge of pretty much everything, that he must respond personally to every problem that pops up. The leader is accordingly positively applauded for strong leadership if he emasculates his own party and manages to reduce Parliament to a rubber stamp. Blair, Cameron and even Miliband have received admiring editorials whenever they have sought to concentrate power within their own hands. The same applause greets a CEO like Sir Fred Goodwin who reduces his own board to yes-men and his subsidiary companies to impotent spectators of his brilliance. In their more malign form, the mass media can act as a recruiting sergeant and cheerleader for an aspiring dictator.

But surely the new media are different. Leaving aside the mega fortunes that accrue to their providers at Microsoft and Apple, surely the Twitter and the blog offer all of us, for the first time ever, the chance to answer back and have our say, unhindered and unscreened by higher authority. The Internet is gloriously free of control from above, except in dictatorships such as China, whose fear of the Net is testimony of its power.

So the conventional argument runs. And it is all true, as far as it goes. But two unkind questions have to be asked. First, who's listening? Do the powers that be pay any more attention to most of our outpourings than they do to the twittering of swifts in the evening sky? And second, don't the other applications of IT easily dwarf its delightful uses for private conversation and debate? In data gathering, monitoring, surveillance and control, electronic devices offer a marvellous cheap replacement for the old armies of clerks, agents and spies.

We walk around the streets under the unblinking scrutiny of CCTV. Even our rubbish bins are under constant surveillance, as are our bank balance and our credit rating and the validity of our car insurance, MoT and vehicle licence. Staff at call centres have their toilet breaks electronically timed; our performance at work is measured by every possible means. Within any industrial or commercial organization, new technology now makes it possible for the central *apparat* and the man or woman who heads that *apparat* to analyse the performance of every branch and every manager from minute to minute and to crush all local initiative and independence. Just as the railways they built helped a handful of British soldiers and civil servants to run a huge empire, so computers help the chairman's writ to run instantaneously to every corner of his empire. This is not the place to assess the pluses and minuses of Big Brother's hyperactivity. But what cannot be denied is that the new technology offers new opportunities for control alongside undreamed-of new freedoms. Michels is wrong to single out bureaucracy as the sole driving influence behind the rise of oligarchies. For oligarchy is like ivy; it will cling to any support; and when you cut it back, it keeps on growing again.

War, technology and bureaucracy – these are only some of the most potent oligators. Political theorists and politicians themselves would want to add to this list the ideologies that they or their opponents subscribe to. Socialism, for example, is generally regarded as a powerful centralizing dogma, and one which can degenerate into the rule of a single leader, thus coming to resemble the ideology to which it is most fiercely opposed, namely fascism. Surely these are among the strongest forces generating oligarchy. So they may be. Yet for all the passion that is expended upon such ideologies, I am not sure that they always have the lasting impact of those tendencies which arise out of modern life more or less unconsciously, without being deliberately pursued as a political programme. Socialism and fascism are in full view, after all. They have their fanatical enemies as well as their passionate supporters. When they fall out of fashion, the new broom does its best to sweep their legacy away. But technology and bureaucracy do not fall out of fashion. Nor, unfortunately, does war.

In the next part of this book, I will discuss how the oligarchic tendencies in modern Britain have infected politics as thoroughly as they have infected business. The combination of the two processes in their respective realms provides the essential precondition for oligarchy. For what oligarchy requires to become effective is a symbiosis between money and power, a daily interweaving of business and politics. The two sets of oligarchs must feed off each other to live and breathe. I do not claim that we have as yet reached a complete state of mutual dependence, but we are certainly heading in that direction.

Part Two

THE EROSION OF DEMOCRACY

The party's over now

On the surface it all looks much the same. In the gentle light of these islands, the landscape of our politics appears little changed in its fundamentals over our lifetime. The institutions that we grew up with are still there: the political parties, the local and general elections, town hall and Whitehall, the two houses of Parliament, the Cabinet and the Prime Ministers, the trade unions, the BBC.

And yet over the past forty years, mostly without our intending it or, to start with, even being aware of it, the reality has changed. The practice of politics, the relationship between people and politicians and the way in which decisions are taken – these things have progressively altered, in some cases almost beyond recognition. I am not talking here of the strictly *constitutional* reforms of the Blair–Brown years: the establishment of the Scottish Parliament and the Welsh Assembly, the Human Rights Act and the new powers enjoyed and exercised with relish by our judges. These reforms are important, and some of them have relevance to what I am talking about, though others do not. But the impact of these reforms is dwarfed by the processes of erosion that have taken place. And what has eroded is the participation of the people.

Let us try to trace the extent of that erosion and the course it has taken, and then consider what might be its cause or causes. I will try to avoid any nostalgia for the good old days. Conversely I will steer clear of any facile enthusiasm for the new 'modernized' institutions and practices. We will attempt to set out as coolly as we can what has actually happened.

The place to begin, I think, is the 1960s. Let us take a look at the middle and later years of that decade. In culture – music, fashion, moral behaviour – these years are taken as the beginning of a new era, looser, less buttoned up, less deferential. But in politics, by contrast, they were the last flowering of the old system. Nothing much had really changed since the Second World War, and not a lot since the First, except that the Labour Party had replaced the Liberals as one of the two great parties.

And it was those great parties that dominated the scene. Between them they controlled everything and supplied the men and women of the governing class. Both the Labour Party and the Conservative and Unionist Party were huge. According to some estimates, they were as big as any voluntary organizations in the free world. Even their offshoots had enormous memberships. At one point, the Young Conservatives were claimed to be the largest youth organization outside Russia and China. Conservative Central Office professed not to know the precise number of the party's overall membership, because the constituency associations guarded their independence and their figures so jealously. At what was probably its high point, though, in 1951 Central Office did shyly admit to a total number of 2,850,000 members. The best estimate of Robert McKenzie in the second edition of his classic *British Political Parties* (1963) was that the party then had around 2,250,000 members.

The Labour Party, by contrast, kept a meticulous public tally of its membership. Between 1947 and 1990, that figure never dipped below five million. In 1965, it had reached 6,440,000. In 1979, when Mrs Thatcher came to power, it hit a high point of 7,236,000. Individual membership (those who were not affiliated through the trade unions and other organizations) had topped a million in the early 1950s but had gradually eroded to 666,000 in 1979. The shortfall was more than made up by the growth of members affiliated through the trade unions, which were then going through a golden period of expanded power and wealth.

Conservatives mocked the Labour Party's claim to such enormous numbers. The nine tenths of its membership who belonged through their trade unions were, the Tories said, mostly sleeping members who took no active part in the Labour Party but who could not be bothered to fill in the form to contract out of the automatic political levy which was paid through the union. At Labour Party conferences, the trade union leaders wielded massive bloc votes, often in disregard of their members' actual views. And it is true that between 1928 and 1946, the period during which members of trade unions had to 'contract in' for membership of the Labour Party, the number of trade union members was much lower, hovering around the two million mark. Yet even in those years the total membership, composed of people who had actively opted to join the party, steadily rose towards three million.

After the war, the Attlee government changed the law back to what it had been before the General Strike of 1926, so that millions of trade union members found themselves also members of the Labour Party, whether they liked it or not. But we should not ignore these involuntary members. They were, willy-nilly, part of the Labour world, and through their branches engaged in some sort of refracted dialogue with the party's leadership. Toss in the then much smaller Liberal Party and the other fringe parties, Communists, Nationalists and so on, and it is fair to estimate that in the 1960s somewhere around ten million people in Britain were members, in one way or another, of one party or another – roughly a fifth of the population.

These giant bodies were formidable presences in the life of
every town and county in Britain. Almost every constituency
party maintained its own offices with a full-time party agent,
equipped with a secretary who herself might be a formidable
character (they were always women then), often more energetic
and ferocious than the agent himself (they were mostly men). A
Tory agent might have been a regular officer in one of the services or gained a wartime commission as a Territorial. Labour
agents more often had trade union connections, having perhaps
served as a branch official, although some of them had done well
in the war too. Agents of either party might sit on the local bench
as JPs, and on the committees of local voluntary organizations.
The party offices often adjoined or occupied the same premises as
the local Labour or Conservative club. These clubs were affiliated
to the party, although many of their members might not be supporters of the party at all but would simply go there, with or
without their spouses, to have a drink and play snooker, whist,
bridge, darts or bingo. In this way, the party was plugged into the
social life of the neighbourhood and had connections beyond its
paid-up membership.

Many MPs too had local connections then, although there
were always a large number of carpet-baggers. A Conservative MP
might be an old friend or a relation of the association chairman or
some other local potentate. Labour MPs would be sponsored by
one or more of the trade unions which were strongly represented
in local factories and offices. The Islington North constituency,
for example, was in the gift of the Transport and General Workers
Union which dominated the Archway bus depot. The constituency also had a strongly Irish flavour, so that a bus driver of
Irish descent was a shoo-in, just as a former miner had a strong
chance in the coal fields of South Wales or Yorkshire.

Yet these local networks of influence did not necessarily put the
new candidate, once elected to Parliament, under continuous

direct pressure from his masters in the constituency. Local pressures were on the whole less intense than they are today. Quite a few MPs rarely visited their constituencies at all. Duncan Sandys, who was Tory MP for Streatham or Norwood most of the time between 1935 and 1974, claimed that he visited the place, only a short hop across the river from Westminster, but once a year, to address his association's AGM (being Winston Churchill's son-in-law may have helped him to get away with this sporadic contact). Most MPs were a little more assiduous, but not many of them regarded it as their sacred duty to hold a 'surgery' in their constituency once a fortnight or even once a month. Conversely, most of their constituents did not then regard their man or woman at Westminster as a glorified welfare officer, though *in extremis* your MP was certainly the person you complained to about an injustice you had endured. Any sensible MP stayed aware of the feeling of his constituents on important issues of the day, but this did not take much doing. For the MP and his or her constituents were part of the same world. They breathed the same air, and even when they differed, they usually knew what their comrades were thinking.

I am not romanticizing these old days. There were considerable drawbacks to the relationship. The fog of party commonality often obscured what was going on in the new world outside. The shared outlook could lead to a shared complacency – about Britain's industrial decline, for example, or the poor standards of Britain's state schools. And when any Prime Minister tried to embark on reform, he or she quickly found out the truth of Disraeli's remark on his deathbed to his socialist interviewer, H. M. Hyndman: 'It is a very difficult country to move, Mr Hyndman, a very difficult country indeed.'

The elaborate hierarchy which these mass parties generated, and which that membership was numerous enough to finance quite handsomely, was also a force against change. The Area or

Regional Agents and the political officers and trade union officers and women's officers who provided a layer of officialdom between the constituencies and the party's National Executive Committee (NEC) reinforced the general conservatism, with a small c, which kept its grip on both major parties. At a higher level, the message would be transmitted from the backbench MPs to their area whips who would report to the Chief Whip who would report to the Prime Minister (or Leader of the Opposition) that 'our people won't have it'.

At the same time, though, this consensus for the status quo was an unmistakable signal that the party still ruled. Even a member who did nothing for his party except to pay the minimum annual subscription could feel confident that his was among the voices which were keeping the party on the right lines. The party would, so far as it prudently and practically could, defend their interests and respect their prejudices.

If the leadership showed signs of backtracking or backsliding, there was always the party conference. These enormous rallies, several thousand strong, held at the seaside just before Parliament returned from the summer recess, were occasions for heroic drinking and feverish plotting. But they also offered the leaders a platform to show that their hearts were still in the right place. And they offered the rank and file a chance to give the leadership a sharp reminder, even an embarrassment, a fright or a humiliation. In the more democratic and meticulous Labour Party, the party's constitution also allotted the party conference the leading role in the formation of party policy.

From this constitutional role derived the furious battles over nationalization and the British nuclear deterrent (and to a lesser extent over Europe) which tore the party apart year after year from the 1950s to the 90s. The memorable phrases from those battles still resound in our ears: Nye Bevan's 'I will not go naked into the conference chamber'; Hugh Gaitskell's 'I will fight, fight and fight again to save the party I love'. Veterans of these occasions can still reel off, like so many battle honours, the years and the names of the resorts at which this or that vituperative and agonized debate and nail-biting vote took place – Brighton or Blackpool, Southport or Scarborough.

It was not often that in the end the party conference did actually make the policy. On the contrary, what went into the party's manifesto for the following general election was usually more or less what the leaders wanted to go in. Only in 1983, when the leadership of Michael Foot was itself left-inclined and so was the majority on the party's National Executive Committee, which had to approve the final document, did the party's programme come close to fulfilling the heart's desires of the activists. And it turned out to be a disaster: 'The longest suicide note in history', as Gerald Kaufman immortally dubbed the document.

As for the Conservative Party, commentators like to quote Balfour's characteristically nonchalant remark that 'I'd rather take advice from my valet than from the Conservative Party conference'. But Balfour was a poor and short-lived leader of his party, and his remark a piece of clubman's bravado. Conservative leaders in practice were just as careful as their Labour counterparts to take account of the instincts and antipathies of their rank and file. On the rare occasions when the leadership defied those instincts and antipathies, it had the devil of a struggle to get its proposals through Parliament, because so many of its backbenchers could defect, comfortable in the knowledge that many if not most of their constituency supporters would applaud. Edward Heath had to battle through these Commons nightmares not once but twice: on the abolition of resale price maintenance, where his small shopkeepers saw their profit margins disappearing in a wave of price-cutting, and on the European Communities Bill.

It remained well worth belonging to the Conservative or Labour Party. You were part of a shaping and inhibiting community which, most of the time, managed to keep its leaders within the bounds of what you thought right and legitimate. If the leaders should happen to stray from the true path, they could be tugged back into line, or, failing that, they could be punished by such a relentless body-battering that they became fatally weakened and could be replaced by more sympathetic figures. The spectacle of intra-party conflict might distress floating voters, but it never seemed to upset party activists themselves. On the contrary, the major parties both maintained high levels of membership throughout their bitter internal struggles.

As long as members continued to feel that, sooner or later, their views might prevail, they mostly stayed paid-up. The only noteworthy sudden drop in registered party membership occurred in the Labour Party between 1979 and 1980 when an internal inquiry revealed that the party had not been as meticulous as it claimed and had assumed a minimum membership of 1,000 even in those constituencies where in reality it was virtually defunct. Recorded individual membership fell from 660,000 to 348,000 as a result, but trade union membership was unaffected by the new count, so the overall drop looked unremarkable.

The postwar party conferences were marvellous spectacles for the onlooker. For thirty years and more, as a political journalist I would attend one or more each year, often all three and sometimes the Trades Union Congress as well. They were often riotous and never boring. How we relished the feverish caucusing in the corridors outside the conference hall. The trade union delegations might swing their entire hundreds of thousands of votes this way or that on the say-so of one delegate at the back of the scrum who had not heard the question properly. It was a chance too for people outside the trade union movement to hear their most electrifying orators like Arthur Scargill. The Labour MPs were usually penned in an enclosure to the right of the platform looking like defendants in a Communist show trial. There might be hissing and booing as a member of the Cabinet stumbled out of this holding pen to make his way to the platform to speak for no longer than the time allotted to the dungareed Young Socialist from the sticks. Conservative party conferences were more deferential, except when it came to the debates on Europe, immigration or capital punishment. From any of these the liberal-minded minister or shadow minister would return to the conference hotel white and shaking.

All these encounters were given lavish coverage by the media. The BBC broadcast the debates entire, consoling itself for the long periods of tedium by the occasional flare-ups that could be clipped for the news bulletins and by the thought of the credit it was thereby stacking up with the politicians.

But gradually from the 1990s on, and more intensively after Tony Blair became Labour leader and impressed everyone with his dazzling success, the parties began to take professional advice. Media experts, not yet dubbed spin doctors, persuaded their clients that these televised punch-ups were repellent to the general public. The sooner the conferences were drained of any real passion and stripped of any pretension to power, the better. One of the things the public was thought to dislike particularly was the sight of raw trade union power as exercised through the bloc vote. These conspicuous embarrassments denied the party the overwhelming popular support it would otherwise enjoy – or so the media wizards argued. For the Labour Party, these anxieties were intensified when the Gang of Four (Roy Jenkins, Shirley Williams, David Owen and Bill Rodgers) broke away in 1981 to form the Social Democrats. These old supporters of Hugh Gaitskell, from the moderate wing of the party, fiercely opposed the party's general drift to the Left on economic policy, but their specific complaint was 'the way the party is run', what they denounced as a sort of mob rule which ignored the moderate views of most Labour voters.

After coming agonizingly close to taking second place in the general election of 1983 in terms of votes, the SDP suffered its own internal splits and faded from view, but its legacy was a far greater awareness inside the Labour Party of how it looked to the outside world. And so throughout the 1980s and 90s the leadership set about systematically castrating the party conference – and also diminishing the power and independence of both the local associations and the National Executive Committee. After their shattering defeats by Tony Blair, the Conservative leadership started doing much the same thing. Stanley Baldwin used to claim that if it became known that he was interfering in the selection of a candidate, his preferred nominee would not have a chance of being chosen. But now both Transport House and Conservative Central Office began to interfere quite openly in the selection process: pushing their own preferred candidates onto compliant associations, banning other candidates whom they considered too extreme or too dim. Special efforts were made to make the party appear more representative of the general population, by infiltrating as many female and black or Asian candidates as possible. Eventually, Labour began to insist on all-women shortlists in some constituencies. The Conservative Party's list of candidates was regularly pruned and reselected to weed out unsuitable candidates.

As for the conferences, the Conservatives' was robbed of what small pretensions it had to advise on policy; there were to be no more contentious motions debated and no votes taken. The Labour conference was neutered in two ways. Between 1992 and 1994, John Smith in his sadly brief tenure as leader instituted 'OMOV', one man one vote – thus destroying the trade union bloc vote, but as a consequence also dramatically reducing the total membership from millions to hundreds of thousands. At a stroke, the number of votes typically cast at a Labour conference dwindled from about half the number of people who might vote Labour at a general election to perhaps five per cent. The new system did ensure that the votes represented the real views of real people, but they were the views of far fewer people, so that their weight was sharply reduced. In future, the leadership could appeal more directly to the presumed views of Labour voters over the heads of its 'unrepresentative' activists. At the same time, the policy motions were no longer filtered through the National Executive Committee, where the majority had so often proved recalcitrant to the views of the leadership. In future, policy was to be sidetracked to the new National Policy Forums. These were packed with trusty loyalists and could be relied on to serve up to conference a string of policy menus which would cause no embarrassment. Votes were still taken at conference, but they were now taken on anodyne motions and had no constitutional impact on future policy. The once glorious annual shindig dwindled into a corporate PR opportunity.

It is hard to exaggerate the overall impact of the changes in the way the Labour Party operates – some of them begun under Neil Kinnock and John Smith but all of them hammered home under Tony Blair. Throughout the 1970s and 80s, the National Executive Committee had tormented successive Labour Party leaders. Now it has become the leader's pussycat. As Meg Russell puts it in *Building New Labour* (2005):[48] 'The regaining of a loyalist majority on the NEC saw it become a willing partner in its own political decline.' It has returned to its original role, of merely 'mobilizing support within the Party for whatever was decided by the Cabinet'. The party's General Secretary and Treasurer and their staffs now tend to report direct to the leader rather than to the NEC. The NEC is once more, as it was in the 1950s, 'no more than a minor offshoot of the Downing Street command post'. [49]

At the same time, the selection of parliamentary candidates has been brought as firmly under control of party HQ as it has in the Conservative Party. Potential candidates may still be nominated by local trade unions or branches of the Constituency Labour Party, but since 1998 they have been subject to pre-approval by a central panel, and then, if selected, have to be endorsed by the NEC. Those rejected by the panel may still seek selection, but the knowledge that they still have to be endorsed by the Party *apparat* is a powerful damper on the ambitions of militants and trouble-makers seeking to become MPs.

The third source of influence for Labour Party grassroots members – and in theory the most potent one – was the party's annual conference. Here too after the Blair years, that influence has been harshly shrunk if not quite eliminated. In Meg Russell's words: 'The period since the late 1980s has seen a complete transformation of the Labour Party conference.'[50] The upshot of all the alterations in the rules for selecting delegates and motions for debate is that 'conference has become a less aggressive, more representative and generally more supportive "showcase" for the party leadership'. Local constituency delegates now have a larger share of the dele-gates' votes and the trade unions a smaller share, but conference as a whole has power over less. The crucial change has been the reform of the conference agenda. Instead of often fiery and ac-cusatory resolutions being submitted direct by local parties and trade unions, the main focus of debate is provided by bland policy documents which have been carefully blended by the National Policy Forum under the directions of the leadership, with little or no opportunity for input from local activists. The leadership pre-cooks the agenda as deftly as a TV chef declaring 'Here's one I made earlier.' The whole emphasis is 'primarily on top-down edu-cation about policy rather than bottom-up democratic control'.[51] The myth that Conference is sovereign over policy remains offi-cially intact, but all concerned are now well aware that it is only a myth.

These moves made it seem less worthwhile to belong to either of the big two political parties. If you could not freely choose your own parliamentary candidate, nor bring forward to conference your own policy demands, what was the point? As numbers dwindled, there was another, somewhat perverse consequence, especially for the Conservatives: the remaining members tended to be increasingly elderly and crotchety. Their faces were not presentable to the media; nor were their views. The more their power was reduced, the less suitable they seemed to exercise what power remained to them. As the broadcasters scaled down their coverage of the conferences, those responsible for organizing them felt nothing but relief.

Only in the election for the party leader did it appear that party members were actually gaining power. The Conservative Party had in 1998 instituted a new system of electing their leader that followed Labour in letting all party members vote in a final run-off, rather than confining this to their MPs. But as the candidates who got through to the run-off were those who had come out top in earlier ballots, which had been confined to MPs, the party at Westminster was still the dominant voice in the selection.

The same objection applied to the fashionable efforts to widen the selection process for MPs. The Conservatives began gingerly experimenting with 'open primaries', in which the final choice of candidate was open to any voter in the constituency, whether party member or not. What could be more democratic, more inclusive, more exhilarating? And it really was a thrill when Dr Sarah Wollaston was chosen to be the Tory candidate for Totnes in August 2009, receiving 7,914 votes, her nearest rival getting 5,495 votes – numbers not far short of what might be clocked up in a parliamentary by-election. If the vote had been confined in the old style to association members, the total vote would have been only a few hundred.

But of course, if widely adopted, the open primary would be another nail in the coffin of the mass political party. Why bother to subscribe, let alone canvass or attend meetings, if any old local resident can blow in and usurp the most cherished right of the local party, to select its candidate for the House of Commons?

Open primaries were not much clamoured for by local associations. On the contrary, the main pressure came from the party leadership, which was eager to show itself responsive to popular demands for greater democracy. That may sound surprising. Why would the centre want to encourage local trouble-makers and mavericks to be selected on a groundswell of local enthusiasm? But of course in a crucial sense these open primaries are not really open at all.

The potential candidates have first of all to go through the rigorous processes of approval by Central Office or Labour Party HQ. They are winnowed down to a shortlist of three or four by a committee of the local association, still under close supervision by Central Office. Only then do they go before the public. Contrast this highly controlled process with the practice in many American states where a complete outsider can get on to the ballot paper at the primary election and romp home on a wave of popular idealism or disgust and unseat the official favourite for the nomination. The American system has other drawbacks, notably the need to raise millions of dollars to make a showing. But it is genuinely open, in the sense that anyone can run in the final vote.

Certainly the experiments in open primaries have done nothing to halt the decline in party membership. The facts are stark. By the end of 2007, membership of the Labour Party had fallen to 177,000, thought to be the lowest figure since the party was formed in 1900, and scarcely forty per cent of the 405,000 reached in 1997 in the first days of the Blair government. Membership of the Conservative Party had fallen to 290,000 when David Cameron took over. His leadership might have restored the party's standing in the polls, but it did nothing to stem the collapse in party membership, which has fallen further to 250,000 or possibly less.

Even if you add in the Liberal Democrats (who probably have more members than the old Liberal Party could boast) and the Greens and the Nationalists, it is doubtful whether the total membership of all the parties put together amounts to much more than half a million. This is one twentieth of the figure that we saw throughout the 1950s, 60s and 70s. As a proportion of the total population, membership has fallen from 20 per cent to 1 per cent within a generation. The big parties have been literally decimated, like the unluckier Roman legions who were reduced to one tenth of their original strength.

But at least the Romans died in battle. The great parties have withered without a whimper. At first glance, it may seem curious that the party leaderships seem so little distressed by the disappearance of their rank and file. On the contrary, it often seems as if they greet the absence of activists with some relief. No longer do they have to fend off the unrealistic demands of their followers or quell embarrassing rebellions. These days party management, outside the House of Commons at least, is a much less exhausting task. The new conventional wisdom is that elections are won and lost in the broadcasting studio, not in the local party offices. Being good in interviews is more important than being good at organization. The money flows in direct to the centre, from a handful of millionaire donors, and it stays in the centre.

Nor is the withering of the party structure much mourned by newspapers and television. Journalists always found that aspect of politics tedious and provincial. In any case, the new focus on the media means that reporters are flattered and fed with titbits and made to feel like big shots, whereas they used to be patronized as lowlifes in dirty raincoats. How much easier to appeal to the public through a few selected media favourites over the heads of the party activists if there are scarcely any party activists left.

Thus belonging to a political party has become almost a freakish activity. If you visit a by-election campaign these days, you are likely to find that most of the canvassers are people who hope to become politicians themselves and are earning their stripes by knocking on doors.

At the same time, these hollowed-out parties actually have more power than they used to enjoy. It is the official party hierarchy which draws up the party list for Scottish and Welsh and European elections. It also does so now for local elections in Scotland and would probably do so when and if we have an elected or partly elected House of Lords, for any new electoral machinery introduced in the UK from now on is likely to be done on a party-list form of proportional representation. The party bosses also nominate sympathetic spirits to sit on the ever-mushrooming quangos which administer all sorts of institutions that either never existed before or were previously under the control of elected bodies such as local councils. The weaker the parties become in terms of their membership, the more patronage they have in their gift. We shall return to the rather vexed question of quangos later, but for the moment all we need to note is that who sits on them is increasingly decided by a very small number of people who run their shrunken parties: the party oligarchs are quango kings.

How then does the internal withering of the political parties impact upon national politics and upon elections in particular? Are the party leaders successful in using the media to appeal to the public more directly? Has the disappearance of the mass party left the crucial bits of the system more or less unaffected? Is the picture brighter when we turn to general elections?

Don't vote, it only encourages them

We have straight away to confront the uncomfortable fact that over the past decade the turnout at general elections has plummeted, quite sharply and unexpectedly. Since universal suffrage was introduced at the end of the 1920s, turnout had remained remarkably steady, at roughly 75 per cent. It reached a peak of 84 per cent in 1951. Given that the electoral register is always a little out of date, that comes close to every able-bodied person turning out. When an election looked like being a close-run thing, as 1951 did, turnout would rise to nearer 80 per cent. It did so again in 1964, 1979 and 1992. When the outcome looked more foregone, then the figure might slip back to nearer 70 per cent. But nothing prepared us for the sudden fall to 59.4 per cent in June 2001 and 61.3 per cent in May 2005. It is as if a considerable slice of the electorate, 15 per cent or thereabouts, had suddenly listened to the siren voices of the 1960s anarchists whispering 'Don't vote, it only encourages them' – or in the variant devised by Ken Livingstone, 'If voting changed anything, they'd abolish it.'

Was it a coincidence that election turnout should hold up for so long and then fall so precipitately soon after party membership had begun to experience that unstoppable decline? And if so, what had caused these parallel declines? And what, if anything, could or should be done to reverse either or both of them? Has popular participation in and enthusiasm for politics become a lost cause, doomed to become the preserve of a minority of obsessives, rather like religion in the eyes of the secular majority?

There was a growing feeling that the plummeting turnout was a symptom that something had gone badly wrong with British politics. Just as the Rowntree Trust had sponsored memorable inquiries into poverty and housing in the early years of the twentieth century, so a century later Rowntree sponsored an inquiry into the reasons for the decline in popular participation. Baroness Helena Kennedy was appointed chairman, and I was asked to join the team. For nearly a year we travelled around Britain, listening to anyone who wanted to come and talk to us.[52]

A host of reasons has been advanced for the decline. On the Power Commission we heard almost all of them – all except the argument I have just advanced, that it is their own leaders who have deliberately deprived the parties of meaningful power. We were often told, for example, that people today have become apathetic about public affairs, particularly where party politics are concerned. They lead frenetically busy lives, full of other, more tempting and absorbing diversions. It is not surprising that dreary old political controversies should fail to attract their attention when private life offers so much more. They have simply less time to spare. They are too busy to loiter in the public square.

Yet people today do manage to find time for all sorts of causes that their parents and grandparents would not have stirred out of doors for. They will march for or against blood sports or the Iraq war. They are passionate about preserving the environment. The memberships of the National Trust and the Royal Society for the Protection of Birds run into millions, several times the membership of any political party. And is it seriously argued that voters today are less concerned about the state of their local hospitals or about standards in their schools? There is uproar whenever the closure of a popular school or hospital is proposed, or a new airport runway is planned, or when planning permission is granted for a developer to build on the field at the bottom of the lane. Far from being numbed into apathy, large numbers of us have a hair-trigger conscience and a lively sense of indignation that can be mobilized at a moment's notice.

Nor can it be said that British people today do not vote in such numbers because they are more or less contented with their lot. One or two MPs did put this point of view to the Power Commission, but they were drowned out by the volume of evidence in the other direction. In all the surveys and focus groups that were conducted for the Commission, as well as the witnesses we heard directly, the overwhelming message was of how frustrated and dissatisfied people felt. If you take MPs' postbags as a rough measure, dissatisfaction has risen steadily as popular participation in politics has declined.

So what other reason or reasons might there be for the non-participation? The most influential view among political sociologists is that participation rose in step with a sense of class allegiance and class antagonism and has declined with them. Tribal loyalty used to be the motor that drove voters to the poll. The motor was driven by the representatives of class locally; squires or trade union officials not only egged on their respective tenantries to vote the right way, they literally drove them to the polling station. This lifelong allegiance to the class you were born into has, it is said, melted as social mobility has increased. People now exercise a good deal of personal control over the social class they come to occupy. They no longer feel an instinctive loyalty or gratitude to their class of origin. Nor do they feel any need to rely on 'their' party to defend their interests.

This explanation elides into another, more popular way of

putting it, which is to say that 'They're all the same nowadays'. Both parties are competing for the centre ground and hope to scoop up a quantity of votes that in the old days might have gone automatically to the other side: Labour under Blair and latterly under Brown sought to appeal to Middle England; the Conservatives under Cameron have begun to portray themselves as the true defenders of the poor. In any case, neither side can afford too flagrantly to favour their traditional supporters, for fear of alienating the uncommitted. Large parts of the parties' manifestoes are interchangeable. In a blind tasting, I certainly could not be sure of identifying which party some passages came from.

At first sight, this explanation seems rather more plausible. Lack of difference breeds indifference. If none of the three main parties seems to offer anything distinctive, why bother with any of them?

Yet there are difficulties with this line of explanation too. For one thing, parties have been pilfering one another's kitbags ever since Disraeli claimed in 1843 that Peel had 'caught the Whigs bathing and walked away with their clothes'. In the mid-1950s, when election turnouts of party memberships were still sky-high, the parties were thought to have converged so much that the *Economist* coined the term 'Butskellism' to describe the sim-ilarities between the Tory Rab Butler and Labour's Hugh Gaitskell. Moreover, it was the 1960s, 70s and 80s which turn out in retrospect to have been the years of maximum social mobility. Since then, statistics suggest that the scene has frozen up some-what. The chances are greater now that young people will finish up in the same social class as their parents and grandparents. Over the same period, income inequalities have increased and polarized at each end of the scale, so that in economic terms (and I would argue, in socio-cultural terms too) class differences have hardened again and have become more visible and painful. This might suggest that tribal loyalties could reawaken and that quite a few people might return to the party which had traditionally represented their interests; as a result, voter turnout and even party identification might be expected to revive. But it hasn't happened yet. Now and then, it is true, party leaders do make a swerve back in the direction of what is now called a 'core vote strategy' – to stir up the old allegiances – but there is not much sign that this tactic works, and the leadership usually soon reverts to the centre ground which they ultimately think is likely to be more profitable.

We can argue the toss one way and the other about these hypotheses, but there is one hard factual type of evidence which does not suggest that the parties are much closer to being identical today than they were a few decades ago. That is the evidence, not of what they say in their manifestoes for the future but of what they have actually done when in office. There is no doubt, for example, that the rich did very well under Mrs Thatcher and that inequalities of income did increase for the first time since the war. Conversely, there is no doubt that schools and hospitals and welfare generally were lavishly treated by Blair and Brown (after the first few years in which they stuck to the Tory targets for public expenditure as they had promised at the 1997 election). If you disregarded the rhetoric and looked at the record, you could reasonably assume that both parties had kept quite a bit of their traditional attitudes and aims. The daily experience of voters would confirm the differences quite acutely.

So I do not think that the 'they're all the same nowadays' argument can be a decisive explanation for decline in participation. If you are primarily worried about the high levels of taxation, then you would still have good reason to vote Conservative. If your main worry is whether enough is going to be spent on schools and hospitals, it remains a rational choice to vote Labour. Either way, there are still good concrete reasons for turning out to vote.

It seems likely, therefore, that voters may have a quite rational reason, or set of reasons, for not joining political parties and for not voting at general elections. It may be that they do not participate because they have come to believe that their participation makes no difference. Ordinary citizens, especially the worst off, may conclude from their experience that power has become separated from the electoral process and operates at such a remote level that they can have little or no influence, whether as party members or voters. In the most concrete instances, they can see that key decisions such as the selection of candidates, which used to be entirely within the province of the local party, are now so controlled and guided by the centre that the role of local party members is close to a charade.

Nor are these charades confined to the party political bits of the system. The quangos now control many activities which used to be either regulated by elected bodies such as local authorities or were left to private initiative and control. The quangocrats are conscious that they have been selected not elected, and they are conscious of a 'democratic deficit'. So they engage in elaborate and costly exercises in 'consultation'. These are now mandatory in many public services, and management consultants, PR firms and focus group operators make a good living of finding out what 'the people' think. But ultimately the quangocrats are in charge. They embark on the project, phrase the questions and interpret (and sometimes disregard) the answers given. Again and again, on the Power Commission we were told, sometimes by the more honest quangocrats themselves, how little confidence these exercises in consultation inspired in the public, how they were a poor substitute for real decision-making power and how citizens had come to feel 'consultation fatigue'. We have already seen how the quangocrats are rewarded by sizeable and growing salaries for what is often part-time work. They like to describe themselves as 'stakeholders', but their position really corresponds to that of those well-connected personages in the eighteenth century who held public sinecures. The modern stakeholding world has developed a further space for party patronage, while the popular base of the parties has continued to dwindle. This too is a classic instance of creeping oligarchy.

Closing the local

We ought also to take a look at what has happened to local government itself. This is not a pretty sight. For what we see is, for the most part, a withered and castrated remnant of what used to be a vigorous and independent part of British life.

Go back a mere forty years, and you will see local councils in relatively rude health, and still retaining much of the power they and their predecessors – the burgesses and magistrates – had enjoyed for centuries. Prince among those powers was the power to tax. Borough and county councillors had an unrestrained right to levy their rates on businesses and domestic households at whatever level they fancied. They possessed, too, the power to borrow money for public works on the open market by issuing bonds, as well as borrowing from the government through the Public Works Loan Board. As they were reliable repayers and seldom feckless, savers readily bought these bonds, and there were few instances of default.

True, all the activities of local councils had come to be limited and specified by Act of Parliament (though some of those activities predated the statute that regulated them). Councils might, very occasionally, be found by the courts to have strayed beyond their legal powers and would be declared to have acted *ultra vires*. But in regard to the activities that were permitted to them, local councils enjoyed a remarkable degree of freedom. In education, for example, they could decide whether their schools system was to be comprehensive or divided into grammar and secondary modern, or at secondary level, by age into upper and lower schools; they hired and, less often, fired the teachers; they had a good deal of freedom as to what subjects were to be taught and by what methods. Civil servants in the Department of Education, then only a modest sliver of a building on the approaches to Waterloo Station, were brought up to regard the school curriculum as 'a secret garden', into which they tiptoed at their peril.

In some public services, such as the police, the government had built up over the decades the right to advise and even dictate on certain matters, such as police pay and training and the appointment of the Commissioner of Police in London. But as late as 1982, I was on the receiving end of a litany of complaint from the then Home Secretary, Willie Whitelaw, about the repeated frustrations he had experienced in trying to make the police follow his bidding.

I am not arguing that, as a result, our schools and police forces then were always more efficient and responsive to the demands of citizens and parents. All I am saying is that those services then were undeniably *local* services, and if you wanted to complain about their shortcomings, you went to the local council, not to Whitehall or to some consultative quango. And that local council commanded a good deal of power to shape its services as it wanted, to improve them where necessary and to raise more money for those improvements.

That local power rested, as most political power rests, on financial independence. And it is this financial independence which was steadily and purposefully destroyed over the course of the twentieth century. The transformation from near-total independence to near-total dependence had a damnable symmetry about it. In 1900, about 90 per cent of local government's revenue was raised locally, through domestic and business rates and through fees for services provided. There was a police grant from central government, some special grants for education, not much else. By 1965, after a rapid growth in local government expenditure which had to be brought to a temporary halt – Tony Crosland, the local government minister, famously said 'the party's over' – local councils were still raising about half of their total revenues. Move on thirty years later, to the last years of the twentieth century, and more than 90 per cent of local government's revenue was provided by central government. The 90–10 ratio had been completely reversed to 10–90, and the town hall had become a puppet theatre.

How did all this happen? The simple answer is that Whitehall crammed the councils with cream. At first the process was more like a seduction. At the same time as central government was laying fresh powers and duties on the local council, it offered attractive grants to pay for them, encouraging councillors to believe that these welcome douceurs would enable them to keep the rates down and get re-elected. All too often, neither of these things happened. As hyper-inflation took hold in the late 1960s and 70s, the local rates went up as fast as the grants, and local government became virulently unpopular. Worse still, a handful of 'loony Left' councils handed out even more in subsidies to their voters. Local government in general got a name for extravagance – largely undeserved but convenient for central government which hoped to deflect the blame. In Opposition, Ted Heath was prompted to prove that he would be even tougher on local government, and he twisted the arm of his young local government spokesman, a newcomer called Margaret Thatcher, to issue a promise that the next Conservative government would find a fairer and less burdensome alternative to the rating system.

Thus the Alderman's Daughter found herself landed with the role of Destroyer of the Rates, something I fancy she might never have dreamed of assuming off her own bat. With her characteristic thoroughness she stuck to this new role even after she became Prime Minister and devised, first, rate-capping – plausible no doubt as a temporary measure to put the lid on the loony Left but which, as its opponents had forecast, would turn out to be a permanent fixture. At the same time, the business rates were nationalized into what was called the Uniform Business Rate, which ever since has been set by the government at the same level for the whole country.

Not content with this, she devised a full-blown replacement for the rating system: the iniquitous and disastrous community charge, or poll tax. The principal drawback of this tax (as of all poll taxes going back to the one which caused the Peasants' Revolt in 1381) was that its flat rate bore down so disproportionately on the lower income groups. The only way of making it even faintly workable was to levy it at a very low rate, so that it raised pitifully small amounts of revenue and forced government to increase the central grant to unheard-of levels. Thus the local basis of council revenue was destroyed. Even after John Major had replaced the poll tax with the considerably fairer council tax, locally raised revenue today raises barely a quarter of what councils spend. The Cameron Conservatives have promised to restore much greater freedom to local councils, but so far these freedoms look likely to be hedged and limited, and unlikely to bring back anything approaching the old independence.

The great defect of the council tax, as opposed to the domestic rates, is that it is progressive only up to a certain point. Above that point, it morphs into a flat-rate tax. Currently all houses in England valued above £320,000 are in the top band H. As a result, for my own house in Islington, where I have lived for more than forty years, I am currently paying almost exactly the same council tax, in cash terms not real terms, as I paid in rates when we moved in. That is why Vince Cable, the Libdem Business Secretary in the Coalition, has suggested some sort of 'mansion tax', an additional tax to be paid on houses valued over £1 million – which would of course include the dwellings of every single oligarch. But it would include the dwellings of middle-class Conservative voters too, which is why the Tories will not have it. It would in fact be simpler and fairer to introduce three or four higher-rate bands in the council tax system. But that would involve a revaluation of all such properties, which would be even more anathema to the Tories. Yet any serious localism must involve a far greater degree of financial independence for local councils, and that must involve just such a reform of the council tax. Why should the rich be expected to pay their fair share nationally (as they mostly do) and not locally too?

The trouble is that the function assigned by national politicians to local councils today has altered from that of local government in the old broad sense – 'little parliaments' as Joseph Chamberlain, the greatest of Birmingham's lord mayors, called them – to something much more modest and secondary, the function of 'delivering services' and, as often as not, delivering them on behalf of central government. In delivering these services, local authorities are expected to meet targets carefully prescribed by Whitehall. Under Labour, they were also assessed like schoolchildren by the National Audit Office and, like schoolchildren, awarded stars for doing well. Schools and hospitals too have had to meet similar grades and targets set down for them.

All this may or may not improve standards of service. What is certain is that the new system visibly and painfully subordinates local government to Whitehall. For these targets and assessments are defined as the 'drivers' of the town hall; the desires of local people and the agitations of their elected councillors on their behalf are marginalized. This is made all the clearer by the pressure on local authorities to adopt 'a Cabinet system'. This local cabinet is expected to act in relation to Whitehall like the subsidiary board of a conglomerate in relation to its main board. The opinions of those councillors who are not members of the Cabinet are sidelined.

At the same time, the number of fresh duties imposed on local government continues to increase. As well as the voluminous new legislation, a stream of guidance notes from the Ministry directs the local authority to 'develop policies' on, if we take health alone, obesity, smoking, drugs and pollution. Some of these fresh duties derive ultimately from the EU, particularly since public health became one of those matters which can be decided on majority vote without a national veto. A recent example is the EU policy on waste disposal and recycling which has pressured councils to go over to fortnightly rubbish collections. But what is characteristic of all such extra duties is that the powers to implement them tend to have a built-in override, by which the minister has the power not only to overrule the council but to redraft the ways in which those powers are to be exercised.

We are seeing something like the return of the notorious 'Henry VIII Clause', which Lord Chief Justice Hewart inveighed against eighty years ago in his polemic *The New Despotism* (1929). A Henry VIII clause was one which gave the minister the power to make an order which 'may modify the provisions of this Act so far as may appear necessary or expedient for carrying the order into effect'. And the making of any such order was to count as proof that the law had been complied with. In other words, the minister could change the law however he fancied, and the fact that he had changed it was itself proof that the law was what he said it was – the kind of convenient rule of definition favoured by

Humpty Dumpty: 'When I use a word, it means just what I choose it to mean – neither more nor less.'

Such breathtakingly wide ministerial powers are now familiar in almost every aspect of local government, not least when the subject is an intrinsically local one, such as planning. Let us say that developers apply to develop a sizeable new estate on the edge of a market town. The town council may protest vigorously against the plan, but of course the proposal has to go to the planning authority at county hall. Yet even if the county endorses the town and rejects the plan, the developers will automatically appeal. The minister then appoints an inspector to hold an inquiry. The inspector is instructed to have regard to wider interests and may very well find in favour of the developers, and even if his verdict is ambiguous, the minister may approve the scheme in his judicial capacity.

But even this does not go far enough for the government's liking. Under a new law, on major planning decisions such as the siting of a nuclear power station or a new airport runway, the local planning system may be bypassed altogether and the decision handed to a new Infrastructure Commission, the decision of which will in effect be final. Much the same unfettered powers are already in the hands of another quango, the Environment Commission, which among other things decides when to take expensive measures to resist coastal erosion and when to let the sea flood in. One could hardly conceive of a more fundamental decision than to decide where one's native country is to begin and end. Yet this decision is taken out of the hands of local people and handed over to an agency that may have entirely different priorities, for example a predilection for preserving wetlands.

It will be said, 'Oh, if you leave it all to the local councils, you are conceding victory to the Nimbys and nothing new will ever get built.' But there are quite a few cases on record in which the government has ruled *against* new developments, even when local opinion was in favour. To take a small but not untypical case: a village in Devon, called High Bickington, put forward a project for building thirty-six dwellings for low-income families, plus sixteen homes to be sold on the open market, a school and a multi-purpose community centre – thus creating a new hamlet on the human scale. The district and county councils approved the plan. So did the Rural Affairs Minister in London. But the Government Office for the South West, the regional quango, rejected it on the grounds that it unduly expanded the boundaries of the existing village. A costly and laborious public inquiry ensued. The inspector found that the project would produce *too many* affordable homes in the area – a complaint I have never heard in my life before – and the latest departmental creation, the Department for Communities and Local Government, confirmed the inspector's finding. So, after five years, not a brick was laid. These planning sagas can last ten years or more. The notorious wrangle over the housing project at Micheldever, Hampshire, seems to have lasted most of my adult life. At no point has Whitehall considered the possibility that if local councils, at the lowest practicable level, had the responsibility for housing their hard-up young couples, they might well find their way to their own solutions, especially if they were encouraged to issue their own bonds to finance the building, rather than having to depend on the caprice of central government.

Whitehall complains scornfully when local authorities fail to meet the targets they have been set, while refusing them the financial elbow-room to meet those targets in the way they think fit. For central control is exerted in various different ways. Direct legal obligations obviously have greater force than guidance notes or government targets. Non-compliance with a statutory duty will carry a legal penalty, but failure to meet a target may also be punished, by the government withholding a grant or by its choosing other authorities for its largesse. A council that fails to follow government guidance may render itself liable to challenge in the civil courts by outraged private citizens or groups. I am not trying to argue here whether this network of central controls produces, on balance, better or worse decisions. I simply want to point out that the freedom of action that local authorities used to enjoy has mostly disappeared.

In the case of institutions that were largely under the control of local government in the old days – the police, the schools, the local authority hospitals – their chief constables, head teachers and hospital managers have exchanged one form of control for another, that is, from town hall to Whitehall. The old form of control was often slow-moving, pernickety and sometimes influenced by the ideology of the locally dominant political party. But it did not interfere so relentlessly in how schools and hospitals and police stations were run. What was taught in schools, the clinical practice in hospitals, the methods of policing were largely left to the discretion of the professionals. Doctors and headmasters and chief constables were implicitly trusted, to a degree which became apparent only when that trust was withdrawn. In fact, trust never used to be much of an issue at all.

Perhaps the first occasion on which it received public prominence was in Professor Onora O'Neill's 2002 Reith Lectures on the subject (published as *A Question of Trust*). Those lectures were, I thought at the time, more of a cry from the heart than a fully worked out analysis of the problem. In particular, O'Neill did not engage with the question of democratic responsibility: if public money is being spent in huge quantities on these services, does not the government have a duty to scrutinize whether the money is being wisely spent and whether the service is as good as it could be? But the underlying argument of Professor O'Neill's lectures remains more valid and pressing than I grasped at the time: hitherto, the judgment and experience of professionals had been regarded as the guiding force in their field. Now the professionals were to be second-guessed at every turn by a small number of central bureaucrats. Was this really the path to excellence?

Here again the oligarchs had taken the reins, claiming to have a better understanding of the speciality in question. Their overriding aim was to eliminate unevenness of provision, so that standards would be uniform everywhere and there would be no 'postcode lottery'. But if you eliminate unevenness, you eliminate diversity, often the most precious quality in any field of endeavour, since without it there is no room for innovation. It is 'best practice' from a diversity of practitioners which is the motor of improvement.

In schools, the transfer of control was especially striking. For the Department of Education had previously taken very little part in either the management of schools or the curricula that were taught in them. Now a stream of guidance notes poured out of the massive new offices of the department, which began to change its name at regular intervals, as though to advertise its new prominence. What had once been the Board of Education now became the Department of Education and Science, then Education and Employment, then Education and Skills, to finish up at the time of writing as the Department for Children, Schools and Families. This last change of name reflected an important aspect of the department's swelling ambition: not merely to devise, in its clotted educationspeak, all the modules, levels and grades which were to enable it to assess at every stage the academic achievement of every child in the country, but also to weave an ever-thickening web of pastoral care around the child. To plough through these documents is to immerse yourself in an impenetrable soup of jargon, but no teacher is safe until he or she has mastered this stuff and is ready for the new Ofsted inspection, an ordeal far worse than the occasional visit of HM Inspectors in the old days and one which has driven several worried teachers to take their own lives.

These intrusions did not begin with New Labour. Blair's ministers merely inherited and elaborated on the apparatus left behind by the Conservatives. The real beginning can be traced back to Kenneth Baker's Education Act of 1988. That was the beginning of the overly prescriptive curricular demands and the testing of every child at the ages of seven, eleven and fourteen.

Ironically, Labour also copied the Conservatives in the way it eventually reacted against the bureaucratic monsters it had created. In their last years in office, the Conservatives began to construct new semi-independent institutions, which were to be partly exempt from the endless nagging of Whitehall and would be free, within limits, to frame their own courses and structures and, for hospitals, their own clinical practices. Most conspicuous among these half-free models were the City Technology Colleges and the Trust Hospitals. On coming to power, Labour, suspicious of these institutions as halfway houses towards privatization, abolished their independent status and reintegrated them into the state framework. But then in its later years, Labour too had second thoughts and revived these admirable models under the new titles of City Academies and Foundation Hospitals. These were eagerly welcomed by the Conservatives, who not unreasonably claimed parentage of them. So there appeared to be emerging a consensus that interference by Whitehall could go and had gone too far. Some degree of local control was highly desirable. Yet this revival in localism was rather hesitant and often seemed more token than reality. As Chancellor, Gordon Brown was especially insistent that the new schools and hospitals should remain firmly under Treasury control. To date anyway, the oligarchs have not let go, and it remains to be seen whether they really ever will.

Of course local government is only a tiny part of local life. Most of us give only fleeting thought to the council – when it fails to grit down our street after a snowfall, when the dustmen haven't come, when the local library turns out to be shut on a weekday. But what we do notice and feel the lack of more painfully is when some familiar part of life disappears from our neighbourhood, when the nearest shop or primary school or post office or garage closes, when the only cinema for miles shuts down, when the pub or chapel is turned into a private residence. All these things and more have happened in our lifetimes, and most of them have happened quite recently.

In my childhood, Chitterne, our quite remote village on the Wiltshire downs, possessed a resident policeman living in one of the two police cottages, two pubs, a general store, a post office, a blacksmith's forge, an electrician's workshop, a racing stable, eight working farmyards, a Methodist chapel as well as a parish church. All except the King's Head, the parish church and three of the farms have now gone. In a way, the most painful of these losses is the conversion of the farmyards into pleasant courtyard homes for people who must either be retired or commute into the nearest towns, Warminster and Salisbury, for there is no work to be had in the village any more.

I do not sentimentalize the village as it was. There was poverty and illegitimacy; relations between the classes, and particularly between the farmers and their workers, were not all sweetness and light. Ronald Blythe's masterpiece *Akenfield* describes an East Anglian village of nearly a century ago, but the hard, bleak tone of life he describes carried more than an echo for me. In its material aspects, life in Chitterne is surely easier now. But what Chitterne like other villages and towns has lost is a good deal of its freestanding quality. Decisions and deliveries come from a long way off. There is the sense of being at the end of the line, the remotest link in a chain of command which stretches all the way back to the Head Office and the Ministry. The branch managers of the bank or building society have no free authority to deal with you.

We used to mock the French for their over-centralization. General de Gaulle himself said that it was one thing he could never hope to get rid of. Yet since his death in 1970 France has steadily decentralized, while Britain has moved in the other direction. A couple of years ago, at a conference in Amsterdam, I heard the famously charismatic Luc Ferry lament the impotence he had felt when he was France's Education Minister. Time and again, M. Ferry said, he had found himself quite unable to alter what actually went on inside schools. I told him that we in Britain always imagined that at any moment of the day the Minister of Education in Paris would know exactly what pupils in the Pyrenees were learning. 'Not a bit of it,' he replied. 'You just pull the levers and nothing happens.' By contrast, his British counterpart, whether it be Labour's Ed Balls or the Conservatives' Michael Gove, blithely intervenes in every minute of the school day, including what the children should have for lunch and how they should disport themselves in the playground.

The hard reality is that, structurally, nothing has changed. The lines of oligarchic command remain in place. And the oligarchs still itch to shorten those lines of command by closing down the extremities as uneconomic and inefficient. The Health Minister wants to close the cottage hospital. The bishop wants to close the little churches and amalgamate the smaller parishes. The Home Secretary wants to amalgamate police forces, and the Chief Constable wants to close local police stations. The brewers want to sell off even more pubs for private homes and make more money by selling their products through the supermarket. The official pressure continues to work against the local and against the human scale.

A terrible squash on the sofa

Oligarchy used to have its consolations. It was at least the rule of the Few, not the rule of the One. Power might be concentrated in the centre, but it had several distinct and often competing voices. There were debates and arguments within the inner council; one faction or family might dominate for a time, but then a rival might gain more or less effective control. The dictates issuing from the central council chamber might alter, perhaps soften in the hope of securing popular endorsement. Those who had been hard pressed by the previous dispensation would have a fresh opportunity to make their discontents known.

Within the British System too there were several powers at the centre: Number Ten Downing Street, the Cabinet, the Ministries, Parliament, the High Court, the public bodies and nationalized industries. Quite a few of these powers were interlocked rather than separated as in the American system, but they certainly possessed distinct voices and the capacity to nudge public policy this way or that, sometimes to overturn it completely. Even within the nerve centre of the whole operation, the Prime Minister and the Cabinet, there was traditionally room for several views. The PM, after all, was supposed to be only *primus inter pares*, first among equals. In earlier days, his power had not in theory extended much beyond the right to hire and fire ministers and to organize the agenda and conduct the meetings of the Cabinet. But that had long undervalued the reality. As far back as 1915, the great constitutionalist A.V. Dicey had lamented in his introduction to the eighth edition of his classic *The Law of the Constitution* (1915):

> The sovereignty of Parliament is still the fundamental doctrine of English constitutionalism. But the authority of the House of Lords has been gravely diminished, whilst the authority of the House of Commons, or rather of the majority thereof during any one Parliament, has been immensely increased. Now this increased portion of sovereignty can be effectively organized only by the Cabinet which holds in its hands the guidance of the party machine. And of the party which the party majority supports, the Premier has become at once the legal head and, if he is a man of ability, the real leader.

John Morley, the leading Liberal politician of that era and biographer of Gladstone, put it more bluntly: the Prime Minister's power was 'not inferior to that of a dictator, provided that the House of Commons will stand by him'.

But in 1915 and for many years after 1915, there were severe constraints on the exercise of that dictatorial power. There was first of all the Cabinet. The Cabinet could make its anxieties known and reshape legislation, not only in its weekly meetings but also in the network of Cabinet committees, which examined current problems and went through proposals for new legislation, often in considerable detail. The Prime Minister would naturally try to ensure that his allies were in a majority on any crucial committee and would often take the chair himself. Even so, meeting by meeting as the weeks wore on, the committee would often wear down or remould the original proposal, so that its eventual impact might be rather different. The minutes of Cabinet meetings drawn up and circulated by the Cabinet Secretary (in the old days by the PM himself) might make the proceedings sound somewhat bland and consensual, but both Cabinet and Cabinet committees had a genuine and substantial role in shaping new laws and policies.

But when Tony Blair became PM, much of this elaborate machinery was scrapped or left to rust in idleness. In *The British Constitution in the Twentieth Century* (2003),[53] Anthony Seldon compared the workings of the Cabinet over the course of the last century by taking snapshots at twenty-year intervals. His conclusion was that 'the Cabinet system in 2000 had changed utterly when compared with its position in 1900.' In terms of power and influence over events, the Cabinet had become a shadow of its former self. The only decision taken by the Blair Cabinet that Seldon could identify was the decision taken to go ahead with the Millennium Dome, and that was the exception that proved the rule, because a clear majority of ministers present opposed the Dome, but Blair simply overruled them. The volume of decisions going through Cabinet had declined enormously, as had the number of Cabinet committees. Proposals tended to be sent down the committee route only if they were relatively unimportant and/or if Blair himself had no interest in them.[54]

Nor were members of Cabinet kept adequately informed of the government business going on outside their own departments. The veteran government adviser Sir Christopher Foster wrote in his book *The End of Cabinet Government?* (1999) that 'In contrast to what I remembered of the 1960s and 1970s, I cannot overstate my astonishment at finding, with rare exceptions, that in the 1990s Cabinet papers are no longer circulated'.[55] Obviously if ministers are not fully briefed, or briefed at all, they cannot take an informed part in the discussion. While they all remain collectively bound by Cabinet decisions, those members whose departments had not been directly involved could scarcely be said to have had any share in the decision-making. In such circumstances, one can hardly talk of Cabinet government at all – at least not with a straight face.

For more than a century, observers had been exploding and re-exploding the myth that the Prime Minster was no more than the first among equals. But this looked like a further leap in his pre-eminence, an unprecedented squirrelling of power within Downing Street, with outlying Cabinet ministers being reduced to mere spectators and yes-men.

For what looks like an ordinary eighteenth-century town house, Number Ten is surprisingly elastic. It can expand laterally to the left, into Numbers Eleven and Twelve, and backwards into the Cabinet offices, which have their main entry on Whitehall but have many rooms and corridors behind their façade. And expand it certainly did during Blair's premiership. The number of staff employed at Number Ten grew from a couple of dozen to about 150; the number of special advisers alone trebled from eight to twenty-five.

But numbers were not the only criterion of the extra muscle that had been built up in what now amounted to a full-grown Department of the Prime Minister. The biggest increase had been in media management operations. This was concentrated around the Number Ten Strategic Communications Unit led by the passionate, devious and intensely partisan Alastair Campbell. This unit not only blared out Blairite propaganda 24/7 but also instigated a system of rewards and punishments for the mostly compliant lobby journalists. Previously, by contrast, the Number Ten press officers had tended to be career civil servants who had some allegiance to objectivity and restraint; this applied even to the peppery and pugnacious Sir Bernard Ingham who, for all his reputation as a doughty Thatcherite, worked in sweet harmony with his deputy Romola Christopherson, who was anything but.

The power of Campbell's personality ensured that the Prime Minister's Office gave unprecedented priority not only to making Blair himself look good but to 'eye-catching initiatives', to quote Blair's own phrase, which would enable him to dominate the news agenda rather than contribute to a long-term strategy.

Significant influence was also drained away from the permanent Civil Service and into the political core of government by making the Prime Minister's personal advisers also heads of the Defence and Overseas and the European Secretariats of the Cabinet. These officials, along with Campbell and Jonathan Powell, the PM's Chief of Staff, had been brought in from outside. They were now, in an unprecedented move, given power to give instructions to civil servants. Soon, they began to brief incoming ministers as to what was expected of them. The Cabinet Secretary, previously the Grand Panjandrum of Whitehall, now became little more than a glorified Establishment and Human Resources Officer. There was no attempt to disguise this move to a much more presidential system. Jonathan Powell (whose brother Charles had occupied a comparable *éminence grise* role under Thatcher) unashamedly called it 'a change from a feudal system of barons to a more Napoleonic system'.

Now I have more than a smidgeon of sympathy with the itch to introduce a more coherent system of decision-making. In the old days, it was uphill work to get any new proposal moving, especially when it involved more than one department. A great deal of time was wasted on departmental turf wars. The Prime Minister often felt isolated and under-informed. A more tenacious and serious-minded executive than Tony Blair might have made good use of the new concentration of power, if only he had not allowed it to go to his head and to slip into an extraordinarily slap-dash and chaotic style of government.

This came to be known as 'sofa government', not only because Blair and his advisers preferred to spend a lot of time on the sofas in Number Ten rather than at formal meetings, but because their confabulations had such a casual, unstructured quality, which appeared to suit Blair's notoriously short attention span. The trouble with his hatching his plans in the company of a couple of cronies, without a proper agenda or often a private secretary in attendance to take notes, was that so many ideas, the good as well as the bad, dribbled away into the sand. Lasting results were few, not least because so few people outside the inner circle were given a chance to point out snags and possible improvements. Both the Hutton and Butler reports, as well as the Chilcot Inquiry, made it clear what calamitous results could follow from a personality-centred, paper-free method of doing business.

But my purpose here is not to rehearse in detail the well-known critiques of Blair's government. What I want to emphasize is how such a style vastly reduces the number of actors who are allowed to contribute to the discussion and the decision. The worst example was the way in which the Secretary of State for Defence and his department were cut out of the loop during the preparations for the Iraq war. Most flagrant of all, the Defence Department's Intelligence Department was excluded from the preparation of the 'Dodgy Dossier'. The concentration of power within Blair's personal court starved the Prime Minister both of information and of critical views.

Such a huddle of trusted and like-minded advisers within a single office is liable to produce and reproduce the same effects in a variety of circumstances. They will reinforce one another's views and resist alternative views from outside, whether these come from opponents or supposed allies. They will increasingly come to believe that any disagreement with their views is due to faulty communications. All that is wrong is that they have failed to get the message across. Fresh efforts will therefore be made to improve those communications, by hiring more staff in their media department, by themselves spending more time on pumping out the message rather than on implementing and refining the policy, and by devising new material to support their case, without paying too much attention to accuracy or proportion. Hence the Dodgy Dossier. The crime of this document was not that it turned out to be wrong in claiming that Saddam Hussein still possessed weapons of mass destruction. Intelligence departments all over the world believed so too, but none of them had any reliable recent evidence to support that very natural assumption, because it was so difficult to obtain from such a closed society as Iraq under Saddam. The crime was rather to inflate such thin and mostly out-of-date evidence as they did have into an unqualified certainty. 'Without doubt' Saddam was developing nuclear weapons, Blair told the House of Commons. This 'sexing up', to use the much maligned Andrew Gilligan's phrase on the BBC, was not an exceptional lapse in the heat of the moment. It was a logical and predictable result of the centralization of power and information, the natural outcome of the squash on the sofa and a classic symptom of oligarchy.

Sir Humphrey takes a back seat – or does he?

When I was at university in the early 1960s, all my thrusting fellow students wanted to get into the BBC, if they were creative types, or into the Civil Service if they weren't. To pass into the Treasury or the Foreign Office was the summit of ambition. The more dashing candidates opted for the new departments that the Wilson government was founding, the Prices and Incomes Board or the Department of Economic Affairs, which was shortly to give birth to George Brown's National Plan. This was where it was at, to use the phrase just coming into style. When the recruiting sergeants for the BBC came down to talk about the glittering prizes that awaited those with sharp swords, their sessions were crowded out. By contrast, the banks and multinational corporations, whose 'milk rounds' were to be just as crowded in later decades, were far less fashionable. First-class minds who wanted to make a splash in the world then automatically gravitated towards government service.

The higher reaches of the Civil Service to which the ambitious undergraduate aspired were called 'the administrative class'. But the pretensions of that class went way beyond what the outside world called admin. Its members regarded themselves as policy-makers and decision-takers. They were architects who designed the policy for their ministers, not the jobbing builders who merely executed it. For ministers were here today, gone tomorrow. During their brief stay, they might tweak the department's policy this way or that, but once they had gone, Sir Humphrey resumed his sway and pursued the line he had always intended to pursue. When *Yes Minister* hit our screens in 1980, senior civil servants were among the most avid viewers and would hurry home to catch the latest episode at 8.30 or 9pm (for being the nation's guardians in the Platonic sense, they worked impressively long hours). What to the rest of the nation might appear as satire would to them seem more like an amusing description of the way things actually were – and the way things ought to be.

The Civil Service had come to think of itself as an inbuilt brake in the system. Its function was to restrain the headlong impulses of inexperienced, ignorant or ideologically deranged politicians. Whether or not it had historically been designed for that function, experience had slotted the service into the role. For Sir Ivor Jennings in his classic study *Cabinet Government* (1936), the Civil Service was as much part of the British Constitution as the Cabinet and the House of Commons, and its restraining role was a blessed safeguard for the nation: 'The check upon incompetence arises not merely from the reaction of parliamentary and public opinion, but also from the competence of the Civil Service. The minister has at hand the best opinion available.'[56] Permanent Secretaries through the ages could be forgiven for nodding sagely in agreement. Of course, that opinion might shift gradually over time, for the Civil Service formed part of the prevailing consensus, and that consensus was liable to shift too. But any incoming minister who sought to depart too abruptly from the consensus found that the mandarins would tug pretty sharply at his dog-lead.

The Civil Service had acquired this high and central role during two world wars, which had demanded intense planning and control from Whitehall. That role was further souped up by the fashion for corporatism that had followed the first war and for nationalization that had followed the second. The trend reached its peak when Ted Heath's Cabinet Secretary Sir William Armstrong became known as 'the Deputy Prime Minister' for his part in designing Heath's policy to control prices and incomes. Shortly after, as though to punish this hubris (though it was hardly his own fault), Armstrong suffered a massive nervous breakdown.

The eventual failure of the prices and incomes policy was a blow to the morale of the Civil Service, but nothing to the shattering damage inflicted by Thatcherism in general and Margaret Thatcher in particular. Whereas Heath had elevated his Cabinet Secretary to near-parity on Mount Olympus, Mrs Thatcher got rid of her first one, Sir Ian Bancroft, and was less than enthusiastic about Bancroft's successor. From now on, permanent secretaries were liable to find themselves sidelined and even ridiculed by ministers and their imported advisers.

Nor was Tony Blair any more respectful, though he had better manners. For the first time, senior civil servants, as we have seen, found themselves taking orders from or being brushed aside by the new Prime Minister's political appointees. More crucial though less conspicuous, the normal processes of sifting and shaping policy through a pyramid of departmental and interdepartmental committees and thence on to Cabinet committees and finally Cabinet itself – all this began to wither on the vine. It had been the basis of the Civil Service's power, that they had been the ones shaping the policy right up to the final stages. Now new policy proposals began to issue not from the relevant department, or even from working groups of ministers and civil servants, but from the sofa at Number Ten and the various Downing Street units that serviced the PM. These wheezes and diktats were delivered in a capricious but demanding style, half thought through, but ungainsayable. The system became both more centralized and more chaotic.

A report from the Institute for Government in January 2010, looking back over the previous twenty years, concluded that, despite Downing Street's strengthened grip, there was 'a conspicuous lack of a single coherent strategy for government'.[57] Downing Street and the Treasury possessed 'few tools beyond the brute force of political edict'. The office of the British PM now held a concentration of formal power greater than that of almost any other country in the developed world. Barmy ideas and knee-jerk reactions to passing events poured out of Number Ten. Yet the fragmentation and lack of co-ordination at the centre of the Civil Service – the Treasury, Number Ten and the Cabinet Office – lead to an administrative centre that is relatively weak. 'This curious situation has created a strategic gap at the heart of government which inhibits the ability to set overall government priorities and translate them into action.' This damning critique was compiled from interviews with a considerable number of former senior civil servants. However intensely able, these ex-mandarins might have become embittered after years of not being listened to, I suppose. Yet the same impressions have been received by outside observers – journalists, businessmen, academics, the more honest MPs. The new way of doing things simply fails to deliver the goods. As John Reid said of the Home Office, on the basis of his experience as Home Secretary, 'It is not fit for purpose.'

The effects on the quality of the resulting legislation and executive government orders were soon all too palpable, reducing even the government's well-wishers to despair. The morale of the civil servants themselves plummeted, their self-esteem melted. 'So much the better,' might be one's first reaction. The unquestioned power and influence of the mandarins in the postwar years had made them often seem complacent and inward-looking, resistant to new ideas and hostile to learning either from the past or from the experience of other nations. It might do them good to be taken down a peg. Their minds might open up a little.

Unfortunately, as so often in life and politics, the process went too far. Middle-ranking civil servants, at the assistant secretary level, lost the will to argue and criticize. Anything other than instant compliance and deference might cost them their next promotion. Even this had its good side when a department gave up its traditional opposition to some overdue reform. But what could not be denied was that the new deference reduced the number of active players. No longer did ministers have to worry what their departments would think of the latest bright idea from Number Ten. They knew that Number Ten would get its way without too much trouble.

The career paths of senior civil servants became of much less interest to the outside world. You could measure the draining away of power by the loss of column inches. No longer did newspapers bother to speculate who might be the next ambassador to Washington or Paris or how the succession struggle at the Treasury was shaping up.

In all these senses, then, Sir Humphrey did indeed seem to be taking a back seat. But in another sense, he exercised power more directly than he had at any time since the glorious days of the Second World War. His influence might be reduced over the new Bills that the Legislation Committee was putting to Cabinet, but there was another new trend that favoured his input. His department now issued an ever-growing quantity of regulations and orders off its own bat, most of the time without scrutiny either by the Cabinet or the House of Commons. In theory, both bodies could demand to have a look at the new regulations, either by the PM or the Cabinet Secretary suggesting that they be circulated for collective discussion, or by some MPs objecting to them – 'praying against' is the technical term – thus forcing a debate and a vote in Parliament.

But the sheer volume of regulation had become far too great for this to happen, except in a tiny minority of cases. Where the regulations emanated from the European Union, as an increasing number now did, there was little point in questioning their exact form, since under the European Communities Act they had to be railroaded through in one form or another. Obsessively tidy-minded or dictatorial departments accordingly felt free to 'gold-plate' these orders from Brussels, secure in the knowledge that there was unlikely to be effective opposition. All sorts of activities, institutions and venues, from dance halls to abattoirs, now fell under national or European regulation, where previously, if regulated at all, they had been subject to often lackadaisical inspection by the local authority.

Thus our daily experience of government became oligarchic in two ways: in the intrusiveness and all-pervasiveness of regulation from the centre, both London and Brussels, and in the reduced number of officials and politicians who had any active role in imposing and devising these regulations. Compared with the 1950s, the hot breath of government was right down our necks. No doubt shepherds and peasants in pastoral societies had experienced a far ruder shock when rules and officials from the city first intruded on their sleepy lives. But it was the same type of shock that we experienced, and we too began to feel remote and impotent. And partly as a result, we too felt less inclined to take an active part in the politics of our own country.

Permanent recess – the decline of the House of Commons

It would still be possible to make a case that senior civil servants became overmighty during the grim years of war and planning, and that now they had been put back in their boxes, returned to their proper limited sphere of power and influence. You could argue that no great damage had been done by reducing their prominence. I do not think that this argument really stands up if you look honestly at the poor standards of execution and the low quality of legislation that have been evident in recent years. Think of the debacles over the Child Protection Agency, the Single Farm payments, the billions wasted on cattle slaughter in the foot-and-mouth epidemic, the failure of the government's vast database scheme, the Millennium Dome, the millions wasted on anti-truancy schemes etc., etc.

But even if you are ready to overlook these and other fiascos, no such excuse is available for the fading away of the House of Commons. By any reckoning, this must be counted a catastrophe. For Parliament is crucial to our democracy; its history is longer and more unbroken than that of parliaments in other European countries, and its veto over public expenditure has been a central part of our politics since the Tudors. If Parliament is not working, then the life goes out of the whole system. The muscular interplay between the executive and the legislature becomes a limp and sap-less thing. If there is no questioning, no holding accountable, no resisting the government's will, no forcing dud ministers from office, then we must be sliding towards a sort of authoritarianism, a flabby and chaotic sort perhaps, but authoritarianism none the less.

The erosion of the influence of the Civil Service has taken place mostly in private, behind the closed doors along the corri-dors of the Ministry. By contrast, the decline of the House of Commons is painfully visible. You can see the unmistakable symp-toms of it in the newspapers, where the proceedings in the Chamber are no longer reported, and on the television screens, where all the talk is of the Prime Minister and his or her relations with a few other senior ministers, not of Parliament and what goes on there, except on rare momentous occasions such as the debate on the invasion of Iraq. Think of all those hours of broad-cast material piling up on BBC Parliament which so seldom make it on to the news bulletins. How MPs agonized when the ques-tion of broadcasting their proceedings came to a head. Would being on air vulgarize and trivialize their debates? Would MPs be tempted to play up to the millions watching them on TV? In the event, there are no millions, and the debates roll on pretty much oblivious of the cameras.

Or think of the basic facts of the modern MP's life. His work-ing hours, for example. At first sight, he appears to be working far harder than MPs in his father's day. He disappears from his tax-payer-funded London residence into the warrens of the Palace of Westminster at much the same time as other office workers, between 8.30 and 9.30am, let us say. He may not emerge from the Palace until long after ordinary people are tucked up on the sofa or have gone to bed, at 11pm or even later. At the weekend, he will be trotting round events in his constituency and listening to his constituents' complaints in his regular 'surgery'. He, or more conscientiously and poignantly she, sacrifices family life to this endless grind. Yet look a little closer, and you will note that the bulk of those hours, both in and out of Westminster, are spent on constituency work. The typical MP may in fact only spend from Tuesday to Thursday at Westminster, for regular Monday and Friday sittings are a thing of the past. Even in the middle of the week, the House's hours are less demanding. All-night sittings, or even sittings into the small hours, are rare indeed. After a mid-morning start, business generally comes to a prompt end at 10pm. These 'modernizations' of the House's timetable are supposed to be family-friendly and attract more 'normal' people into Parliament. Perhaps they do or will in the future. But as far as political power goes, the new hours vastly strengthen the government's control over the House. No longer is it common practice for MPs to 'talk out' contentious Bills or filibuster into the middle of the night. A few heroic MPs do carry on this ancient democratic tradition (which dates back to ancient Rome and Cato the Elder, who would regularly obstruct legislation he disapproved of by speaking until nightfall when the rule was that sittings had to be suspended). These days, MPs' speeches in debate on Government Bills are time-limited to five or ten minutes. It is only on Private Members' Bills that the backbencher has a genuine opportunity to obstruct an obnoxious proposal.

On major Bills, the timetable motion or 'guillotine', which strictly rations the amounts of hours to be spent on a Bill at the committee stage, in recent years has been routinely deployed, instead of being a last resort. In 1997–8, Blair's first session, the guillotine was used eighteen times on thirteen Bills. That experimental practice became a permanent fixture. Once a Bill had passed its Second Reading, a government with a decent majority could be assured of its trouble-free passage through the later

Committee and Report stages. The brutish guillotine has recently been replaced by a more civilized procedure, which allocates time to the various portions of a bill in accordance with their importance, but the overall effect is much the same: the government is still assured of getting its bill through in the time allotted.

Those who are optimistic about the future of Parliament like to point out that rebellions by backbench MPs are far commoner these days and often involve more of them. The spectacular rebellion by Labour MPs against the Iraq war was by some counts the greatest in parliamentary history. Without support from the Conservatives, the invasion would not have been approved. To that extent, the power of the whips to bring backbenchers into line on an unpopular Bill has clearly diminished. The military discipline that used to be inflicted by former half-colonels in the Conservative Party and by former trade union officials in the Labour Party has lost some of its authority. But this is usually of secondary importance, so long as the Bill proceeds on its agreed timetable for consideration and approval, according to the motion steamrollered through the House by the whipped majority. If the government ever lost a timetable motion, let alone a motion of no confidence, then it would have lost its control over the House and would have to drop the Bill and perhaps resign. But timetable motions are not lost.

For the House of Commons has lost control over *time*, which is the Parliamentarians' greatest weapon. Only by persistent obstruction and delay can Parliament deny its assent and force the government to think again. The government's will to proceed can only be worn down in a battle of attrition. Without mastery of time, Parliament is nothing – a fig leaf, a rubber stamp, a ghost of past glories, just as many parliaments in other countries already are.

It is an irony, and an embarrassing one, that in this supposed age of democracy the last 'time lords' are in the House of Lords.

There, business proceeds at an unconstrained pace and timetable motions are unknown. The Upper House may consider a Bill for as long as it takes. And a clause or even a whole Bill which is repugnant to them will be rejected, twice if need be, thus forcing the government to invoke the Parliament Acts of 1911 and 1949, and pass the Bill into law after being approved only by the House of Commons. And this can happen only after a year's delay has elapsed.

I do not romanticize the House of Lords. Too many of its members are deaf or decrepit. Its debates are seldom the feasts of wisdom and expertise that its supporters claim; they tend to ramble in a self-indulgent, often myopic fashion. But at least members of the Upper House do retain that crucial attribute of any effective Parliament: control over their own business. Their power becomes all the more palpable as the date approaches by which a general election must be held. The government will shy away from putting forward any Bill which is bound to founder in the House of Lords and therefore doomed to die with the death of the Parliament, for there will be no time to present it a second time, let alone to deploy the Parliament Act. No government wants to go to the polls with its legislative programme in a public mess.

True, there have been some improvements in the way in which the Commons operates. There are, for example, the select committees which now cover every field of government, from children to agriculture. The proceedings of these committees do receive a fair bit of publicity and may be featured in news bulletins and newspaper reports. When a session looks like proving controversial, the committee room will be crowded out. Yet we must also notice certain defects in the system as it has developed so far (its full flowering dates back only to Norman St John-Stevas's years as Leader of the House in the early 1980s). Our select committees occupy as yet nowhere near the huge power and influence of their counterparts in the US Congress. Unlike Congressional committees, they have no power to examine upcoming Bills. The most they can do is retrospectively to examine whether an Act has worked well or badly. In fact, most of their verdicts are retrospective, on how public money has been spent rather than on how it is going to be spent.

Moreover, the chairman and members of our select committees have had to be more or less acceptable to the whips, for it is the whipped majority of the whole House that have ultimately decided their selection. The whips are quite content if a nonentity or a waffler occupies the chair of an important committee for years on end. Seldom are these chairmen household names. If they should become so because of their vigorous interrogations, the whips may try to turf them out, as they tried, unsuccessfully, to remove the doughty chairman of the Transport Committee, Gwyneth Dunwoody.

The reports from these committees tend to be debated, if at all, in the Chamber long after they were published, by which time they have ceased to carry any urgency. In general, the procedures of the House are averse to topicality. It is hard for an MP to raise a matter of urgent moment, unless he or she happens to be called in the bear pit of Prime Minister's questions, where questions seldom extract an answer which is serious or germane. If you look down the agenda for a typical week in the Commons, you may be surprised by the fact that the great two or three issues of the day are not on it, while the business is stacked with trivial or ritual debates. Nor does timetabling of debate on government Bills ensure that at least the key clauses are thoroughly gone over. Hours may be spent bickering over unimportant parts of the bill, while the crucial bit has to be rushed through in order to keep to the timetable.

Now it would not be difficult to devise reforms which remedied these drawbacks. Select committees would have their chairmen, and perhaps their members too, elected by secret ballot of all MPs. They would have the right to examine new Bills and present their reports to Parliament in good time. A new Business Committee, on which the whips would be represented but where they would not be in the majority, would have the duty of going through new Bills to see whether they were seriously necessary and did not simply repeat existing legislation (as so many criminal justice bills do, for example), whether they were properly drafted, and whether there would be time enough to fit them into the programme for the current session. There could be an upper limit on the number of Bills to be presented each session – and so on. Such solutions have been put forward by various committees of the House, by think tanks and by party task forces. Many such solutions can, for example, be found in the report to David Cameron of Kennneth Clarke's task force on the constitution. As a member of this committee, I was continually struck by how much of what we were saying was common ground across all parties – and indeed pretty well trampled ground too. As with classic recipes, the best methods for breathing life back into our politics and for reviving the vigour and independence of Parliament tend to be common property.

So far the government of the day has usually played a dead bat, fending off these bouncers into the long grass. In Opposition, by contrast, both major parties have expressed enthusiasm, but such things tend to be postponed or forgotten as soon as they get into power.

The cause of reform is not helped by the extent to which the media have lost real interest in Parliament. In the 1950s and 60s, the broadsheets and some of the popular papers too carried a full page of coverage of the day's doings in Parliament. The speeches of the minister and his shadow would be reported at some length. So would the meat of a new White Paper or Green Paper. Anyone who read the newspapers regularly would acquire a quite detailed grasp of what was going on in Parliament. Today only the parliamentary sketch survives. A satirical description of the day's proceedings is assumed to be all that the readers deserve or that they can be bothered with.

This decline of outside interest in what goes on in the Chamber is mirrored by a decline in MPs' attendance there. Apart from question time and the winding-up speeches at the end of the debate (when MPs have to be there because they are about to be called on to vote), attendance at debates has been patchy for years. Now it is vestigial. And contrary to expectations, the broadcasting of proceedings has done nothing to halt the decline. In the early days of the broadcasting, the whips would see to it that their front-bench speaker was 'doughnutted', surrounded by eagerly attentive supporters. Now he is lucky if all the benches behind him contain enough MPs to fill a single doughnut.

An MP may rise in the hope of catching the Speaker's eye for a variety of reasons: to please his party's whips if he is a loyalist or his outside supporters if he is not, to provide material to recycle to his local newspaper, to hear the sound of his own voice. The one thing he cannot hope to do, unless he is remarkably conceited, is to persuade his fellow MPs, for his audience will typically consist of two or three members who are nervously hoping to be called next and concentrating on what they are going to say, the whips on either side whose only aim is to avoid embarrassment and the minister who will be leafing through his brief to find the approved response. Anything less like the tense and lively debates which often do sway their audiences in the outside world would be hard to imagine.

It would be hard to imagine too a Prime Minister these days, who like Stanley Baldwin would wander into the House by himself at odd moments and sit down on the front bench to take the mood of the Chamber. Modern Prime Ministers such as Thatcher and Blair avoid the Chamber as far as they possibly can, and when they do appear, they sweep in with an entourage and a general air of wishing to be somewhere else as soon as possible. It was noticeable, for example, that David Cameron and Nick Clegg left the Chamber as soon as the backbenchers began to speak in the debate on the EU referendum on 24 October 2011 – what would in other times have been a real House of Commons occasion with the front benches full.[58]

Parliament's loss of prestige is signalled in other ways too: in the disappearance of parliamentary characters who owed their prominence not to the offices they had held (for many of them never held office at all) but to their colourful rhetoric, their cheeky pranks, their taunting of the ministerial timeservers of the day, even their outlandish physical appearance: personalities such as Sir Gerald Nabarro, Bessie Braddock, Eric Heffer, Michael Foot, Enoch Powell. A few still survive, such as the mining MP Dennis Skinner, but they depend on an arena that no longer commands public attention and so fewer people these days have heard of them. Now would-be personalities must make their mark on *Question Time* or *Have I Got News for You*. The *lion comique* of these arenas is Mr Boris Johnson, and it was through his mastery of them that he rose effortlessly to become Mayor of London, not for anything he did or said in the House of Commons, for he did and said very little there. The oxygen of publicity has dissipated from the Chamber.

On certain special occasions, such as the Budget (although the publicity is now shared between the Budget itself and the Pre-Budget Report several months earlier), the House is still crowded, the most ordinary remark is greeted with the traditional oohs and aahs and the feeblest sally acclaimed with uproarious laughter. But these seem now more like revivals of ancient rituals rather than an expression of genuine vigour and authentic drama. The glory has departed.

Stuck on the Eurostar

Departed to where? Well, for Eurosceptics there is only one answer. They lament incessantly that everything is decided in Brussels now. Look, do not even the Eurocrats themselves boast of this? As President of the European Commission, Jacques Delors went to a British party conference in Bournemouth in 1988 and famously prophesied that within a few years, 80 per cent of our legislation would come from Brussels.[59] Not quite true even today. It just feels that way.

Earlier, Lord Denning in a famous judgment had described the Treaty of Rome as 'like an incoming tide. It flows into the estuaries and up the rivers. It cannot be held back.'[60] He made this remark only two years after the 1972 European Communities Act had been passed but was already transforming English and Scottish law. The case was one which beautifully illustrated the new grip of European law on British life: the British cider maker Bulmer was seeking a declaration from the court that they could legitimately use the word 'champagne' to describe their premium fizzy apple drink. They were opposed by Bollinger and Lanson, representing the great champagne houses of France. Bulmer prevailed on appeal, and every nicely brought up eighteen-year-old can still ask for champagne cider on her first night out. But the case is quoted and remembered for the defining role of Denning's judgment in anchoring British law within the European system, so that decisions of the European Court of Justice could be referred to and invoked in legal proceedings as easily as decisions of the House of Lords.

A pedant might point out that Denning had chosen the wrong metaphor. The incursions of European law were not exactly like a tide, because tides go out again. There is something singularly irreversible about European law, which derives in part at least from the way in which it is made. I am not arguing here whether European law in general is better or worse made than English and Scottish law. Nor am I asserting that it is intrinsically good or bad that some of our laws should be made by a legislature which sits on foreign soil and where our own representatives are necessarily in a small minority. The same is true, after all, of many conventions and treaties which have pretty much the force of law. What is most relevant here is the difference that adding on a European legislature to our own makes to the total system of law.

Firstly, it means that there is simply more of it, more laws, more directives, more regulations. And all of the ones that come from Brussels have to be dutifully re-enacted by our own Parliament without amendment or improvement. At the same time, British MPs and governments do not pause to consider whether they might ease their foot off the pedal and make fewer laws, now that there is an extra stream of law coming from the EU. Not a bit of it. There are few more disheartening spectacles than to gaze at the shelves of a law library and see how the volumes of British statutes have grown steadily fatter, year by year. Denning once pointed out that when he had been called to the Bar in 1923, the laws passed that year filled a single volume of 500 pages. By 1978, the year's output filled three volumes of more

than 3,000 pages. The laws made in 1996 consumed four volumes
running to 4,096 pages. And so on and on.

Second, the making of European law is in general further
removed from public opinion than is the making of national law.
It is generated by the bureaucracy of the European Commission.
The commissioners are political appointees who have to be
approved by the European Parliament, but this formal process
scarcely connects them to public feeling, either in their own
country of origin or across the EU. On the contrary, their
appointment is regarded as a disconnecting from their old vulgar
political world and their enlistment into a supranational institution
with its own ideals and purposes. Now and then, some commissioners are accused of smuggling in their own national interests
(the French ones are prime suspects here), but the experience of
working in the same organization, the same building, for years on
end, insulated from the hot breath of the electorate, inevitably cre-
ates an *esprit de corps*. And so it turns out that European
law-making proceeds, for the most part, in a sincere spirit of
indifference to what voters actually want at that moment.

Now it is true that the proposal issuing from the Commission
is placed before the European Parliament, or sometimes the other
way round, when a proposal comes initially from the Parliament.
And it is by this process of 'co-determination' that the new proposal is licked into shape before it goes to the Council of
Ministers. Because it is elected by the citizens, the European
Parliament ought in theory to be injecting some political realism,
but the majority in both the two main alliances in the Parliament,
the Socialists and the European People's Party, have a strongly
federalist mindset. Any measure that widens and deepens
European integration is likely to have an easy passage, regardless of
what voters back home may think. It is therefore not until the
new proposal reaches the Council of Ministers that raw national
politics comes into play. If the measure is a controversial one, the

minister must fight his corner, or he will be savaged when he gets home. But if he is in a minority, and the issue falls into one of the fields where a simple majority is enough – health and safety, for example – he has no hope of resisting. It is too late.

It is for that reason that European law is so singularly irreversible. It requires a huge effort for a discontented government to muster a majority in the Council to instruct the Commission to think again and undo the damage. Under the Lisbon Treaty, there is a new procedure by which national parliaments can club together and demand that the Commission reconsider a proposal which they do not care for. We live in hope that this provision will actually be deployed and that the Commission will acknowledge that a proposal which has been sent back to them is therefore dead and cannot be revived without a complete rethink. It remains a good idea, but I wouldn't bet on it happening to any significant extent.

And even if this admirable clause does now and then succeed in making the Commission a little more responsive to public opinion, it is not intended as a device to prod the Commission to reconsider a law or directive which is already in force. For here we run up against a doctrine that is peculiar to the EU and makes it unlike any other type of government and legislature I can think of.

This is the doctrine of the *acquis communautaire* – the Community's acquired property or deposit (there doesn't seem to be an exact equivalent in English). The EU's volume of law is thought of almost like a geological deposit, which gathers size and weight over time. It represents a possession that is intended to be permanent and not to be chipped away at. By comparison, English law is in no sense unalterable. It is more like the collection of a restless art connoisseur who buys works of art and then sells some of them again when he wearies of them. At any moment, Parliament can revoke any one of the laws that it or any of its predecessor Parliaments has passed. Similarly, the high court can reverse or reshape any of its earlier judgments or doctrines in the light of fresh views and information; the laws of confidence and of privacy, for example, bear little relation to what they were like a generation or so ago. A new British administration will almost certainly want to reverse several of the Acts passed by its predecessor that it regards as having turned out badly; it may well have promised such a repeal in its election campaign and so be committed to go ahead. Such reversals are rare indeed in the affairs of the EU: first, because, there is no single-party government to be turfed out and replaced by a government with different views. Nor does a new set of commissioners come in panting with eagerness to undo its predecessors' work. On the contrary, the new lot is more likely to take pride in carrying that work a stage further forward.

This attitude was born of the insecurity felt by the founders of the Common Market in its early days. Any such reversal then would have been acclaimed by the EEC's opponents as a sign that the whole project was beginning to unravel. The bus or train (choose your transport metaphor) had to keep travelling forward. The body of law that was being built up was the visible evidence of the Community's growing permanence and authority.

Finally, because it was a completely new way of doing things, the EEC, later Community, later Union, had inherited no inhibitions. There were no historic limits that it had inherited. It had no tradition of leaving whole spheres of life either to private initiative and choice or to local institutions such as town and county councils. It had the exhilarating freedom of being able to make it all up as it went along.

True, to placate suspicion of any overweening ambition, the EU has always declared its commitment to 'subsidiarity' – the principle that decisions should be taken at the lowest possible tier of authority. But as Eurosceptics were not slow to point out, this term derived from the Catholic Church, possibly the most centralized international organization in history. 'Subsidiarity' clearly implied that it was only by the indulgence of the central authority that this or that power was to be devolved down the line. All power ultimately resided by rights at the centre. Compare with this, for example, the Constitution of the United States, which states clearly that those powers that are not explicitly allotted to the federal government belong to the states and have their ultimate home there.

The Commission's energetic publicity machine is swift to react whenever the EU is accused of interfering in a grotesque or overbearing manner, stipulating how curly a banana or a cucumber may legitimately be or how low a lawnmower's blades may be set. These are myths or wild exaggerations put about by rabid Europhobes, we are told. Well, sometimes they are and sometimes they are not. But the EU's spokesmen never dream of declaring that, in any case, the EU has no right to make such intrusive and detailed regulations. For the province of its rule-making and law-making is in theory limitless.

So belonging to the EU brings us under a system of law that is new to us, both in kind and in degree. It is far more abundant, much less responsive to public opinion, more or less irreversible and, within its spheres of competence, unlimited.

Yes, there are some important areas of policy from which the EU remains barred at present and which continue to be left to national governments. But as seen from Brussels, these look more like temporary exemptions and concessions to national prejudice rather than a long-term constitutional division of powers. Where spheres of action are already shared between the EU and its member nations, or where the boundaries are fuzzy, the Commission pushes forward with energy and ingenuity, supported by the judgments of the European Court of Justice, which enthusiastically exercises its remit to 'complete' the Treaty of

Rome and its successor treaties; that is, to interpret them in a way that leads to greater integration.

The pressure is always to expand the power of the Euro-oligarchs and to reduce the diversities and independences of nations and their national and local parliaments. I use the word 'oligarchs' here for the first time in a European context, but with some confidence that it is the right word. For oligarchs they are indeed. They belong to a ruling elite that cannot be ejected by the voters and whose membership changes only through being refreshed by co-opting others like themselves. They are a circulating elite, precisely in the sense defined by Pareto. They are also oligarchs in the sense that there are relatively few of them to lay down rules for the greater part of a large and populous continent. Indeed, when charged with extravagance, the Commission itself likes to point out how small its staff is, certainly compared with the size of national bureaucracies.

There are certainly areas of life in which the EU has enhanced the liberty and opportunity of the citizen quite considerably: free movement of goods within the Union, freedom for its citizens to travel and settle anywhere within its boundaries and, after lengthy negotiations, to practise their trades and professions however they fancy. The mutual recognition of degrees and qualifications has eventually followed the mutual recognition of trading standards. The latter became possible after the famous 1979 Cassis de Dijon judgment prevented national governments from banning or blocking goods from other member states on spurious grounds of quality, or health and safety; in the Cassis case, the European Court of Justice decided that the Germans could not continue to keep out the French blackcurrant liqueur on the curious grounds that it did not contain enough alcohol to qualify as a spirit suitable for drinking by the harder-headed Germans.

Yet for every case in which the EU has made life easier, there are others where it has imposed costly standardization and reduced freedom of action. I do not say that all such standardizations are absurd or contrary to the public good. Often a national government likes to hide behind the EU's skirts when it does not dare to do something which it knows it should.

Our concern here is not to evaluate the specifics of the output. It is with the way in which EU law is made: how faint is the voice of the people, how few the number of high officials who take the decisions for a continent. At least the oligarchies of old mostly governed small states, often city-states. The area was small enough for the populace to lobby their rulers directly, to jeer and jostle them if they were displeased, and if all else failed, to turf them out, roughly if need be. Only in the second half of the twentieth century have we managed to devise for ourselves an oligarchy on such a colossal scale, in which the machinery of government is so remote from us, and which is so intrinsically irremovable.

I am not asserting that the EU commissioners and their staffs are brutish, or ill-informed or ill-intentioned. Nor are most of their views irrational or callous. It is just that their ideals and purposes do not correspond very closely to the ideals and purposes of most British voters. The Eurocrats believe strongly, for example, in carrying the integration of Europe as far as possible, perhaps until it approximates to a single federal state; a steady majority in Britain believes that European union has already gone far enough and should, in several important respects, be reversed. Again, Eurocrats tend to believe that climate change is probably the most urgent challenge facing the human race and that we must reduce our carbon emissions, whatever the cost. A majority of the British people is much more sceptical of the International Panel on Climate Change's claim that global warming is largely man-made and is therefore dubious that we should embark on costly programmes that may turn out to be misguided or superfluous. Voters in other EU nations have varying views: in the old six nations of the EEC, they tend to be more in sympathy with the

Eurocrats; in the newer member nations of Central and Eastern Europe rather less so.

There is in short no sign of a single, more or less homogeneous European people – a *demos,* as the Greeks would call it – emerging as yet. Jean Monnet and the other pioneers of the EU were well aware of this absence, and they designed its structures so that they could develop without any strong popular backing: a Coal and Steel Community, a Court of Human Rights (not strictly part of the EU, but furthering the idea of European institutions), a Court of Justice, then an Economic Community. With time, it was thought, the voters would become accustomed to these institutions and wonder how they ever got on without them; they would gather a kind of retrospective assent which would grow into a feeling of European citizenship. The lack of any machinery for filtering back public opinion, let alone machinery for allowing the public to block the setting up of these institutions, was not an accidental fault in the design; it was central to that design. Without it, Monnet feared that the whole marvellous project would come apart at the first sign of public opposition.

Even today, the rare occasions on which the voters of a member nation get a chance to speak out loud and clear on the latest European treaty (either because its constitution insists on a referendum or because the government is in deep trouble and has to promise one to survive intact) are greeted with horror and apprehension by the Eurocrats. If the voters say No to a new Treaty, as the Irish have done twice, then they must be made to vote again and say Yes, or they will have all their lovely EU subsidies withdrawn. At the same conference in Amsterdam where I heard Luc Ferry bemoan his impotence as France's Minister of Education, I heard two leading Dutch politicians, the former EU Commissioner Frits Bolkestein and his colleague the Deputy Prime Minister, questioned on what they thought of the resounding No which the Dutch electorate had just given to the new

European Constitution (later resurrected as the Lisbon Treaty). They both said that 'The people were not well instructed.' In democratic politics, the mantra is that the voters are always right even when they are wrong. No such view is to be heard in the corridors of Brussels. There, it is axiomatic that the people are short-sighted, ignorant and ungrateful and must be guided towards their own best interests.

For my part, I have always supported Britain's entry into and continued membership of the EU. My support has been buoyed by a continuing hope that over the years the EU would gradually cast off its elitist oligarchic origins and engage with the people. I have to confess that no such casting-off or engaging has been observable to date. It is hard to see in the operations of the EU any real understanding of how political dialogue between rulers and ruled works. Such dialogue carries on even in regimes which we would not think of as particularly democratic: in tribal societies, for example, where the humblest people have traditional rights of access to their chief and the right to demand judgment and justice from him; or in traditional monarchies, where the ruler is contracted not only to obey the law but also to pay attention to the views and grievances of his subjects and to listen to the desires and petitions of subordinate assemblies and institutions. Compared with such older styles of government, the EU is remarkably *impervious*. Well-funded and determined lobbying organizations can make an impact on the Commission and the Parliament, but ordinary voters and their representative groups find it harder to make their voices heard.

To voice anxiety about this gap is to be dismissed as a closet Europhobe. The democratic deficit does not really worry the Eurocrats. They may acknowledge it as a theoretical problem, but it does not keep them awake at night. By contrast, the thought of any power being 'repatriated' from the EU gives them nightmares. Even now, the fear of unravelling has not quite gone away.

I do not mean to exaggerate the size of the European 'threat' at the moment to voters who abhor the thought of any more integration. The proportion of any member nation's wealth consumed by the EU is still tiny, less than five per cent. The most crucial functions of government – the levels of taxation, the power to make war and peace, the power to judge and imprison malefactors, the relief of poverty – all these remain within the exclusive power of the nation state. In that sense, the EU remains a community of nation states, an *union des patries* just as General de Gaulle insisted that it should be. But that is not what its strategists and cheerleaders want it to be in the long run. It is more the impending possibilities and the limitless pretensions of the EU that unnerve and aggravate the sceptics.

Take the most conspicuous ways in which the EU presently itches to interfere in taxation policy and in criminal justice, both still reserved for the member nations. The EU regards it as deplorable and intolerable that certain islands sprinkled around the coasts of Europe (and far beyond, in the West Indies for example) should offer a haven to people and companies who want to avoid what they regard as penal rates of taxation. Member states, on the whole, are content to allow these anomalies as offering a certain flexibility, which may on balance be beneficial to the economy as a whole. Similarly, the EU Establishment regards it as indefensible that offenders should be able to escape prosecution by decamping from the scene of the crime and stringing out a legal campaign to resist extradition. How cleanly and swiftly a European arrest warrant would cut through these obfuscations. Again, member nations would rather trust their own legal systems than grant foreign policemen the unfettered right to arrest and deport people who may turn out to be innocent.

The Eurocrats have it as an article of faith that there should be no escape from their regime, no concessions to liberty or diversity. The blanket, when fully woven, is meant to stifle.

These two examples are, after all, only forerunners of larger ambitions, to set common rates of tax across the EU and to install a common system of criminal justice. The introduction of Value Added Tax across the EU, or the 'cascade tax' as it was originally called, was designed with this object in mind. Once there was a single system in place everywhere, it could replace in one go national taxes with all their quirks and differences; all that was needed was that it should be levied at a single set of rates with identical rules and exemptions. This, however, was too much for national governments, and VAT rates and rules still vary from nation to nation. Each national exemption, for example the British relief on children's clothes and shoes, was a stab at the Eurocrat's heart. But one day perhaps there will be a single rate across the Union, and there will no longer be any need for twenty-seven Chancellors of the Exchequer to parade their Budgets; a single Finance Minister in Brussels could do the job with no fuss and no questions asked.

In the eyes of committed Eurocrats, the eurozone economic crisis of 2011 did not seem such a terrible thing. For it provided a legitimate pretext for insisting on just such a single economic policy for the whole zone, whipping into line its feckless Mediterranean members. The only way of avoiding a default by Greece and perhaps by Italy or Portugal too, it was argued, was to turn them effectively into provinces of a new Holy Roman Empire with Frankfurt as its capital. What was wrong with the EU as it stood was not that it was an oligarchy but that it was not oligarchic enough.

The EU began as an oligarchy, it continues oligarchic, and the oligarchs see no reason to alter their practices or their ambitions. No previous empire that I can think of, certainly not that of the Romans or the British, not even the French, carried centralization quite so far.

I have left the euro itself to last. It is the oligarch project to end all oligarch projects, entered into in a spirit of careless vainglory and with no thought of who its casualties might be if things went wrong. Now we have suffered the predictable, and widely predicted, crisis that has blighted the lives of the poorest people in the poorest members of the eurozone, just as it was bound to. Any currency area that lacks a single government will be unable to cushion the impact of a recession or a debt crisis upon its backward or depressed regions in the way that the United States or the United Kingdom is able to. A single interest rate can never be appropriate for seventeen hopelessly divergent economies. The risks to the poorer Mediterranean members of the zone (and to Ireland) always outweighed the modest benefits of eliminating the costs of cross-border transactions (which were fast disappearing anyway with the rise of the credit card and electronic banking). The oligarchs in Brussels and Frankfurt, unconstrained by the rancid breath of public opinion, went on preening themselves like modern Charlemagnes while the debts and the unemployment figures went on rising to intolerable levels.

It will be painful for Greece and Portugal, perhaps for Italy as well, to detach themselves from the eurozone. But not nearly as painful as it will be if they remain members. By the time this book comes out, the eurozone crisis may be resolved by several of its weaker members withdrawing from it. Or all seventeen of them may still be limping on together. Neither outcome is appetizing.

In theory, the turbulence has presented a delicious opportunity for those EU members outside the zone to repatriate some of the powers they wish they had never surrendered – over employment law, for example, or fisheries or even waste disposal. That was the glint in the eyes of those eighty-one Tory MPs who launched the biggest rebellion ever on Europe on the night of 24 October 2011. If the Coalition had yielded to their demand for a referendum on renegotiation, the referendum would have been won in a canter. But how much good would it have done? Would the eurozone core powers really be willing to loosen the rules for the UK at a time when they are desperately trying to tighten the governance of their own zone? The Eurosceptics believe that this could be the price that the UK could extract in return for agreeing to a new economic treaty to shore up the euro. But a stitch-up of that kind would hardly enhance the democratic credibility of the EU. What is needed is a new constitutional settlement, which sets out a fresh division of powers that will last and which allows national parliaments a serious role in the decision-making process. A national parliament might for example have the right to seek an exemption from the EU Treaties if there was a 75 per cent majority for the exemption.

But that kind of genuine new settlement (as distinct from the devious tarting up of the status quo devised by Giscard d'Estaing) is a long way off. The high functionaries of the EU have yet to learn the language of democracy, and they do not seem in the least eager to learn.

Part Three

WAKING UP

Glimmerings in the boardroom

There sometimes comes a moment when you have half woken up and have put the night behind you, and you suddenly see exactly what has gone wrong and what you must do to put it right. Everything is as clear as the light flooding in through the window. Unfortunately, this vision of clarity tends not to last. By the time you are up and dressed, you have begun thinking of all the snags. The old familiar reasons for not doing anything of the sort come back to you. All the same, as you plough on through the day, it is worth remembering that wonderful moment when you saw your way clear.

For the past year or so, these little epiphanies have been popping off like flash bulbs at an old film premiere. Political and business leaders are waking up to the possibility of doing things differently. Suddenly they see that it is not inevitable that the drift to inequality and oligarchy should carry on unchecked. There are counter-principles that can be invoked and, with sufficient determination and clarity of purpose, can be carried into practice.

Here are a few ripe examples, culled pretty much at random but none the less significant for that.

Speaking at the 2011 Hay Festival, Sir Stuart Rose, who had just retired as CEO of Marks & Spencer, endorsed the conclusion of the Hutton Review on fair pay, which recommended that private-sector companies should cap the pay of directors at a multiple of staff wages:

> There has to be a variation between what you earn on the shop floor and what the chief executive earns. The question is, by what quantum? One hundred times? One thousand? Two thousand? There's no doubt about it, we have to accept that over the last year or three the division between the lowest paid and the highest has got wider, so that does need looking at.[61]

Sir Stuart took home a total of just over £8 million in 2010. So assuming that the average annual wage at Marks & Spencer is something like £20,000, he must be paid around 400 times the wage of his average worker – which I suspect he would find hard to defend, if it were put as bluntly as that. But we should be grateful, I think, that he puts the question at all. And if it is objected that a retail wizard of his magnitude should be paid appropriately, well, one can only say that when he arrived at Marks & Spencer in 2004 the share price was 366. When he left seven years later at the beginning of 2011, it was 361 (to be fair, there was an exciting surge early on his tenure when the share price nearly doubled, but that eventually fizzled out). Quite possibly, without Sir Stuart, Marks & Spencer would have continued on its dowdy downward path, but what he wrought does not in retrospect look much like a miracle, certainly not an £8 million miracle.

Besides, Sir Stuart mused only on the question of how many times the pay of his shop-floor people his salary should be. He seems to have overlooked his other emoluments. In January 2004, he was lured from Topshop to Marks & Spencer for an annual salary of £850,000, plus a 'golden hello' of £1.25 million – a total remuneration of just over £2 million. His golden goodbye seven years later comes to over £8 million, four times as much. Yet the value of the company has stayed almost exactly the same. In real terms, the company is worth rather less than when he arrived there.

But oligarchs are notoriously reluctant that there should be a 'reverse ratchet' when the value of the company they manage goes down, although they are eager enough to claim thumping pay increases when it goes up. Investors in Trinity Mirror, owner of the *Daily Mirror*, demanded that the chief executive, Sly Bailey, should halve her annual package of £1.7 million after the company's value had halved over the preceding year.[62] This suggestion was not well received. But the fact that shareholders should bestir themselves thus far was distinctly encouraging.

Stephen Hester, the man brought in at RBS to reconstitute the ruins that Sir Fred Goodwin left behind, was lured for less than Sir Stuart Rose, at a salary of about £1.2 million a year, although it was envisaged that he could earn a total of £10 million in pay and bonuses over three years if he hitched the bank's share price to the required level. Yet he was prepared to admit to the Treasury Select Committee that 'If you ask my mother and father about my pay they'd say it was too high.' Mr Hester's father is a professor of chemistry (average salary £68,000), so his son earns at least twenty times what he does and, if RBS recovers, will be earning more like sixty times.

But again, we should be grateful that some inkling of how the outside world feels is at last beginning to trickle into the boardroom. More interesting still, there is even a faint intimation that business leaders are beginning to ruminate on the causes of this accelerating inequality.

Sir Richard Greenbury, one of Rose's predecessors at the head of Marks & Spencer, lent his name to one of those reviews of corporate governance which I mentioned earlier. After the Crash he tells us: 'The system now taken as sacrosanct has let us down – badly, in the case of the banking system, and let us down in the case of GEC.'[63] The latter was a reference to the failure of GEC-Marconi, after a couple of bonus-crazed top executives went on a harebrained spree. The huge cash mountain that Sir Arnold Weinstock had painstakingly accumulated over the years was dissipated on a series of dotcom companies that turned out to be worthless when the IT bubble collapsed in 2001. I speak with feeling on this subject, since I was one of the misguided small shareholders who bought a tiny chunk of GEC-Marconi shares halfway through the slide. I simply could not believe that a great company could just melt into nothing. I know better now.

The only reason why posterity has not covered the names of the CEO, George Simpson, now Lord Simpson, and his deputy CEO John Mayo in quite the same obloquy as those of Fred Goodwin and Andy Hornby is that the misery spread by the collapse of GEC was confined to the company's shareholders, while the implosion of a big bank or building society may threaten the whole financial system. But the harebrained hubris took much the same form: betting the whole company on a series of reckless gambles, buying at hugely inflated prices a bunch of businesses which they did not properly understand. Greenbury is quite right to point out that the danger of the runaway oligarch is not confined to banks.

Ironically, the system which 'let us down' was largely designed, at any rate approved by, the Greenbury Committee. So Greenbury no longer believes in Greenbury. He used to oppose two-tier boards on the Continental model. Now he believes that RBS would have had a good chance of avoiding collapse if it had possessed a supervisory board of outside directors to restrain Fred in his headlong rush to perdition. 'There was a culture of greed in the remuneration policies of the banks. The bonus system was clearly much too generous, not sufficiently testing and drove bankers towards riskier policies.'[64] The remuneration committees were too close to the colleagues whose reward they were determining. And their shareholders, who were mainly the investment institutions, far from restraining the banks, encouraged them to become even more reckless because of their own relentless pressure for profits growth.

For the past eleven years, Greenbury had sat on the supervisory board of Philips, the Dutch telecommunications giant, and he now proclaims himself a convert to the Dutch system of two-tier boards: an executive board of directors who run the business full-time and above them a supervisory board of non-executives – often including representatives of shareholders and trade unions – who monitor the executive board's performance and behaviour. There was no question, Greenbury thought: a supervisory board would have had more authority to deal with any chief executive like Goodwin getting out of control and would be able to hold him to account.

After 400 years, Sir Richard has, so to speak, rediscovered the wheel. For the present two-tier system in Holland is remarkably like the system evolved by the Dutch East Indies Company in 1622. As we have seen, the dissident shareholders, the *Doleanten*, had the company reorganized so that Nine Men (the supervisory board) sat in judgment over the Seventeen Lords (the executive board), recruiting future Lords, scrutinizing the accounts and approving or disapproving its strategy. So the answer is quite simple: bring back the Nine Men. As for bonuses, Greenbury Mark Two has an equally simple solution. In fact, he already had the solution when he was chairing the Greenbury Committee back in 1995. He told his colleagues then that they should adopt the rule that Marks & Spencer had at that time, of limiting cash bonuses to 20 per cent of salary. 'They told me I was living in the dark ages. They said it was ludicrous, that this is the 1990s, people have to be incentivized by bonuses.' But of course the 20 per cent rule is not ludicrous at all. Anyone who doesn't regard an extra fifth of his salary as sufficient inducement to work his socks off ought to be in another job.

It is good news, of course, that Sir Richard should have had the intellectual honesty to question the conclusions of his own earlier self. But I cannot resist pointing out that Sir Richard is now seventy-four years old and retired, and spends his time playing tennis and walking his dog. The number of *serving* executives who have come out in favour of installing a supervisory board to keep them in check and scrutinize their strategies is invisibly small.

Sir Richard is not alone in lamenting his old life. It was not until the end of June 2011 that Sir Victor Blank, the former chairman of Lloyds Banking Group, broke his self-imposed silence and demanded greater pay restraint from bankers. Some of the multi-million pay deals for leading figures in the industry had been 'unconscionable' and driven by greed. Yes, to get the best people you had to pay the market rate, 'but you can't have an ongoing widening gap between the top pay and the average'. It was distressing, he said, to see the pay of top executives continue to soar while the lower-paid were hit by inflation and pay freezes.[65]

This is the same Sir Victor who, while himself paid a mere £669,000 per annum at Lloyds, sanctioned that his chief executive, Eric Daniels, took home over £2 million in pay and bonuses, not to mention an accumulated pension pot of some £4 million. It is also the same Sir Victor who was tempted to put in the disastrous bid for HBOS after an apparently chance remark by Gordon Brown at a cocktail party that the government might be willing to waive the normal rules about competition in order to rescue HBOS. Now HBOS was already

known to be in horrendous difficulties. Blank disputes Daniels's
claim that Lloyds did not have the time to carry out the proper
checks with 'due diligence'. He asserts that 'massive due diligence
was done'. So they knew or should have known what they were
letting themselves in for. There could be no likely benefit to
shareholders for years to come, while there was a huge risk that
in attempting to absorb HBOS they would capsize both banks.
There was certainly no likely benefit to staff in either bank, many
of whom would lose their jobs in the amalgamation. As for any
possible benefits to bank customers, forget it. As we saw right at
the beginning of this book in the case of HSBC's doomed
takeover of Household, the only conceivable benefit would be to
the pay and bonuses of senior managers, not least Daniels and
Blank.

I make this point yet again because in his recantation Sir
Victor protests that 'I've tried from time to time in difficult
situations to get a senior management team to say we'll have a
salary hold and it is a very difficult thing to deliver.' He portrays
himself as a helpless victim of a culture of greed. But what's a
chairman for if he cannot impose his personality sufficiently on
his colleagues to make them say – in Blank's own words – 'I'm
not going to take more, I don't need more'? If there has existed
a predatory mindset among executives in banking (and many
other industries too), how can we exclude from blame those
chairmen and chief executives who relentlessly seek monster
take-overs, even at crazy prices and prohibitive risk? We are
always grateful to see lost sheep trot home, but lost sheep who
have done their share of fleecing others must expect a somewhat
mixed welcome.

These glimmerings that I have mentioned so far have a double
aspect. A moral aspect first: these business leaders are at last prepared to talk about greed and to accept that living in a community
demands a certain proportionate restraint. The entirely valid

argument for rewarding talent must not be allowed to trump other equally valid arguments about justice and fairness.

And the second aspect is a practical one: there exist quite simple remedies, which have been tried before and which have not impeded the majestic progress of great companies like Philips, or indeed the Dutch East Indies Company. We need not be prisoners of the status quo, not least because it hasn't been the status quo for very long or the status quo everywhere else. There are and always have been viable alternatives.

And this leads us on to the other, intertwined strand in oligarchy: the political strand. For the past three or four decades, whenever confronted by what Ted Heath called 'the unacceptable face of capitalism', politicians have been paralysed by fear. They were terrified that if they suggested any serious reforms they would be pilloried as enemies of capitalism – as indeed Heath was. Politicians had been led to believe that they did not, could not, understand how business worked, and that any interventions they undertook would be misguided and counter-productive. Business, and business alone, knew what was best for business.

So it was essential that there should first be some debate, preferably heated debate, amongst businessmen themselves. The problem was not so much the unacceptable face of capitalism, it was the monolithic face. Until leading businessmen were prepared to break ranks and argue about their existing practices, the politicians – in all parties – would continue to lie low. And the cruel truth was that no such argument was going to start until there had been an almighty crash.

Now we have had the crash. We are beginning to have the argument. And very gingerly, the politicians are starting to come out of their burrows.

Nowhere was the taboo against reform more strongly enforced than in the New Labour Party. That traditional crusader against inequality was terrified of being tagged as an enemy of the free market. To avoid this reputation at all cost, Peter Mandelson, the very fountainhead of New Labour, went so far as to tell a gathering of Californian computer executives in 1998 that 'We are intensely relaxed about people getting filthy rich, as long as they pay their taxes.' But of course Mandelson and his friends weren't relaxed at all; they were obsessively tense about the danger of being mistaken for old-fashioned squeeze-the-rich socialists. Even the mildest suggestion that some modest reduction in inequality might be a good thing would be erased from the text of any important speech from the leadership.

So it was a genuine break with the past when Ed Miliband told party supporters at the Coin Street Neighbourhood Trust in Southwark on 12 June 2011:

> My party must change. We were intensely relaxed about what happened at the top of society. I say – no more. We must create a boardroom culture that rewards wealth creation, not failure. To those entrepreneurs and business people who generate wealth, create jobs and deserve their top salaries, I'm not just relaxed about you getting rich, I applaud you. But every time a chief executive gives himself a massive pay rise – more than he deserves or his company can bear – it undermines trust at every level of society, We cannot and we must not be relaxed about that.

For the first time in recent Labour Party history, the party's leader rehearsed some of the data of inequality which I have already set out:

> Back in the 1970s, very high rates of taxation put people off creating greater wealth. The link between pay and performance was broken. There can be no going back to that. But the

danger today is that pay and performance have become detached again. Over the last twelve years chief executive pay in Britain's top companies has quadrupled while share prices have remained flat. And according to the recent High Pay Commission report, just in the last ten years, the pay of someone at the top of a company has gone from sixty-nine times the average wage to 145 times. Things haven't always been this way. It is worth recalling that J. P. Morgan founded his financial company on the idea that the ratio of pay between the highest and lowest paid employee should be no more than twenty to 1. It isn't for government to set maximum ratios but we do need change to encourage the responsibility we need.

So if Labour was not promising a return to the very high rates of taxation of the 1970s and was not proposing to set maximum ratios between the salaries paid to top and bottom earners, what was it proposing? Well, this is what he said, pretty much in total:

So how do we change things to ensure a better link between top pay and performance? As other countries require, we need companies to justify and explain what they are doing. On pay, companies should publish the ratio of the pay of its top earner compared to its average employee. If it can be justified by performance, they should have nothing to fear. We need shareholders to better exercise their responsibilities to scrutinize top pay. And we also need to recognize – as many great companies do – that firms are accountable to their workers as well as their shareholders. Some companies already understand that having an employee on the committee that decides top pay is the right thing to do. We should debate whether this requirement should be extended to all firms. And of course the same should be true in the public sector.

You may think that these proposals as stated do not amount to much. No, they don't. But it is the stating of them that counts. From now on, it is open season for reform. Proposals of this sort may sound timid and vague, but if linked and developed they could produce quite formidable results. Say you revise the Code of Stewardship to include clauses suggesting that (a) the normal ratio of chief executive salary to average shop-floor salary should not exceed 20 to 1 in a medium-sized company and 40 to 1 in a large company, and (b) that no cash bonus should exceed 20 per cent of salary, and (c) that any bonus paid in shares may not be cashed in for a minimum of three years (this last is beginning to become common practice anyway). Then you add another clause urging all companies above a certain size to consider adopting a two-tier board structure. Naturally, as soon as you set up any such supervisory board, it will be eager to follow the Stewardship Code to show that it is doing its job, and so it will see how best it can lock in the limits prescribed by the Code.

I do not think we need be too anxious for the bank balances of senior managers under any such new regime. Even on my illustrative figures, the CEO of a big company could still take home a massive salary: £800,000 (assuming average staff wages to be around £20,000), plus £160,000 in bonuses if he performed well. But there would be a reasonable and known limit to his earnings, his rewards would be determined by agreed principles and not by clandestine exercises in mutual back-scratching. He would not be able to loot the company. This is in fact the kind of package paid to the CEO of my own bank, the Co-op. In 2010 (the year I switched my account to the Co-op), the CEO of Co-operative Financial Services was paid a salary of £590,000 with a bonus of £183,000. He, I hope, is happy. I'm happy. And the bank is doing very nicely, having steered clear of all those dodgy derivatives and kept out of trouble.

I am not in the least sorry to have deserted Barclays Bank,

after having had my account there for fifty years. Barclays doesn't seem to be very sorry either, judging by the fact that I did not even receive a letter when I told them I was leaving. On the other hand, the assistants in the branch where I went to fill in the transfer forms were courtesy and sweetness itself. Was there any way they could help? What was it exactly that the bank had done wrong? As always in my experience, there was a striking contrast between the solicitude of the staff and the indifference of the top management.

Coalition – a new world symphony?

The formation of the Coalition government over those six hectic days in May 2011 is the most interesting political event I have witnessed. Such a thing had not happened in peacetime in living memory, and the way in which it happened was, I think, unique in Britain, though not on the Continent. It was unprecedented that the brightest policy minds in two parties should get together to hammer out, in considerable detail, an agreed programme for the Parliament. By comparison, the 'Coupon Election' of December 1918 was a casual affair. The 'Coupon' was simply a letter of support signed by both Lloyd George as Prime Minister and Bonar Law as leader of the Conservatives, and issued to those Liberals who had supported the Lloyd George Coalition during the war. Where a 'Coupon' Liberal stood, no Conservative challenged him; where a Conservative stood, no 'Coupon' Liberal would challenge him. It was an electoral pact, pure and simple, without any specific policy content. The 1931 and 1935 general elections, by contrast, returned a pre-existing Coalition National government, which had been formed after the budget crisis of 1931. Again no policy content, except that the Coalition supporters had originally been defined by their willingness to support Ramsay MacDonald's budget cuts in 1931. So 2011 was the first occasion in the modern era on which the two parties had come together to thrash out an agreed common programme.

It was not the coming together that was so startling. It is important to nail the illusion that the Coalition was a meteorite that thumped us out of a clear blue sky. It wasn't unpredictable at all. For what it's worth, I predicted it four-and-a-half years before the election, and if even I can see that far ahead, I am sure plenty of other people could too.[66]

The Tories and Libdems had become natural allies, I argued, because both parties had been forced by political necessity to alter their policies and their profiles. And this had dragged them closer together. After the thunderous Noes to the new EU Constitution from voters in France and the Netherlands in May and June 2005, the Libdems had been forced to abandon their dreams of a federal Europe with Britain joining the single currency. At home they were confronted with a new Tory leader who was not ashamed to say that 'I have always thought I was a liberal Conservative' – words that I cannot imagine tripping from the lips of any other Tory leader in the past thirty years. At the same time, the Conservatives had repented of their very unConservative obsession with central control and could make common cause with the Libdems on an agenda for a new localism. On economic policy, it was the Libdems who had undergone the most painful refurb. The liberalism of Jo Grimond seemed to be prevailing over the social democracy of Shirley Williams. The new generation of Libdems looked for answers more to the market than to the government. The party's economic spokesmen, Vince Cable and Mark Oaten, would not, I hazarded, look ill at ease in a Cameronian government. Well, Mr Oaten has gone the way of all flesh, but we had only to pencil in the name of Danny Alexander in his place.

But this congruence of policy became pressing and relevant only because of the accidents of electoral arithmetic. These, too, were clearly visible four or five years ago. The trouble for the Tories was that the electoral system had become so skewed that even if they finished several percentage points ahead of Labour in the popular vote, that might still not be enough for an overall majority. In that case, we might have to contemplate something that had seemed wildly improbable for a generation – a Tory–Libdem coalition. Not since Ted Heath vainly tried to woo Jeremy Thorpe in February 1974 had such an alliance been remotely palatable to either side. The repositioning of both parties made it easier to imagine if the situation were to arise in four years' time – easier perhaps for Libdems than the alternative of propping up an exhausted and discredited Labour administration. And since the first-past-the-post system made it so much harder for the Tories to win that overall majority than for Labour, they might be readier, then and only then, to concede that ultimate Libdem goal of proportional representation. Well, that, give or take a referendum on AV, is pretty much what has happened.[67]

But two things were not predictable. At least I had not foreseen them at all. The first was that the negotiations between the two parties would be so detailed and exhaustive. Every tiny point of potential disagreement had to be identified, clarified and resolved, either by a compromise formula, or by dropping that particular policy, or by the two sides agreeing to disagree. The Libdems would not be compelled to support any Conservative proposal to reintroduce tax breaks for marriage, for example, which meant in practice that no such proposal would be introduced so long as the Coalition continued in existence.

In retrospect, it is clear that this was the only way to make the agreement stick. The two parties, both in and outside Parliament, had been fighting against each other all their political lives and entertained the darkest suspicions of each other's motives. Only if

everything was spelled out and nailed down was there any hope of
sustaining the Coalition for four or five years. Anyone who had
seriously thought about the logistics of coalitions would have
come to the conclusion that this kind of hammering-out was
indispensable.

But the other thing that happened was much more surprising
and could not have been foreseen with anything like the same certainty. At best, it could have been only a gleam in a percipient eye.
What happened was that the two parties found much more in
common than they had anticipated. So much so that what
emerged was not a battered and untidy bundle of compromises,
but rather a much more focused and purposeful document than
either of the individual party manifestos had been. Far from being
a recipe for muddle and drift, as leading Tories had described the
prospect of a coalition during the election campaign, the
'Coalition Programme for Government' exhibited a remarkable
sense of direction and an unexpected enthusiasm. Instead of being
a second best, a *pis aller* reluctantly resorted to, coalition seemed to
have a certain zing to it. The whole was a lot more than the sum
of its parts.

The document started in a way that neither the Conservative
nor the Libdem manifesto had started, with a recognition that
centralization and oligarchy had got out of hand. The opening
paragraph declared that this was the common ground between the
parties:

> We share a conviction that the days of big government are over;
> that centralization and top-down control have proved a failure.
> We believe that the time has come to disperse power more
> widely in Britain today; to recognize that we will only make
> progress if we help people to come together to make life better.
> In short, it is our ambition to distribute power and opportunity
> to people rather than hoarding authority within government.

There would be 'radical plans to reform our broken banking system' and 'a radical redistribution of power away from Westminster and Whitehall to councils, communities and homes across the nation. Wherever possible, we want people to call the shots over the decisions that affect their lives.'

This may just sound like a resonant preamble, but I think any fair-minded reader would concede that the anti-oligarchic theme runs through the whole document. Again and again, it promises the distribution of power to the many, the taming of the oligarchs, the opening up of opportunities to the worst off. If every one of its lines of action were carried through to a practical and effective conclusion, by the end British society would be both levelled up and levelled down; the gap between the richest and the poorest would no longer be widening. The people at the top would no longer be running away with the spoils. And the people at the bottom would become agents rather than patients. Both democracy and capitalism would be reinvigorated.

There would be detailed proposals to foster diversity and competition in financial services, and an independent commission to inquire whether retail and investment banking could be separated. Companies would be made more transparent and accountable. Bonuses would be curbed.

There would be radical devolution of power to local government and community groups. Local councils would regain control of planning and of their own finances. There would be elected mayors and elected police chiefs. Parents and charities would have the chance to set up new schools.

In the public sector, a pay review would ensure that nobody at the top would be paid more than twenty times the average wage. At the bottom, low and middle incomes would have their personal tax allowances gradually increased towards £10,000. The co-operative ideal (pretty much dormant since the Second World War) would be actively supported.

Parliament, too, would be reformed to give backbenchers more control over the business of the House. Petitions that secured 100,000 signatures would be eligible to be debated and to have a Bill drafted and voted on. Local residents would be given the power to instigate referendums on any local issue. They would also have the power to vote down excessive rises in council tax.

You may dismiss some of this as the usual manifesto verbiage, but taken as a whole, it makes up quite a programme. The central theme genuinely is what is claimed in the preamble: decentralization, government by the many rather than the few, and reducing the gap between the rich and the poor in wealth as well as in power. In other words, a programme designed to curb the growth of oligarchy.

I think most people were so stunned that a coalition was formed at all that they failed to take account of what a radical programme it had devised for itself. Even now, two years after its formation, what still dominates our minds is the fact that it has survived this far, and without major disruption. There are squawks from both back benches, but the government has not been seriously threatened, far less so in fact than many a government with modest overall majorities. How long will this charmed life continue? If there is a bust-up, who or what will trigger it? These are the questions that agitate the minds of the commentariat.

Yet the greater and surely more interesting question is whether the Coalition will fulfil its surprisingly radical purpose. Whether it will leave behind a country that is a lot less oligarchic and slightly less unequal, or whether it will be remembered simply as a curious prolonged intermission between majority governments of one party or the other.

What does the record so far look like? Is the reforming drive still active, or is it dribbling into the sand? Has the Coalition managed to operate those levers of power which Tony Blair complained he couldn't shift?

Are we getting anywhere?

The Isles are full of noises. Never have all parts of the UK been more abuzz with talk of reform – political, constitutional, financial and social. The first intimations from David Cameron's Big Society seem to indicate a society that is ready to look at every aspect of its own life and contemplate change. In each significant limb of the body politic, there are significant stirrings: Commission reports, committees sitting, Bills published or passed.

It would be hopeless to try to draw up an overall progress report. The only useful approach, I think, is to examine each area on its own and try to answer one simple question: does what is proposed, or being put into practice, really get to the heart of the problem, or is it merely an attractive palliative? Each sketch will not attempt a comprehensive critique of what is happening. What I hope to do is to identify the central question and ask: does it improve the strength of the system and reduce the power of the oligarchs?

There are five arenas in play: the City (where the trouble started), the political parties, Whitehall and Westminster, the local dimension, and, anything but least, Europe.

The Bankers

Great things were expected of the Independent Commission on Banking. It was set up in June 2010 under the chairmanship of Sir John Vickers, Warden of All Souls College, Oxford, formerly Chief Economist at the Bank of England and Director-General of the Office of Fair Trading, and in terms of intellectual distinction and independence of mind it had one of the strongest memberships of any public inquiry in recent years. In both its interim report published in April 2011 and the final report which came out that September (there's not much difference between the two), the commission gives an admirable account of what's wrong with the banks – and what was wrong before the crash of 2007–8. To start with, not enough competition to provide a better service. The Big Four banks (Lloyds, Barclays, RBS and HSBC) occupy 80 per cent of the market for personal current accounts, and there are only two 'challenger banks', Nationwide and Santander, to spur them into a semblance of offering their customers a better service. The banks are also inherently unstable, since they borrow short, increasingly from each other, and lend long. So when a lack of confidence causes lending between banks to dry up, any bank is liable to implode with terrifying rapidity. As the banks have taken on more risk in recent years, so the ratio of their reserves to their loans has dwindled to perilous levels.

So the first, and pretty obvious remedy is for the banks to hold more capital, to equip themselves with a fatter cushion to absorb shocks.

Then we also need to clean up the derivatives business and all the fancy dealings between customers and prime brokers which at present don't have to be reported to any central authority and can produce hysterical swings in the market that take everyone by surprise, because the dealings which caused them all take place under the Stock Exchange radar.

Vickers also welcomes the decision to split Britain's Financial
Services Authority into two new bodies: the Prudential
Regulation Authority, a new subsidiary of the Bank of England,
which has the power once attributed to the Governor's Eyebrows
of being able to inspect firms, and instruct them to desist from
risky business and put themselves back into shape; and a Financial
Conduct Authority, which takes over the fraud-busting functions
of the old FSA and also, importantly, has a duty to promote the
competition that is sorely lacking.

So far, so good. But now comes the real question, the potential game-changer: do we break the banks up, or do we just
fiddle with the way they operate? There are, after all, really only
two ways to make banks safer. You can force them to hold much
more capital. Or you can separate retail banking – the staid old
high street banks with their cautious lending policies and modest
salaries – from investment banking, with their complex and
risky bank loans and their gilded bonuses. That is the way things
were done in the United States under the Glass–Steagall Act
from 1933 until the 1990s, and in the UK until the Big Bang of
1986.

Well, which is it to be? Neither, says Vickers, or rather 'a more
moderate combination of these approaches'. There would be
'internal ring-fencing within universal banks to isolate UK retail
banking services'; and 'higher – but not very high – capital
requirements, together with measures to make bank debt effectively loss-absorbing'.[68]

How would this 'ring fence' work? The idea is that the retail
section of the big 'universal' bank would be protected in the
event of the crash of the investment banking bit. Each section
would have to maintain its own minimum capital requirement and
the investment banking arm would not be able to raid the retail
arm for cash so as to threaten that requirement, and vice versa.
But subject to those minimum requirements, huge quantities of

cash could slop over the fence in either direction.[69] These sloppings can occur on a vast scale. Even under Stephen Hester's post-Crash leadership, the subsidiary Natwest lent £92.4 billion to its parent company, Royal Bank of Scotland, and other subsidiaries in 2010.[70] As long as the minimum capital requirements were maintained on both sides of the fence, such massive transfers could continue under the Vickers recommendation. So the ring fence is a pretty low fence, the sort a rabbit can easily hop over to reach your broad beans.

Vickers does not deny that these universal banks are a potential menace. His interim report argues very cogently[71] that 'universal banks can damage the stability of the whole system'. First, universal banks can be one way in which problems spread through the financial system. Second, universal banks typically hold less capital relative to assets than equivalent separate institutions. This can heighten risk at times of general economic stress, when banking system resilience is most needed.[72] Yes, sometimes the investment banking operation may be able to cover losses on retail banking, but 'Unsuccessful wholesale/investment banking may bring down the universal bank, including the retail bank.'[73]

This is not just a theoretical catastrophe. It is a catastrophe that we have just experienced. It seems unlikely that we can prevent a repetition by installing a fence that would not deter a rabbit. Vickers's 'more moderate combination' does not seem to me to be an adequate response to the threat that he outlines so clearly.

Like so many publications by government committees, however eminent, Vickers's analysis seems light on the *historical* dimension. For surely the evidence from the last century is overwhelming. The equivalent of 'universal banks' were irrepressibly risky in the years leading up to the Great Depression. Since Big Bang and the repeal of Glass–Steagall, they have been irrepressibly risky again. In between, for half a century, we had sound and stable banks and, after the Second World War, a steady progress of prosperity on both sides of the Atlantic. This period was the Golden Calm of Anglo-Saxon banking.

The benefits to their customers and the wider public of having colossal universal banks are unproven and, here at any rate, unargued. The risks that their existence poses to the stability of the economic system and to the jobs and welfare of the ordinary citizen are unarguable. The only undoubted beneficiaries from their existence are the top executives who run them. The bigger the banks are, the better off the oligarchs at the top.

Of course there must be some cost involved in separating the two sides of the universal banks, although everyone seems to find that cost extremely difficult to calculate. But it seems to me to be an insurance premium well worth paying when you consider the gigantic national and personal costs of the Crash. And once the initial premium is paid, I have no doubt that the actors will adjust their behaviour to maximize the benefits of the new system; that is what people do in a market.

By the same token, alas, the relevant actors in a ring-fenced system à la Vickers will also make the most of their situation under the new rules. The Fred Goodwin of the future will run both parts of his universal bank on maximum revs, threatening the stability of the whole vehicle. Customers and the public will have to trust the vigilance of the Financial Authorities to pull him up when he goes too far. For a year or five, that vigilance will no doubt be maintained. But in the end, either the vigilantes will become slack or the oligarch will find more ingenious ways to pile on the risk or both. Such risks would be much reduced if the two sorts of banking were separated.

Better still if the big banks did not have such overwhelming dominance in the markets. Vickers supports the existing demands that Lloyds and RBS should divest themselves of some of their branches, but won't go any further, arguing, for example, that by now HBOS is so far integrated into Lloyds that it would be prohibitively expensive to demerge it again. But a demerger would be a once-for-all cost that would leave a far healthier competitive situation.

It is not as if Sir John is under any illusions that the present practice of the banks offers anything remotely approaching perfect competition. They make scarcely any pretence of competing for retail customers, relying on the sloth or loyalty of the customers they already have. Nor is it as if they exploited only the masses. They charge extortionate rates for underwriting issues, relying again on the sloth or loyalty of their long-term business customers who don't bother to shop around for better terms. There is nothing the banks hate more than customers who shop around; witness their contempt for people who switch their savings in search of a better rate of interest as 'rate tarts'. Can one imagine a supermarket boss daring to refer to customers who moved to a rival as 'trolley tarts'?

Yet despite their awareness of its obvious imperfections, Sir John and his colleagues seem implicitly to accept that the status quo must, basically, be accepted. They don't of course actually say that 'the market is always right', that 'big is beautiful', or that 'complexity equals prosperity'. But their whole report seems to take it as read that the system which has actually evolved has considerable 'synergies'; that the size of universal banks must, on the whole, be a good thing; and that the sheer baffling complexity of modern banking is an advance on the old days.

But why? Do banks today lend more readily to small and medium enterprises – or on better terms to bigger enterprises? Do they grant mortgages on a more rational basis? Do they reduce the cost of credit to cardholders and people with overdrafts? Do they hell.

Personally, I find it hard to see how a bank can enjoy any further economies of scale once it has passed, say, the present size of the Co-operative Bank, with a reasonable network of branches, the standard array of payment and credit services (BACS, Chaps, credit and debit cards that you can use in any ATM and so on) and a sufficient capital base to handle reasonably large loans. Loans beyond a certain size tend in any case to be syndicated among a number of banks, often a large number. When Rupert Murdoch was desperately seeking to stay afloat in the early 1990s he had to travel the world to pacify no less than 146 banks that had lent him money.

Another thing you cannot help noticing is how narrowly the ICB has interpreted its remit. The Chancellor of the Exchequer asked the committee 'to consider structural and related non-structural reforms to the UK banking sector to promote financial stability and competition'. There are quite a few other avenues to such reforms which fall within those instructions, but the Commission has barely tiptoed down any of them.

First, bonuses, the subject that understandably burns hottest in our minds. Any fool can see that a company that rewards its executives so hugely in bonuses for achieving expansion and driving up the share price is likely to take more risks than a company that pays salaries only. Since the Commission acknowledges that banks are systemically more fragile than other businesses and that bank failures have such a ghastly knock-on effect for the rest of the economy, the Governor could do worse than institute the old Marks & Spencer rule, as recommended by Sir Richard Greenbury: a bank should not, as a rule, pay anyone a bonus larger than 20 per cent of his or her salary.

Because of this systemic fragility, isn't there a case too for insisting that banks above a certain size set up a two-tier board, also now recommended by Greenbury? The supervisory board would have a special interest in seeing to it that the bank satisfied all the regulatory authorities, didn't take any silly or disproportionate risks, that its reserve ratios were sound, and that there was no funny business going on off the balance sheet. That sort of supervisory board might well put a brake on the bank's pace of expansion. So much the better. A bank is meant to be more like an armour-plated Volvo than a Formula One racing car, which breaks up the moment it hits something.

Then if we return to the historical perspective, we may note that one feature of the financial sector during the Golden Calm of the half-century after 1933 was its *diversity*. There were far more banks, both big and small, and there were also a large number of non-profit-making building societies. The principal building societies, except for Nationwide, all demutualized after the Big Bang of 1986 and became banks, often highly aggressive and hungry banks. Some of these new banks, such as the Halifax, Abbey and Alliance & Leicester, were swallowed up by the big banks. Others, like Northern Rock, came to grief in the Crash. Only Nationwide sailed on in splendid mutuality. It is now the largest building society in the world. There seems to be a moral there, not least for the government, which is now the reluctant owner or part-owner of Northern Rock, RBS and Lloyds. Does this not present an opportunity to regenerate the building societies?

Preoccupied with the appalling deficit, George Osborne has ducked the chance to remutualize Northern Rock and has sought out a bidder who will pay a satisfactory price. The Treasury felt that its duty to the taxpayer must come first.

Yet in a longer perspective, a higher public duty might be to restore that diversity which surely contributed greatly to the overall stability of the financial system. Building societies were by their nature risk-averse; they took in savings from the public and lent the money to home-buyers. Only extreme incompetence or outright fraud could bring down a building society. Anyway, there used to be so many of them that the collapse of one caused scarcely a ripple on the millpond. There never was anything complex about the business; there still isn't; and its twin functions, of helping home-buyers and offering a secure haven for small and medium savings, remain as relevant as ever.

Yet again the Vickers Commission and, I fear, the government shrink from interfering. But will a better chance ever come again, to promote mutuals, as promised in the Coalition Programme?

Of course we might be lucky. The 'more moderate combination' which Vickers proposes might see us through the next twenty years. But the odds don't look favourable. And insurance against calamity is, after all, a question of odds.

There is, I cannot help feeling, an instinctive lack of appetite for reform in the City which lies behind the proposals advanced by the Vickers Commission and the response of the government, with the signal exception of Vince Cable. We can hear the dogs barking at the oligarchs. But where's the bite?

Yet there is something to cheer about in the City. At last the politicians have begun to recall the underlying principles of shareholder rights. David Cameron's first initiative in 2012 was to promise that, in future, shareholder votes on directors' pay would be mandatory rather than merely advisory. Some self-styled reformers shudder. Isn't this a ghastly surrender to the Left? But of course it is not. The shareholders own the company; they have every right to exercise effective control over the rewards their managers are dishing out to themselves. This isn't socialism. This is real capitalism. Adam Smith would have loved it.

Some old City hands are still cynical. They argue that investors these days are only interested in the immediate returns from their holdings, which in any case they no longer hold long enough to take a serious role in governance, as they flit from flower to flower without a backward glance. Yet there remains a critical mass of long-term investors who have the power – and increasingly the will – to change things. Large fund managers like Hermes, owned by the BT pension scheme, now operate skilled lobbying arms to engage directly with the companies they are invested in.

Recalcitrant CEOs find themselves under steady and stinging pressure to freshen up their boards, to separate the role of chairman from chief executive, to review the risks they are taking, to reform their pay systems and to follow ethical and ecological codes. Giants like Moody's and J. P. Morgan Chase, which have suffered severe damage to their reputations during the Crash, have reluctantly found themselves forced to take notice. As soon as these pressures become mandatory rather than advisory, 'responsible capitalism' ceases to be a do-gooder's daydream. It becomes a route for sensible managers to restore their firm's reputation, retain its customers and so ultimately revive its share price. It is a route which, I fancy, more and more listed companies will go down until it becomes second nature to them.

The Parties

When Christopher Shale died suddenly at the Glastonbury Festival in 2011, the newspapers at first suspected something tragic or even sinister. Mr Shale was the charismatic chairman of the West Oxfordshire Conservative Association, David Cameron's constituency. Cameron was very fond of Shale and owed a lot to him. Mr Shale had recently written a trenchant and feisty strategy paper about the failings of his Association, and he had just been told that the juiciest passages of this memo had been leaked to the *Mail on Sunday*.[74] Could the embarrassment of the leak have caused Mr Shale to kill himself or at least brought on a fatal heart attack?

Well, no it couldn't. Mr Shale turned out to have died of entirely natural causes, and in any case there was no embarrassment to speak of. Cameron had actually encouraged Shale to write the memo as a blueprint for increasing party membership in West Oxon and elsewhere. Besides, anyone who has been following politics knows perfectly well that Shale's views of his fellow members chime exactly with what the Cameroons think: 'Over the years we have come across as graceless, voracious, crass, always on the take. Collectively we are not an appealing proposition. As a group we don't look much different to how we looked ten or twenty years ago. Everyone else does. The perception is that we are too fond of looking inwards rather than outwards.' Exactly what Cameron's Home Secretary Theresa May meant when she said back in 2002 that the Conservatives had to face up to the 'uncomfortable truth' that they were 'sometimes perceived by the public as the nasty party'.[75]

After Theresa May, I remember Francis Maude when he was party chairman telling the 2005 Conservative Conference in Blackpool how dislikeable and disliked they were: 'People think we are out of touch. People think we are a party that doesn't understand how people live their lives. People attribute some bad values to us. They think things about us that are not what we think of ourselves.'[76] And I remember the frisson of unease that rippled round the hall.

Ever since, it has been central to the project of the 'modernizers' in the Conservative leadership that the party they represented had become socially repellent, verging on leprous. Only if they changed the way they looked and sounded could they hope to attract new recruits. Party members had to think and act more like ordinary people. Far from representing the best of British, they tended to be weird, hidebound and out of date.

This line of patter would have been regarded as bizarre, not to say outrageous by an earlier generation of Conservative leaders. Their ingrained practice was to praise the decency and dedication, the high principles and hard work of the people who had helped to get them where they were. Privately Tory MPs might make jokes about 'the greengrocers and garagistes' who ran their associations, but in public they paid tribute to them as the salt of the earth.

All that has changed. The decline of party membership is attributed, in considerable part, to the futility of joining and the unpleasant experience if you do. There are a dozen better things to do with your time. Again, Mr Shale was merely spouting the new orthodoxy: 90 per cent of the population is 'politics lite'; 'politics heavy is a big turn-off for politics-lite people ... The claimed benefits [of joining the Conservative Party] – the right to attend party Conference, take part in selecting our MPs and so on are of zero interest to most current, let alone potential, members.'[77] By continuing to offer potential recruits more political activity, they were only making them even less likely to join. That was why party membership had continued to decline even under Cameron's energetic leadership, by about one third, from 259,000 to 177,000.

So the much lamented Christopher Shale was merely saying, in vivid language, what everyone else around him has been saying. And not merely saying.

For the most striking feature of Cameron's management of his party is the way in which he has consistently and successfully managed to bleed politics out of party activity.

The most crucial – and most exciting – function of a local constituency party is to choose its parliamentary candidate. In the old days, this was a jealously guarded privilege. As far back as 1935, Central Office had established a Standing Advisory Committee on Parliamentary Candidates, to build up a list of approved candidates, which was sent out, but only on request, to constituency associations that were about to select a candidate. Those associations were perfectly free to draw up a shortlist including people who were not on the approved list, but already in 1949 the Maxwell Fyfe Report was expressing anxiety that, before the 1945 general election, associations were frequently adopting candidates not on the approved list and having them endorsed only after they had been chosen. In future, non-approved prospective candidates ought to be screened *before* adoption – which of course made it much easier to veto candidates that Central Office disliked. But at least the local association was still free to put its own favourite sons and daughters on its shortlist, and choose someone who had not originally been on the approved list.

Not any more. Now anyone seeking to be chosen anywhere has to be on the national approved list and has to undergo an exhaustive examination of their social and rhetorical skills, their political knowledge and, most crucially, of their political opinions – no mavericks, no dark horses, no original local figures. Everyone has to go through the machine.

And even after reaching the approved list, there is no guarantee that you will stay on it after the election. Annunziata Rees-Mogg, the daughter of the former editor of *The Times*, first achieved notoriety when David Cameron jokingly suggested that she ought to change her name to Nancy Mogg when she stood as the Tory candidate for the key marginal seat of Somerton & Frome, where she failed by only 1,900 votes to unseat the sitting Liberal Democrat MP. A year later, she achieved notoriety a second time by becoming the most conspicuous candidate to be axed from the new list of approved parliamentary candidates. Other notable casualties were Deborah Dunleavy who had stood in Bolton North East and Mark Clarke, the candidate in Tooting.[78] Thus the Conservatives in Somerton & Frome, Bolton North East and Tooting were barred from readopting their candidates, however highly they rated their performance in the general election. The suspicion among Eurosceptics is that these three, and others too, were so brutally dropped because of their strong views about the EU. But whether or not this explanation is true, the point of principle is that the freedom of associations to choose the candidate they want has been curtailed one more notch.

The Coalition Programme for Government promised to fund 200 all-postal primaries over this Parliament, 'targeted at seats which have not changed hands for many years'. This commitment has now apparently been shelved because of shortage of funds. But in any case the attraction of this proposal, as of 'open primaries' in which non-members of the local association can also take part in the selection, is much reduced because the choice of candidate is so severely constrained by the pre-screening at national level. This is the kind of 'democratic centralism' of which Lenin would have approved.

Shale's memo, or what we have read of it, makes no reference to this hotly resented take-over of an ancient right and privilege. Nor do we hear anything about the other conspicuous control-freakery: the emasculation of the annual party conference, so that it is incapable of causing serious trouble for the leadership. Unlike at a Labour conference, at a Conservative conference there was never much danger of the leadership actually losing a vote on a resolution, but there could be hot and meaningful debate on a contentious subject, and the party leaders could be left in no doubt of the strength of feeling amongst the rank and file. Not any more. Such resentments now circulate semi-underground, on blogs and websites such as Conservative Home. In those quarters of the ether there has been an indignant reaction to the centralizing of control. But this is not yet as significant as open public debate between flesh-and-blood human beings.

Thus the reasons for wishing to join the Conservative Party have been substantially eroded over recent years. The chances of party members being able to play a significant role have been deliberately reduced in the interests of the party making a forceful and unified impact in the media. I don't think any reasonable person could resist the conclusion that this must have something to do with the further decline in party membership. When I was a member of the Power Commission investigating the reasons for the public disaffection with politics, I lost count of the witnesses who told us that they derived little or no satisfaction from belonging to a political party; and they could well see why so many of their friends thought it a pointless thing to do.

When I read the reports of the Shale memo, there was something familiar about it, something which I struggled to identify at first. But then I realized that much of it was a weird echo of what Ed Miliband had said about the Labour Party only two days earlier: 'Old Labour forgot about the public – New Labour forgot about the party. We can only win if we change. Our political culture must become less inward-looking and decision-making, more open. We have got to change the way we work as a party. We need to build a party that is rooted in the lives of every community in the country.'[79]

So Labour too now regards self-loathing and a little healthy flagellation as the route to success. Everyone in the party was to recognize how introspective and out of touch they had become. Every part of the party had to become open and accessible to ordinary people.

Which all sounds fine. Except that in the very same speech Miliband also announced that henceforth his shadow cabinet would no longer be elected by Labour MPs but chosen by himself. And he warned that there could be no going back to the days when the party's National Executive Committee ruled the roost and when the party's conference took the party's constitution literally and therefore took it for granted that Conference (always with a divine capital C) had the right to dictate the party's policy. Like the National Policy Forum, the body he happened to be addressing, Conference did 'not have sufficient legitimacy in the eyes of members'. The National Policy Forum was the body set up to replace the NEC as the party's deciding voice on policy; its membership was designed to be reliable and docile. Yet now even the Policy Forum is thought too unsafe to be entrusted with substantial power. In the end, the leader alone is to decide on policy, just as only the leader 'can be allowed to choose the Shadow Cabinet'.

Thus a long speech that was supposed to open up the party to its members in practice seems rather to close it down by concentrating all remaining power within the leadership – almost exactly what has happened inside the Conservative Party. When Miliband says he wants 'to open up conference to the public', what he really means is that he wants to make the conference even more of a snazzy media event that manages to be bland and conflict-free and will provide appealing clips for *News at Ten*. The last thing he has in mind is that there should be more passionate debates that may well end in defeats for the leadership and purport to saddle the leader with embarrassing commitments which he thinks will cost votes at the next general election.

The old ways in both parties certainly had their downside. But on a strict analysis of power flows over the past few decades there is no question: the real power is flowing one way, towards the centre. For all the fluffy talk about opening the party out and getting in touch with real ordinary people, our politics is becoming more not less oligarchic. And this trend is accompanied by an unmistakable contempt for the poor souls who persist in staying party members.

Yet can the views and anxieties of party members be dismissed quite so easily as bigoted, crazy and backward-looking? The prevailing and pervasive problems of British politics are in fact more likely to be highlighted by the despised party activists than by the consensus deemed acceptable by the BBC and the better class of newspaper. It is Labour activists who have been hammering away about the growing inequality in our society during the years when the New Labour leadership was terrified of using the word. It was Tory activists who refused to accept that large-scale immigration was an unqualified benefit and kept on worrying about working-class unemployment and social dislocation. Again, the activists are far more incensed about the costs and the high-handed manners of the EU; and about the dangers to competition and employment posed by high taxes. On both sides, problems which the *bien pensants* have only now consented to recognize as problems have been uppermost in the minds of activists for years.

This isn't really an accident. In fact I suspect that this is an inbuilt tendency of oligarchies: to exclude from discussion or remedy those problems which do not inconvenience and may well hugely benefit the oligarchs themselves. Mass immigration is a superb example of this: wonderful for providing au pairs, waiters and fruit-pickers for the elite, not so hot for the workers whose wages are depressed and job opportunities diminished by the competition from the incomers. In the end, this failure to address the real problems of the day is what brings oligarchies crashing down, because when in the end they are brought to address those problems they do so too late and too half-heartedly, to stave off the uprising.

Raw, noisy, unabashed debate and a decisive open system of election at every level – these are the only cures, but they are the last cures that your average oligarch is willing to contemplate.

The conventional explanation or excuse for centralizing power and eliminating conspicuous public dissent is that the nature of twenty-first-century politics demands that the party presents a smooth unified front to the media, and transmits a clear and consistent message. The relentless exigencies of '24/7 politics' are said to require that the whole party apparatus is 'on-message' at all times. Debate, disagreement and mavericks are unaffordable luxuries.

This assertion seems to me false in fact and devious in motive. In many other successful countries, party congresses/conventions/conferences continue to debate policy robustly and, what's more, maintain their right to approve or disapprove any proposed strategic changes in the party's direction. None of this damages the country or its currency or even the ruling party, which may well be driven onto a more popular course by the strength of party feeling. The French Socialists, for example, have come back into the reckoning partly because of their robust intra-party debates and their willingness to hold a nationwide vote, open to all, not just to party members, to decide who should be their candidate for the next presidential election.

Nor is any great harm done by allowing fresh, unapproved candidates to take their chance. That is what makes American politics so full of fizz. Anyone can have a shot at the nomination, and sometimes the most unlikely amateur makes the best candidate.

I spent the best part of a year in the inspiriting company of Helena Kennedy and the other members of the Power Commission. And what we discovered was really quite simple, and only partially obscured because professional politicians refuse to believe it. People are turned off politics in general, not because they don't care but because they don't believe that voting or joining a political party will make the slightest difference. This is an entirely rational judgment, and not the result of sloth or apathy. It is the sucking up of power to the centre that has devitalized British politics. And the remedy is as straightforward as it is distasteful to the elite: give power back to the people.

Parliament and government

It is something of a relief to turn from the desertified wastes of party to a rather more encouraging prospect.

I have tried a little to describe the degradation of Whitehall and Westminster under Tony Blair; the reduction of the Cabinet to a once-a-week coffee morning; the virtual disappearance of Cabinet papers and formal minutes, which formerly provided a structured basis for discussion and action; the Prime Minister's contempt for the House of Commons and his determination to go there as little as possible (one or two other postwar Prime Ministers had felt rather the same, Margaret Thatcher for example, but at least she observed the proprieties); the increasing use of the guillotine to terminate discussion on contentious Bills, sometimes even before the crucial clauses had been reached; the reduction of the Government Information Service to a party tool and the abuse of official statistics for party purposes. All these malpractices came together in the notorious business of the Dodgy Dossier in the run-up to the Iraq war: the entire Whitehall machine was perverted in order to maximize the case for war. If you want to understand just how bad things got, you have only to read Lord Butler's Review of Intelligence on Iraq's Weapons of Mass Destruction,[80] which demonstrated all the failings of 'sofa government'.

Things got a little better when Gordon Brown took over, but there really has been a decisive improvement in the manners of Whitehall and the practices of Westminster since the Coalition was formed in May 2010. The Cabinet has regained some of its old lost importance – though it is still less significant than it was in Macmillan's day, let alone Churchill's. Ministers have to explain their intentions in proper papers, and decisions are properly minuted and transmitted down the line. Not nuclear physics I grant you, but we should be grateful when government begins to behave a little more like any reasonably well run institution – such as a commercial company, charity or cricket club.

The Office of National Statistics has been put on a fresh independent basis. And government forecasting has been farmed out to a new body, the Office of Budget Responsibility. This does not guarantee that the forecasts will be any more accurate, but they may be a little less subject to distortion and wishful thinking.

But it is inside Parliament that we can see the most hopeful signs that power may be a little more dispersed and debate reinvigorated with greater public participation. The chairmen of select committees used to be inserted by the whips and removed by the whips if they gave trouble. Now the chairmen are genuinely elected by the whole House, and the first fruit of this overdue reform has been the election of the sardonic and tenacious Andrew Tyrie as the chairman of the Treasury Select Committee.

Tyrie has already managed to gain for the committee the power of approval over appointments to the Bank of England Monetary Policy Committee and to the head of the Office of Budget Responsibility. He has led the way in forcing the Financial Services Authority to publish a full report into the RBS disaster. In other words, the Treasury Select Committee is already beginning to assume a much more aggressive and investigative role, comparable to that of a Congressional committee in the US. We used to be told that all this would be impossible because the UK doesn't have the same separation of powers as the US, because MPs won't have either the staff or the expertise to carry out these enhanced functions effectively, etc., etc. Well, of course it's all perfectly possible; give these committees the powers and the back-up and they'll acquire the expertise soon enough.

I am equally pleased to see other reforms of Parliament either in train or proposed. We can perfectly well have something like the US War Powers Act, which requires Congressional approval before troops are sent into battle. The objections – that this would inhibit the government's flexibility of response or weaken its negotiating position – are insubstantial quibbles. Anyway, the House did approve Britain's participation in the Iraq war, and by an overwhelming majority. There is everything to be said for adopting it as a standard practice that entry into a war must have prior democratic legitimization.

The same applies to the question of whether any fresh grant of powers to the EU should be subject to a national referendum. Europhiles in the House of Lords tried to erode this clause from the Europe Bill of 2011 by demanding that there be a 40 per cent turnout for the result of the referendum to have effect. The truth was that the Europhile peers did not want any referendum to be held at all, ever, hoping that the EU elite could continue to accumulate further powers without hindrance. But the case for insisting on a referendum when substantial powers are to be transferred from Parliament for the foreseeable future is unanswerable. Such a transfer is not just another Bill or Treaty; it is a major change in the terms of our constitution and requires solemn public consent. The same Europhile peers also disliked Clause 18 in the European Union Bill, which makes it clear that it is 'by virtue of the European Communities Act, 1972' that EU law 'is to be recognized and available in law in the UK'. The idea behind the clause is to make it clear that the British Parliament made that law and could always unmake it again. Statement of the bleeding obvious, argues the distinguished lawyer Lord Pannick in *The Times*.[81] In fact, he says it's worse than that, because the insertion of Clause 18 suggests that without the clause it might be possible to argue that Parliament's powers *had* been removed or reduced by the 1972 Act. This strikes me as what lawyers call a bad point. Making a statement that X is the case does not imply that, if the statement were not made, X would not be the case. There is, moreover, often a lot to be said for a declaratory statement to clarify and reassure where there is doubt and fear. We do have a right to know where we stand.

I have already listed some of the other parliamentary reforms that the Coalition has promised. If properly implemented, they really would open the doors of Parliament to allow the public to be heard, and its concerns debated in good time; at the same

time, they would give ordinary Members of Parliament more say
in the business of the House. I don't doubt for a minute that we
shall be disappointed in some of the outcomes; but I don't think
that we shall be disappointed in all of them. It may sound child-
ishly optimistic, but I really do think that Parliament has turned a
corner. I do not, for example, share the cynical consensus in the
press gallery that the reform of the House of Lords is an idea
whose time still has not come (it was first envisaged in an Act of
Parliament in 1911). Was Nick Clegg's perfectly plausible Draft
not received with rude derision in the Chamber, especially by
Tory MPs? Are not the diehards in the House of Lords getting
ready to resist reform – as they have resisted every reform of their
powers in the past, in 1832, 1911 and 1949? So they are, but the
diehards lost each time in the past, and I think they will lose this
time. I remain utterly unconvinced by the life peers' overweening
assessment of their own brilliance and wisdom. It is not simply
that whenever I peer down at those scarlet benches they seem to
be whiffling and whuffling much as their hereditary predecessors
whiffled and whuffled. It is also the case that other parliamentary
systems seem to manage perfectly well, in fact rather better, with
an elected Upper Chamber. So long as the Upper Chamber is
elected by a different system from the Lower House (which it
invariably is), the democratic mixture is enriched; if the terms of
office are also different from those of MPs, then the perspective
becomes longer and the chances of legislation being improved are
increased.

It is, I think, to the Coalition that we owe this genuine enthusiasm for reforming Parliament. A single-party government
would continue to be in thrall to the whips and their conviction
that the only thing in life that really matters is that we get 'our
business' through. In a Coalition, the tough eggs who believe
that reform is only for wimps and wonks cannot have things all
their own way.

A coalition that commanded, as in this case, 59 per cent at the general election is in that sense stronger than a single-party government, which at best is unlikely to have commanded much more than 40 per cent. It need not feel humiliated and in mortal peril if it loses the odd vote. And it can afford to contemplate reforms which might mean that Bills are chewed over longer and sometimes redrafted quite a bit. In other words, a coalition can afford to let MPs perform the role that they are supposed to perform and not fly into a panic every time they refuse to act as a rubber stamp.

This may not last for ever. If the Coalition begins to fracture as the next general election approaches, it may become more paranoid and peremptory, and government may slip back into its old bad habits.

But for the moment, the sun is still smiling on the Coalition. MPs are, we assume, cleaning their own moats, pruning their own wisteria and no longer claiming for mortgages they have already paid off. And at long last they are beginning to make a show of controlling the oligarchs, instead of joining them.

Localism – the real thing?

So we have said goodbye – for the time being – to the worst days of the Blair style: sloppy decisions casually taken on the Number Ten sofa, with a semi-defunct Cabinet and an ill-attended and mildly corrupt Parliament acting as rubber stamps (I say 'mildly' only by comparison with the far larger dollops of gravy guzzled by members of the US Congress and the European Parliament). The system today at the end of the Coalition's second year works a little more like it is supposed to; political practice has at least come within shouting distance of constitutional theory. So far, so good.

It is nice that decisions are now arrived at through something approximating to the proper processes. But that does not make them the right decisions. The more important question we have to address is whether the Coalition is living up to its thrilling early promise. In particular, is it following through its grand opening declaration that 'the days of big government are over; that centralization and top-down control have proved a failure'? Is power really being redistributed away from Westminster and Whitehall to councils, communities and homes across the nation? Are the people really beginning to call the shots?

This ambitious undertaking was given conspicuous and concrete form in the Localism Act. It is certainly an ambitious piece of legislation, which seeks to reverse a half-century (or more) of creeping centralization.

The most sweeping new power to be given to local councils is 'the general power of competence'. Local authorities will in future have the legal capacity to do anything that an individual can do that is not specifically prohibited by law. If this provision works, local authorities will in future be writing their own scripts rather than mostly following instructions from Whitehall.

Then elected mayors: the government will give all the largest cities in Britain in May 2012 the chance to vote on whether they would like to have an elected mayor. Those cities that vote yes will be electing their mayor the following year, in May 2013.

Parish councils and local communities will be given a chance to take over the running of a local authority service. Committees will also have a right to designate buildings and land – such as meeting halls, swimming pools, markets and pubs – as 'community assets' and would have the right to buy such properties if they are threatened with sale or closure.

Local people will also have the right to trigger a referendum on a local issue that is close to their heart. And the power to cap rises in council tax above a certain level will pass from the Secretary of

State to local people, who will be able to veto an excessive rise in a referendum. Instead of being the passive victims of 'regional strategies', local communities will also be able to draw up their 'neighbourhood development plan', deciding for themselves where new homes, businesses and shops should go – and what they should look like. Local councils would also keep the rents they garner from social housing, instead of having to pass the money over to central government and wait to have part of it doled back again if they behave in ways the government approves of.

All this sounds appetizing. Three quarters of it has been on the menu of fanatical localists like the present writer for years. Much of it is common practice on the Continent and in Canada, Australia and the US. Only Britain staggered quite so far down the centralizing route, and there are a lot of steps for us to retrace.

The one thing the Localism Act doesn't say much about, though, is the one thing that really matters: money. Until local councils themselves raise the bulk of their revenue, all talk of localism can only be a charming *tableau vivant*. You can have all the 'power of competence' in the world, but none of it amounts to anything if you haven't got the cash to exercise that power.

So the business end of localism is the review of local government finance, which Eric Pickles, the rotund yet somewhat menacing Secretary of State, announced in March 2011, with proposals for reform to be delivered by July 2011. The review was to look at ways of reducing the reliance of local government on funding from central government and increase local accountability.

How to do this? First obviously, allow local authorities to keep the proceeds of the business rates – as they did in the old days – with arrangements to redistribute some of the money from rich boroughs like Westminster to poor boroughs like Tower Hamlets. When it comes to other sources of revenue, apart from the business rate, Pickles was rather vaguer, speaking only of 'examining the scope for further financial freedoms for local authorities while standing up for and protecting the interests of local taxpayers' – which might mean anything or nothing. Further enlightenment, I thought, might be expected from the second phase of the Review, beginning in April 2011 and focusing on Community Budgets.

Actually, the second phase sounded worse than the first. When it was 'rolled out', it sounded more like rolling over the local institutions in a distinctly New-Labour-ish way. Each community was to have a single budget which would be 'co-designed with Whitehall'; 'to operate alongside national spending decisions for strategic national priorities'; 'ensure that identified options for a single budget fit with the Government's on-going reform programme'; 'identify and agree national local outcomes that would be delivered'. This is rather like what the bright sparks in the Kremlin used to call 'guided democracy'. You are entirely free to do what you wish, so long as you do as we wish.

Far from opening the way to local councils to reform the council tax in order to increase their revenues, Mr Pickles declared in August 2011 that there could be no question of anything like a 'mansion tax', as suggested by Vince Cable. On the contrary, this was a 'red-line issue' within the Coalition, because it would involve a revaluation of domestic property that would inevitably lead to middle-class people in prosperous areas paying far more council tax, because quite modest homes in such areas were now worth a million pounds or more.[82]

I would like to believe that in the long run localism will come through in a perhaps battered but recognizable shape. Yet if you look out of the window, the weather is not exactly encouraging. In June 2011, a year after the Coalition had come into being, there was little immediate sign of any retreat from 'top-down government'.

On the contrary, ministers seemed to be making as much noise as ever and as eager to micromanage everything in sight as their much-scorned Labour predecessors. Mr Pickles himself was planning to offer incentives to local authorities to make weekly rather than fortnightly bin collections – the reverse of the previous *diktat* which originated with the EU.

Meanwhile, George Osborne had announced a freeze in council tax for another year, making a mockery of the key pledge in the Localism Bill to allow local people to vote on council tax rises. Ministers have also introduced laws to stop councils from imposing 'disproportionate' cuts to the grants they make to charities. No question of allowing the councils themselves to decide what is 'disproportionate'. Number Ten has appointed Mary Portas, the Queen of TV shopping, to create a national blueprint for saving the high street. Forget all that stuff in the Localism Bill about local people themselves saving their pubs and post offices. The Prime Minister weighed in to back national guidelines for councils and broadcasters to prevent the sexualization of children. Even as I write, the Prime Minister is threatening to strip local authorities of their powers over adoption if they fail to arrange for a minimum proportion of children to be adopted from care each year.[83]

And even in the Localism Bill there are stern provisions to enable the government to ram through its pet *grands projets* – nuclear power stations, the high-speed rail line through the Chilterns, not to mention a large programme of house-building on public-sector land. Yet it is not so long since the Tories were jeering at Labour's Infrastructure Planning Commission for overriding establishing planning procedures. Surveying the entire field of government, Rachel Sylvester, the most perceptive of *The Times*'s political columnists, cannot avoid the conclusion that 'in reality, a year in, power is being concentrated ever more narrowly at the centre.'[84] All political parties are decentralizers in Opposition and centralizers in government. Once you have power, it is very hard to give it up, especially when you find that you are still held responsible for the decisions made by the local people to whom you have passed them.

The brutal truth is that we are *not* all localizers nowadays. Within the Conservative Party in particular, the conversion to localism is often skin-deep. The last Tory governments, after all, not only capped the domestic rates, and then replaced them with the disastrous poll tax; ministers also toyed with the idea of abolishing local government altogether, privatizing every service possible and running the rest from Whitehall. Even in the past few years, I often stood amazed listening to senior Conservatives talk of local government as if it were the enemy (regardless of the fact that they controlled the majority of local councils). Matthew Parris, formerly a Conservative MP, from his pulpit in *The Times* under the headline 'Put local councils in the dustbin of history'[85] expresses joy that the Coalition's flirtation with local government is coming to an end. 'England is too small and the English too urban, too miscellaneous, too footloose and too busy for place-based subdivisions of a national democracy ... Our elected local representatives don't have many levers of power; and we wouldn't like it if they did.' The reason we wouldn't like it if we did have effective local democracy is summed up in the media cliché: 'postcode lottery'. We simply will not tolerate different areas having different levels of service.

Now there are several answers to that argument. The first is the Libdem answer, which is that 'postcode lottery' is only a rude rephrasing of 'postcode democracy': people should be allowed to choose the level and type of services they pay for. The second answer is that we already do in fact have considerable variations in service from one area to the next; this is as true of schools and hospitals as it is of directly provided council services. And you don't often hear people complaining that 'Our traffic wardens/libraries/binmen are not as good as South Loamshire's.'

The third answer is that freedom to vary and experiment will promote best practice; without competition, standards of service droop and drop.

But the really extraordinary thing is that these Tory nationalizers seem quite unaware how freakish their attitude is. Nowhere else in the civilized world are politicians (of almost any party) so ready to junk local government. In most countries, such a programme would be regarded as insane.

I cannot imagine any serious commentators in Germany or Australia or the USA talking as Parris does, of blocking these 'intermediate institutions of government with their spurious pretensions to democratic legitimacy'. Almost everywhere else in the civilized world, it is precisely these intermediate institutions that are seen as blocking the overweening oligarchic power at the centre and as giving local people something good in itself. Joseph Chamberlain, who created modern Birmingham and was as robust a Conservative as any, said: 'I am inclined to increase the duties and power of local authorities, and do everything in my power to constitute them real local parliaments supreme in their local jurisdiction.'[86] And supreme too financially, for in Chamberlain's day councils like Birmingham raised 90 per cent of their own income.

If you were brought up in the 1950s as a good little Conservative, you were taught to regard Douglas Jay's pronouncement that 'the man in Whitehall knows best' as the wickedest and silliest thing any Labour politician had ever uttered. Now this heresy appears to have entered the bloodstream of the Conservative Party.

The unrepentant centralists mistake a fleeting embarrassment for a permanent obstacle. They fail to understand the extent to which they are the victims of their own centralism. Yes, if you persist in assuming responsibility for every detail of services provided and intervening with guidance and control at every little glitch, then the media and the public will quite reasonably assume that it is you who are to blame when things go wrong. It is only when the service is clearly managed, funded and supervised by someone else that you will escape the blame.

The oligarchic mindset is still firmly entrenched in the minister's office as it is in the boardroom. The localist revolution has a long way to go. In fact it has barely begun.

Europe – the unexpected reveille

But perhaps the most unexpected waking up over the past two years took place in Brussels in the small hours of 9 December 2011. We ourselves woke up the next morning to learn that David Cameron had used the British veto for the first time. The Prime Minister had every right to refuse to sign up to the proposed new EU treaty. He had had little part in its framing, he would have had endless trouble pushing it through the British Parliament, and the treaty would have done nothing to solve the immediate problem of protecting the weaker eurozone countries against default. But the treaty was merely the trigger. What Cameron did, whether he had intended to do it beforehand or not, was to signal that Britain was entering into a more uninhibited relationship with the EU, in which the views of the British Parliament would in future come first, or at any rate not be lightly overridden.

Within days of the Cameron veto, senior civil servants were meeting Eurosceptic policy groups they would have not previously been seen dead with. They were asking advice, not because they had become overnight converts to Euroscepticism but because they needed to talk to someone who had done serious work on the repatriation, or at least renegotiation, of powers – work which had hitherto been virtually taboo in Whitehall.

In a subtler way, too, the terms of argument had changed. Ever since the Conservative Party had torn itself apart over the Maastricht Treaty in the early 1990s, political leaders in Britain – not least Cameron himself – had steered clear of Europe as far as possible, regarding it as a troublesome and unprofitable area. Now, almost overnight, there was the prospect of real dividends to be had from close attention to the subject.

Almost as significant was the evidence given by the Lord Chief Justice, Lord Judge, to the joint parliamentary committee on human rights on 15 November. The British courts, he told the committee of MPs and peers, much to their surprise, had not been 'sufficiently flexible' in the way they had interpreted the judgments of the European Court of Human Rights and other supranational courts. Those judgments were only decided on the particular facts of the cases before them. They were not 'precedents for anything'. Lord Judge thought there had been 'a tendency to follow them much more closely than I think we should'. It was for our own Parliament to make or alter the rules as to how we should deal with such things.

In other words, just because we were members of these European institutions, we were not to think of ourselves as impotent puppets. We need not be afraid of speaking our minds or of adjusting the rules of interpretation to suit our traditions and inclinations.

This is not a mass outbreak of Europhobia. Nor is it the first step on some irreversible exit path from the EU. It is simply to state that if the EU is to grow into a genuine community, it must allow the individual voices of its member nations room to breathe and speak. If the EU remains an arrogant and unresponsive oligarchy, it cannot hope to survive, let alone flourish.

Inequality – the underlying question

So we come back to the question that raised its awkward head at the beginning: inequality. The brute reality is that none of the reforms we have been discussing, or even a fair selection of them taken together, will answer the present unease and discontent, so long as inequality continues to grow in Britain year by year, sometimes faster, sometimes slower, but always stretching the gap between the richest and the poorest.

It may seem surprising that it has taken so long for the debate to get around to this flagrant fact: that inequality of income in Britain has been increasing pretty steadily for the past thirty years and shows no sign of slowing down. Isn't this just the very question that you would expect to inflame every question time, in the media, in Parliament and in the pub? Yet it seems to be a rather slow burner. Only in the last few years, especially after the Crash, has it begun to show any sign of sizzling, although the facts have been visible for miles and for years. Why is this?

For both the big political parties, there have been tactical reasons for not bringing up the subject. The New Labour project was to convince voters that the party had changed utterly. All vestiges of old-fashioned socialism had been wiped away; there was to be no question of 'levelling down'; the rich were not to be squeezed until the pips squeaked. In fact, they were not to be squeezed at all. On the contrary, the thrusters and go-getters were egged on to thrust harder and go-get more. By making themselves richer, they would make the rest of us richer. Equality was simply not on the agenda.

The Conservatives had slightly different but closely allied reasons for not wishing to talk about equality at all. They had only recently, under Margaret Thatcher, established themselves as the party of freedom and opportunity. In particular, they had won millions of votes among the lower middle and upper working classes, or the Cs and Ds as the sociologists call them; the people who did the right thing and worked hard to better themselves and their families were to be encouraged and rewarded. It would muddy the message if the Conservatives suddenly started worrying publicly about the growth of inequality. Politics, often reviled by its enemies as a devious and subtle art, is in many ways a rather simple pursuit. The rule is: only one message at a time.

But that is not the only reason why the politicians kept quiet about inequality for so long. The truth is that inequality is a tricky terrain. I am not sure whether to describe it as a quagmire or a minefield. Perhaps it is both, rather like parts of the battlefield of the First World War: a treacherous swamp that is at the same time sown with unexploded bombs and crisscrossed by ancient trenches, some now crumbling and unoccupied, others still fiercely defended, sometimes occupied by enemy forces since the battle lines have swung to and fro. Arguments about equality have gone on so long, and aroused such fierce feelings, that anyone venturing into this particular no-man's-land needs to tiptoe.

Much of the confusion is due to the assumption shared by many of the combatants that equality and inequality are simple and easily defined concepts, whereas they seem to me to be slippery and complex.

At the same time, the subject cannot really be avoided altogether. Because equality is not and cannot be the exclusive preoccupation of the Left. We have to remember that equality is a core principle of Western civilization. This is true both of our dominant political tradition and of our dominant religious tradition. The equality of citizens was a basic element in the rise of the Greek city-state. This was, by our standards, an impaired form of equality; it did not include women and slaves, and in some of the earlier cities it did not include the poorer citizens either. In Rome under the Republic, there were Roman citizens and there were other subjects of Rome who did not qualify for that citizenship. Despite these important defects, equality was the founding principle, and this equality was always capable of extension. Cato the Elder won plaudits for extending the benefits of Roman citizenship to some of the 'lesser breeds'. In the same way, the equality of all human beings in the eyes of God was a crucial founding principle of Christianity.[87]

Very slowly over the centuries, certain egalitarian practices gained hold: the equality of all men before the law, then, much later, equal right to political participation. In this country, that process was not completed until 1928, when women under thirty were enfranchised – the 'flapper vote'. Female suffrage was fiercely resisted, we must remember, not just by the unenlightened but by some of our finer minds, such as the great constitutionalist A.V. Dicey. The achievement of these legal and political equalities levelled up all adult citizens in their relations with the authorities and the political system, but economic and social equality remained a long way off.

The equalities that are already achieved, or half-achieved, came from that deep urge to recognize the equality of all human beings as citizens and as children of God. We can see, for example how the abolition of slavery and, in our own time, the fall of apartheid derived very largely from those impulses. And the same is true of the progress towards sexual equality: the movement for women's rights arose first out of the wider pursuit of political equality and equality before the law, then, over the decades, extended into such areas as the workplace and social security. It started with the suffragettes and ended with equal pay and pensions for women.

It is when we go on from all this to look at the questions of economic and social equality that the plot thickens. Equality before the law and giving all adults the vote, even gender equality, are relatively simple enterprises. We all know what needs to happen for those goals to be fulfilled, even if it takes a long time to get there.

But as soon as you move on to the questions of social and economic equality, things instantly are less simple. And those politicians and philosophers who claim that here too there are simple answers run slap into what I would call the Berlin Wall. It is Sir Isaiah Berlin's lasting contribution to political philosophy to have pointed out that no single principle of social action, however irreproachable, can hope to enjoy unchallenged supremacy. Other principles, no less morally desirable, may come into conflict with it, and there is no inherent reason to regard any one of the principles at stake as intrinsically superior to the other, or to expect that any such conflict can be easily resolved. Two principles may be stubbornly contradictory in their effects; the best you can do is to work out a compromise between them, a trade-off, so that you obtain as much as you can of each, or as much as is desirable for each in the particular context. Equality often conflicts with liberty, for example. The government cannot engineer greater equality in economic relations without damaging the freedom of the more thrusting citizens to get ahead.[88]

Just as principles may conflict, so may goals: the goal of income equality may, for example, conflict with the goal of a dynamic economy. Say we increase income taxes to a level at which all incomes after tax are approximately equal. Any rational person will then conclude that there is no point in striving to increase his or her income in this society. He or she will, therefore, either take life easy or emigrate, and the general level of prosperity, which is being shared out with such exquisite precision, is likely to decline – slowly at first, but inexorably. It is also obvious that equality of opportunity may lead to inequality of result: if you let the greyhound off the leash at the same time as the dachshund, the result is unlikely to be a dead heat. The worst of the trouble is not only that equality may clash with other values that we have set our hearts on; it is that different kinds of equality may clash with one another. The most obvious case is that equality of opportunity is likely to lead – in fact is almost designed to lead – to unequal outcomes.

In turn, those unequal outcomes are likely to engender an inequality of respect. This is what Michael Young showed so brilliantly in his famous satire, *The Rise of Meritocracy*. When it was published in 1958 (but only after eleven publishers had rejected it), people who hadn't read the book didn't realize it was a satire, and assumed that it must be in praise of meritocracy. Who could be against a society in which people rose on merit? But what Lord Young of Dartington, as he rather ironically later became, was out to show was that in a society where all the top places are awarded on merit the losers have no hiding place and no excuses. Indeed, it was quite soon after the book was published that we began to imitate the American habit of talking about 'losers', not just to describe someone who had lost a tennis match but to designate someone who was a hopeless failure in life.

So equality of opportunity has its costs. And so too do our efforts to equalize the life chances of the poorest, or at least that is what has happened so often in Britain. The result has been an insidious inequality of *treatment* which has corroded the lives of the better off and the aspirations of the worst off. We build differently when we are building for the poor. You do not need to look twice to distinguish a council estate from a private estate: the open stairways and walkways of the tower blocks in those pointless grass wastelands – no spec builder in his right mind builds like that with private tenants in mind. In the same way, nobody (with the possible exception of A. S. Neill at Summerhill) ever set up an independent school on the lines of a typical comprehensive school of the 1960s: no competition, no uniform, no discipline to speak of, a curriculum usually without any serious attempt to teach the classics or modern languages. My point is not that such comprehensive schools were necessarily worse than the public schools; they were just totally different. Even serious sport became increasingly confined to fee-paying schools, so that, years after the distinction between Gentlemen and Players was abolished, the England batting order has become dominated by players educated at independent schools.

If you look at inequality of income alone, you will not grasp the full extent of social dislocation in Britain. You must consider also the inequality of treatment and the inequality of respect. In an earlier book, *Mind the Gap*, I tried to set out the ways in which the institutions that the working class had created for themselves had been undermined or destroyed by intervention from above: the derision heaped upon the Nonconformist churches, the strangulation of the voluntary welfare and friendly societies, the take-over of the poor schools and much more. Even the castration of the trade unions, necessary though it was if British industry was to move at all, was a deprivation too.

It is only in our own time, though, that a sharpening inequality of income has been accompanied by a pervading contempt for those who are at the bottom of the ladder and may have less chance of climbing a few rungs than their parents had – and less inclination to try, too. The problem is not just that social mobility has slowed down in recent years. Even if equality of opportunity were more fluid and effective than it is today, it would not be enough. A reasonably contented society must also have a sense of relationship between all its citizens. The whole point of Bernard Shaw's fable, *Pygmalion*, is that there must be a place by the fire for the undeserving poor too.

But the political reality is that it has always been equality of opportunity that has been the driving force in Britain, certainly since the Second World War. Lessening inequalities of income has never been the top priority. This is not how the story is usually told, certainly not on the Left. The heroic narrative of the Labour Party and its allies is that the progressive forces in British politics won a gruelling struggle to equalize incomes through the tax system. The ideologists of inequality on the Right were routed (or at least had to pay lip service to the endeavour); and as a result net post-tax incomes today, or at least until the last few years, while by no means equal, are or were a great deal more equal than ever before.

This, I am afraid, is not quite how it happened. It was war, not socialism, that was the great leveller. Income tax was first introduced on a serious basis to pay for the Napoleonic Wars. And ever since it has been in wartime and only in wartime that income tax has been raised to punitive levels.[89]

So it is an interesting fact, but one which neither Labour nor the Conservatives has any reason to make much of, that the party of the working class has played remarkably little part in establishing our modern taxes, especially in their more punitive aspects.[90]

It was the coalitions in the First World War (half Liberals, half Conservatives) and in the Second (dominated by Conservatives) that pushed those taxes to their highest levels. Whatever the rich themselves may think, it was never Labour, despite Denis Healey's ferocious threat, which made the pips squeak.[91]

Huge quantities of money had to be found to pay for the war, and it was right that those who could afford to should pay the most. It is not clear that income equalization for its own sake had ever taken such a firm grip on British politics as its enthusiasts fondly imagined. Tax rates remained high after each war and came down so slowly only because high levels of public expenditure had become entrenched.

For what had taken root was something that fits better into the category of equality of opportunity. Every citizen had a right to a decent start in life. There were to be 'homes for heroes' provided by the postwar council housing drive, the last enduring act of Lloyd George's coalition. And there were to be schools and hospitals fit for heroes and the children of heroes too.

All through the 1920s and 30s, a succession of health and education Acts were passed, mostly by Conservative or Conservative-dominated governments because Conservative governments happened to be in power for most of the time. Then, during the Second World War, the Churchill coalition produced blueprints for amalgamating the existing network of publicly provided schools and hospitals and pensions into nationally controlled and funded services – through the 1944 Butler Act, the Beveridge Report and the Willink Committee. I mention all these not to undermine the Attlee government's proud claim to have actually introduced these national services. I merely wish to point out how the two world wars had introduced a new consensus, a new ethic if you like, that the state had a duty to ensure for all its citizens both a decent minimum standard of living and a start in life that would enable them to make the best of their talents. But even then governments remained reluctant to put up taxes to pay for the new ethic. It is noticeable, for example, that the Labour government did not put up the rate of income tax when the National Health Service (NHS) and National Insurance (NI) schemes came into operation in 1948, but did so only in its last year of office, and then it was to pay for the Korean War. Equality of opportunity, rather than equality of outcome, was clearly the guiding principle.

Even after the war, reducing inequality scarcely seems to have been a high priority. As a matter of fact, inequality of income did gently abate during much of the early postwar period, but this was probably because the top earners were still attuned to austerity and had not yet learnt to ask for more, while manual workers, millions of them still working in the old heavy industries, were protected by their trade unions. Government policy did not have much to do with it. After all, the standard rate of income tax was being steadily reduced by both Labour and Tory governments.

As for New Labour, whatever else may have been a priority, equalizing incomes certainly was not. The gap between the richest and the poorest continued to widen, except perhaps in Gordon Brown's last years in office. Ministers did not seem much worried about the growing polarization of incomes at both ends of the scale or about the emergence of the oligarchs at the top end. John Hutton, then Business and Enterprise Secretary, said in 2008:

Rather than questioning whether huge salaries are morally justified, we should celebrate the fact that people can be enormously successful in this country. Rather than placing a cap on that success, we should be questioning why it is not available to more people. Our overarching goal that no one should get left behind must not become translated into a stultifying sense that no one should be allowed to get ahead.

The truth is that none of the main parties has ever thought seriously about moderating the rise of income inequality. As a result, when that inequality approached its present dizzying heights, we tried to pretend it didn't really matter, largely because we didn't have a clue what to do about it.

Abdul and Sir John

I don't think that this complaisance will do any longer. The unchecked growth of inequality has begun to corrode our sense of belonging. George Osborne continues to proclaim that, in tackling the deficit, 'We are all in this together.' This mantra is increasingly met amongst the less well off with a resounding raspberry. It is so clearly the case that, proportionately, they are afflicted by the crisis and the cuts far more than the well-to-do, who are protected by their professional cartels and the *omertà* of the boardroom. And it no longer seems adequate to excuse inequality as the inescapable consequence of market forces. For we were told that over time market forces would trickle all the way down to reach the worst off. That is not how it looks to the worst off today.

The trends and processes that have generated and accelerated this inequality are not God-given or natural. They are often the outcome of neglect, thoughtlessness and indulgence. They can be reformed or reversed. What's more, I believe that this can be done without damaging whatever dynamism the British economy may possess. Extremes of low pay and high pay are not necessary or indeed greatly relevant to a decent rate of economic growth.

Nor need a careful and sustained examination of inequality lead inescapably to the knee-jerk reaction: increase taxes. On the contrary, for a generation after the war, we continued to become more equal while taxes were going down. In the first decade of the twenty-first century, we have continued to become more unequal while taxes have gone up quite a lot. If taxation is part of the answer, it does not look like the whole answer. It is not the relative taxation of Abdul and Sir John Bond that has made the earnings of one 400 times that of the other. If we go back to where we started – the Barbican in May 2003 – Abdul the cleaner, on roughly £10,000 a year, was paying very little tax. It is the Coalition's ambition today that he should pay none at all. We should aim to return to the situation before 1939 when only the middle classes and above paid income tax.

Sir John, on the other hand, paid a great deal of income tax in that year, probably £700,000 on his salary, and much the same again when he cashed in his other incentives. The fat cats have contributed hugely to the revenue ever since Nigel Lawson reduced their top rate to 40 per cent. I don't think much was gained when, as a gesture during the banking crisis, Alistair Darling raised the top rate to 50 per cent. Even less would be gained by hoicking it any higher; the present trickle of rich decampers would become an unhealthy stream. There might well be a net falling off of revenue from the rich. Lawson's 40 per cent looks like the right ceiling, enough to bring in substantial revenues, not too high to scare off the entrepreneurs.

The trouble is that the debate about inequality has mostly been a sterile wrangle about the top rate of income tax. The real question is about *wages* not tax. Why are the Sir Johns paid so much and the Abduls paid so little?

At first sight nothing has changed, or naught for our comfort. Today Stuart Gulliver earns over £6 million a year for running HSBC, where Sir John earned £4 million – a 50 per cent increase. Average wages and the national minimum wage have both increased by not much more than 30 per cent, so the CEO is streaking ahead. In fact if we assumed that Abdul was still cleaning the offices at HSBC and was still earning about 50p an hour more than the national minimum wage, as he had been in 2003, he would now be pulling in £14,500 a year for a 40-hour week. On these assumptions the ratio between his and Gulliver's pay would actually have worsened a little, to 428 to 1.[92]

But that is not in fact the present situation. For down in the jungle of Canary Wharf something has stirred. And it stirred partly because of Abdul.

What happened was this: at the turn of the millennium, Citizens UK and several other campaigning organizations launched a campaign for a 'Living Wage'. What they were seeking, especially in London and other areas where the cost of living was high, was the introduction of a minimum wage higher than the official national minimum wage, one which was actually enough to live on. Church leaders, the TUC and trade unions representing low-paid workers, such as Unison, joined the campaign and began to badger MPs and the bosses of large companies. The campaigners bought shares in HSBC and interrupted the 2002 AGM in May with their demands. This secured them a meeting with Sir John Bond in June 2002. Sir John, as you might expect, rebuffed this first approach. He could not countenance interfering with market rates in order to pay his cleaners more.

Enter Abdul. It was not simply the commotion he made at the 2003 AGM, or even the demo that was staged both inside and outside the Barbican Hall. It was the fatal conjunction between Abdul's demands and the arrival of Bill Aldinger on the board. Five pounds an hour for Abdul and no sick pay; £35 million for Bill plus free dentistry for life and the glittering array of other perks. The contrast was simply too embarrassing. No doubt Sir John could foresee these awkward encounters damaging the reputation of 'the World's Local Bank' at every AGM until the end of time. And so halfway through May 2004, two weeks before the next AGM, he caved in. Cleaners' wages at HSBC Canary Wharf were to rise by 11 per cent to £6.10 an hour; they would also receive eight days extra holiday, ten days sick pay, and a 30 per cent increase for those working nights. Notice that these terms were hammered out in negotiation directly with HSBC, not with OCS Cleaning, the firm that had the cleaning contract and actually employed Abdul. The bank was taking responsibility for terms and conditions of contract workers whom it did not itself employ. Barclays Bank had already in February struck a very similar deal with its contract cleaners at the new Barclays HQ in Canary Wharf. Other companies opening in the area were soon persuaded to follow suit, notably the contractors working on the London Olympic site. Candidates at the 2005 General Election were asked to declare their support. So were the candidates for London Mayor. Boris Johnson carried on Ken Livingstone's commitment to the London Living Wage. This is now a settled part of the political scene. Backsliders who fail to make good their promises are speedily hassled back into line; this has happened both to Barclays and the Olympic Delivery Authority.

The current London Living Wage, announced by Boris Johnson in May 2011, is £8.30 an hour. The national minimum wage for October 2010–October 2011 is a mere £5.93 per hour. The difference therefore on a 40-hour week is getting on for £5,000 a year: between £12,330 and £17,260. This is a tremendous hike. In many cases, it would lift the recipient out of the cat's cradle of welfare benefits, so that he or she becomes independent and self-supporting.

Can the employers afford it? Will this well-meaning reform have the downside of destroying marginal jobs? That was always the fear of Conservatives and market economists when the national minimum wage was introduced. To their bemusement and (in most cases) pleasure, no such effect on employment was observed. So much so that the Coalition spokesmen such as the Immigration Minister Damian Green have now begun to use the minimum-wage experience as an argument as to why putting a cap on immigration would have no such bad effects either.

But this is not the end of the possibilities opened up by the Living Wage idea. As soon as you lift the lowest workers above the poverty line, you free them from the demoralizing effects of the welfare state; there will no longer be any question of it being better to stay on benefits. But you also make it possible to help them further when funds allow. For someone earning as much as

£17,000 will be paying a fair bit of tax, even when and if the Coalition finds the funds to push the personal allowance up to £10,000 a year. And that offers an opportunity further down the line to continue concentrating tax cuts on the lowest paid. Such an enticing prospect must obviously await the day when the public finances have been licked back into shape, which won't be today or tomorrow.

The prospect is there, none the less. In the long run, we may be able to inch our way back to the pattern of the old days before the war when most low-paid workers paid no income tax at all. We can hope to say farewell to the Budgets, all too common in recent decades, when the Chancellor's actions have added hundreds of thousands of people to the number of Britain's taxpayers. That figure has risen from 26.1 million in 1990/91 to a peak of 32.5 million in Gordon Brown's first year as Prime Minister, before dropping back to 29.9 million by 2011/12.

I must also point out the interesting character of the Living Wage Campaign. It is a voluntary movement, not sponsored by government or party. And it seeks volunteers to do business with, not legislation to be pushed through Parliament. Only those employers who can obviously afford to sign up are exhorted to join. Small shopkeepers struggling to stay afloat are not to be conscripted into paying wages they cannot afford. The more modest back-up of the official national minimum wage is there on the statute book to stop outrageous sweating. But there is no doubt that as the years go by, the Living Wage, if widely imple-mented, will lift most boats off the mud and stop the polarization of wages at the low end of the scale.

This is not the way we are accustomed to think. When some-thing needs reform, we have been taught to look to government and to legislation. The voluntary model, with its codes of conduct and mutual agreement between the participants, has looked frail and insignificant in comparison with the ministerial steamroller.

Yet the polarization of income was not imposed, or even unwittingly assisted by government. It has arisen spontaneously out of the custom and practice of businesses and the group think of businessmen. I am sure that it can be reversed only by retracing the way it came. Narrowing the gap will be as much a matter of moral pressure and best practice as of laws and regulations.

The old Wages Councils set minimum wages in a variety of low-paid trades such as retailing, hairdressing and clothing between 1909 (when they were called Trades Boards) and 1993 (when they were finally abolished). They were established by statute, but they were independent of government, and the levels they set were agreed between representatives of employers, employees and independent members who might have the casting vote in cases of deadlock.

The Living Wage Campaign offers a comparable, but more informal model. What it does is to open up a conversation, pursued at first through a megaphone, by marches and demos, and then morphing into face-to-face exchanges. At first Sir John refuses to meet the campaigners, then he does meet them but refuses to meet their demands, then he meets their demands by engaging directly with the cleaners (as opposed to merely buying their services through the contractors). Finally at the campaigners' anniversary meeting (in November 2006), Sir John is honoured and thanked for his recantation.

David Cameron's Big Society is commonly thought of as an endeavour to promote voluntary and charitable enterprises. But of course, if it is to mean anything, business has a duty to embrace it wholeheartedly too. At the very least, large employers ought to engage much more with their local communities. When the enormous Canary Wharf development was first proposed, one of the key arguments for going ahead was that it would regenerate the desolate wastes of the Isle of Dogs and offer thousands of jobs to the wider East End of London. It was not much of a surprise that when the high-rise towers were complete most of the bankers who occupied them trooped in every morning on the Jubilee Line from the West End and its adjacent dormitories.

But what was a surprise, and much lamented, was that so few of the low-paid jobs were taken up by the local inhabitants. At Canary Wharf, as elsewhere in London, most of the cleaners and sweepers and Tube staff and traffic wardens were of immigrant or immigrant-descended stock, often living some distance away. The new development reproduced the uncomfortable divide between the underground and late-night toilers on the one hand and the masters of the universe on the other, between the Downers and the Uppers as I called them in an earlier book.[93] As long as the low-paid jobs remain so low-paid, that divide will continue and deepen.

Lifting the floor can only lift the spirits of those unskilled workers who can find nothing except unappealing jobs at rock-bottom pay. If we bring back into play those thousands of discouraged workers who drift in and out of those jobs and finally subside onto incapacity benefit complaining of stress, then we can hope to reduce welfare bills and we can also impose a cap on immigration with much less fear of incurring labour shortages. But the Living Wage is the first step on the way back, the indispensable beginning of the virtuous circle.

What we are proposing is modest in money terms. It's important to make that crystal clear. Whatever changes are made at the bottom as at the top, the whole pay scale will not suddenly concertina in some spectacular fashion. That is not the intention. We intend merely to bring the Uppers and Downers into some kind of relation. At the BBC, the new Chairman, Chris Patten, is out to introduce a 20 to 1 limit on the ratio between the Director-General's pay and that of the average BBC staff member. Just what J. P. Morgan advocated a century ago. It seems likely that this will become common practice throughout the public sector, and the semi-public sector too, where large sums of public money are involved, in the running of universities, for example. And we have already outlined a similar scheme for large public companies, where a supervisory board would monitor a 40 or 50 to 1 ratio, depending on the size of the company.

This is not some crazy outburst of egalitarianism. Under the new dispensation, Abdul and the other cleaners will still be earning £17,000 per annum at the most. The successor to Sir John Bond will still be earning something close to £1 million including bonuses, sixty times as much.

But a limit will have been set. Britain will no longer be getting more painfully unequal. The direction of travel will have been gently reversed, without significant damage to incentives or performance. Can anyone seriously pretend that an ambitious BBC trainee would not still be thirsting to become Director-General at a salary of £400,000?

And there is a loftier benefit too, a moral one. The top earners will have been taught that the boardroom is not an island and that even in Canary Wharf it is a happier fate to live in some sort of community with your fellow citizens rather than to tower over them in frosty and insecure isolation. We need once again to remember the other great book written by that much maligned genius, Adam Smith. *The Wealth of Nations* cannot continue to grow without a *Theory of Moral Sentiments*.

The riots and after

Then came the riots. Between 6 and 10 August 2011, riots broke out in run-down areas across a dozen English cities. The riots began in Tottenham, North London, after the police had shot Mark Duggan, a suspected gangster, in questionable circumstances. Duggan's death provoked a peaceful protest march on 6 August. The following night, rioting spread through Tottenham to other London boroughs such as Brixton, Hackney, Croydon, Lewisham and Ealing. Outbreaks of copycat rioting then began outside London, beginning in Birmingham, Bristol and Nottingham.

The police, who had been accused of not providing nearly enough officers and of initially standing back while property was looted and set on fire, then poured into London. The next day, some 18,000 officers were on duty. As a result, London was more or less quiet on 9 August, almost eerily so. But rioting now spread to Leicester, West Bromwich and Wolverhampton in the Midlands, and to Liverpool, Manchester, Bury and Salford in the North West. The disorder then faded out, with a few final sporadic incidents reported in the provinces on 10 August, notably in Birmingham and Greater Manchester. Five people had been killed, three of them in a single hit-and-run incident. Sixteen people were initially reported as injured, although the final figure was probably two or three times that. Damage to property was estimated at £200 million, and many small shops would take months to reopen if they ever did.

The speed with which the riots spread bemused and terrified the public. So did the unnerving abandon with which the looters smashed shop windows and stole anything that took their fancy, from bottles of mineral water to plasma televisions. The rioters seemed so weirdly relaxed. Youths were seen in sports shops sitting down to try on trainers for size before scampering down the street with their loot, outrunning the heavy-footed coppers. The severe sentences handed out by magistrates to most of the 3,000 people arrested were greeted with approval and relief by a public whose nerve had been as brusquely shattered as the shop windows. Several of the stiffer sentences were swiftly overturned on appeal, though. A woman who was jailed for five months for receiving a pair of shorts, although she herself had taken no part in the riots, was set free.

In the flood of comment that followed these alarming scenes – the worst seen across England since 1981 – a considerable number of contributory causes were suggested. These included: feeble policing generally and initially feeble police tactics in coping with the disturbances; moral decay and the decline of the two-parent family; youth unemployment; the Coalition's recent cuts in public expenditure, especially the axing of the educational maintenance allowance and the trebling of the maximum university tuition fees; resentment against the obscene greed of the bankers and other billionaires who paid little or no income tax; the use of Blackberry and Twitter and other social media to spread news of the nearest riot; the unsettling thoughts provoked by the Arab Spring; the aggressive tactics of the police in dealing with young people on the street (which looks rather like a contradiction of the first explanation); mass immigration and, allied to this, the black gangsta culture and its imitation by non-black teenagers (this last suggested by the historian David Starkey on *Newsnight*, a suggestion for which he was excommunicated from polite society).

So there was no shortage of explanations. If even half of them were even partly relevant, it would be amazing that rioting on a large scale had not erupted earlier and even more violently than it did.

Rather than trying to sort out these jostling contenders, it might be better to start by considering the undisputed facts. Obviously, these were by no means the first riots to break on British streets. A variety of religious, racial and political resentments have generated violent disorder over the past two centuries. The religious riots ranged from the anti-Catholic (the Gordon Riots of 1780 and the endless sectarian riots in Northern Ireland, carried over to a lesser extent to Western Scotland) to the anti-Semitic (Merthyr Tydfil in 1911, Liverpool in 1945 and the disorders provoked by the Mosleyites in the East End of London in the 1980s). The most notorious race riots were in Notting Hill at the end of the 1950s and in Brixton and Toxteth in 1981, but there was another severe epidemic of violence between resentful white youths and Asian immigrants in the summer of 2001 in the old Northern textile towns – Oldham, Burnley, Bradford and Leeds.

Such racial or religious motives were very little in evidence in the August riots of 2011. If black and Asian youths were in the majority, there was also a substantial minority of white youths rioting alongside them, looting and throwing bricks and petrol bombs with a brio uninflected by racial feeling. True, the hit-and-run driver and his friends who killed the three Asian shopkeepers defending their property may have been partly fuelled by anti-Asian feeling, but they were undoubtedly fuelled by anti-shopkeeper feeling.

It is also an important qualification that all the riots did take place in areas with a high immigrant population. The riots did not really spread to Scotland and Wales, where fewer immigrants live (though there was a minor outbreak in Cardiff, which does have a considerable immigrant population), or to North-East England. Nor was there much rioting in rich or even middle-class areas, although that is where there would be more goods worth stealing. The August Riots were thus quite unlike the demos Against the Cuts the preceding March, which processed through downtown areas, and in the case of the march organized by the TUC in London spiralled out of control into a pitched battle with police in Trafalgar Square. There were plenty of students and middle-class agitators in action that day. The same is true of the riots against globalization that have occurred in cities where the G7 were meeting, such as Seattle, Genoa, Turin and London, doing extensive damage to shops and other property in city centres. The August rioters, by contrast, were mostly trashing their own shabby parts of town.

Nor, it seems, were the August riots primarily directed against the police, although it was the police shooting of Mark Duggan that sparked them off. There were some pitched battles with police, but the abiding image of the riots is rather of youths rampaging down the streets with police officers far behind and often out of sight. The police were initially so ineffective precisely because they came prepared and massed for pitched battles, rather like an army that has been practising for the trench warfare of the last war and is taken quite unawares by the new tactics of rapid movement.

Police harassment of the young was no doubt a contributory resentment, but the police themselves were only partly the enemy, and in a sense that sometimes appeared only semi-serious. The rioters referred to them as 'the Feds', which makes them sound more like the enemy in a video game, rather than as 'the Pigs' as an earlier generation of rioters did, which suggests a fiercer hatred. Injury statistics tend to indicate a lesser level of violence in general, and anti-police violence in particular, in the August riots by comparison with the single battle of Trafalgar Square on 26 March, in which eighty-four people were reported injured, including thirty-one police.

Much was made of the more or less middle-class young people among those arrested in August: a girl from Surrey who lived in a million-pound gated mansion, several university students and another girl who was an 'ambassador' for the Olympics with a glittering CV. These cases were convenient for those on the Right who sought to identify a nationally shared moral decay as the leading cause of the riots. They were convenient, too, for government ministers who, like the Prime Minister, sought to argue that the riots 'were not about poverty'. Curiously, the cases of middle-class rioters were also handy for Harriet Harman and other Labour politicians who sought to link the riots to cuts in university finance.

But these cases appear to have been highly untypical. An analysis of more than 1,000 cases brought before magistrates' courts across England found that only 8.6 per cent of those going through the courts were either students or employed.[94] Over ninety per cent of them were unemployed. Over ninety per cent of them were also male. And two thirds were under the age of twenty-five, but only 17 per cent were under the age of seventeen, although the 11-year-olds caught on camera were so prominently featured and aroused such anguish about the future generation. Thus the rioters were predominantly young adults, male and unemployed. They were not graphic designers or sociology students or commis chefs. They were out of work.

A month after the riots, the Justice Secretary Kenneth Clarke brought to light a fact that had not previously been noted: that three quarters of the rioters had criminal records. Thus most of them were not giddy first offenders, dragged along by the thrill of the scamper through the streets. They were young adults who had already disengaged from society, alienated enough to break the law again without much care for the consequences.

What was so alarming was not the absolute numbers of the rioters – they were only a tiny percentage of their age group – as the fact that there were hundreds of thousands of young men in the same boat. To the pessimists, the rioters looked like the advance guard of a far larger army of the excluded and forgotten. The unemployment figures released in August showed that out of the two-and-a-half million people out of work, 20 per cent were aged between sixteen and twenty-four. And it won't do either to argue that most of them are out of work solely because the welfare state has encouraged them to loll on the dole. The system certainly does offer perverse incentives and needs urgent reform to encourage people back into work, as outlined by Iain Duncan Smith. But any such reform could offer only a partial solution.

For the other thing is that jobs in the riot areas are in extremely short supply. According to the TUC analysis, in the London borough of Haringey, which includes Tottenham, not only are there 10,578 people out of work and claiming benefit, but there are a mere 367 job vacancies – that is, nearly thirty claimants for every vacancy. Much the same was true of other riot boroughs in London, such as Hackney and Lewisham. Unemployment among young people generally is running at around 20 per cent, but the rate is higher in these places and especially among young blacks. I do not for a moment deny that there are plenty of jobs to be had in other parts of London for anyone with the energy to get on a bike (the fares are prohibitive), even if it means nicking the bike. EU immigrants, from Poland and the rest of Eastern Europe in particular, were not to be found among the rioters and not often among the unemployed either. For anyone who is ready to do anything and work any hours there is always work. But the most tough-minded observer could not deny that the picture for an ordinary, not very dynamic young person growing up in Tottenham is discouraging.

All over the country, opportunities for unskilled young men do not grow on trees, and finding openings to acquire skills is not easy either. The number of applicants for training places at Network Rail outnumber the places available by 40 to 1, 8,000 to 200; BT had a hundred applicants for every one of its training places; Marks & Spencer has 1,600 competing for forty school-leaver places. As the columnist Jenni Russell points out, 'decent apprenticeships are as hard to win as places at Balliol College, Oxford'[95] – and less well supported by the State too. Is it not extraordinary that we have poured so many millions into universities and prided ourselves on the ever-growing number of young people going to university, but we have begrudged a hundredth part of that public expenditure to set up technical schools for the less academic?[96] Yet technical schools were promised as the third leg of the school system as far back as Rab Butler's 1944 Education Act. And if you wanted to identify one single cause of Germany's amazing and unshaken technical pre-eminence from Bismarck's day to our own, it would be her tremendous technical high schools and colleges.

It is not surprising that young men of low educational attainment, with no skills and low expectations should feel disenchanted. Although these were not race riots, it is, I think, significant that they all happened in areas of high immigrant concentration. For the young of all races in such areas when unemployment is high are likely to feel that the dice are loaded against them: the immigrants because they feel they are the last in the queue, the whites because they think they suffer unfair competition from the immigrants. Second- and third-generation black and Asian youths may feel both types of resentment. All are likely to lack much in the way of social attachments, to church or trade union or sports club or youth club. This isolation is likely to be deepened if they come from a single-parent family, where the mother may be struggling so hard to bring up her family that she too feels a similar isolation. As all observers agree, the gang is the only social alternative.

Gangs are nothing new. Towns in the Middle Ages were often terrorized by gangs of marauding apprentices. But at least when the apprentices sobered up, they were corralled within muscular social institutions – their indentures to their masters, the disciplines of the city and the Church. Gang life was not the whole of life. It was not a permanent disengagement. It was an occasional break-out.

But to have nothing to break out from is a different and disorienting experience. Disengagement has its compensations. You could not miss the glee on the faces of the rioters as they roamed through the broken glass, lords of the street for a couple of hours. Such joys have never been confined to the underclass. Evelyn Waugh reminded us in *Decline and Fall* how terrifying could be the 'sound of English county families baying for broken glass'. All who take part in such brief bacchanalia are temporarily out of their skulls, disengaged or *dégagé* in the French sense, relaxed, at their ease.

The downside of disengagement only sinks in the morning after, when 'on the bald street breaks the blank day' – the empty hours ahead, perhaps the empty years. Who is there to feel loyalty to or to show respect for, except your contemporaries who are in the same boat?

The truth, I think, is welcome to neither side in the political argument. It is that both Right and Left are more or less correct in their analysis. The collapse of many working-class families, white and black, is likely to leave adolescents in those families even more adrift than adolescents generally are. But it is also the case that young men who have a job to lose are less likely to riot than those who don't have one and cannot see much prospect of getting one. At the same time, the unbridled greed of the oligarchs and their indifference to the normal obligations and restraints do engender a sense that society has lost its recognizable moral shape and, with it, its legitimacy.

None of this begins to excuse riot, thieving or violence against the police or anyone else. But it does give us a clue as to who is most likely to riot and why. It may also lead us to the intimation that our society now may be fractured in a way that it was not in the past, however severe the poverty and inequality of that past.

For we now seem to have not one but two detached classes, one at the bottom, the other at the top; each of them much smaller in size than the great mass of the predominant middle class but none the less unsettling by its presence, or rather by its curious absence.

For what is true of the underclass is, surprisingly, often true of the overclass too: the powerless are as unconnected to the rest of us as are the oligarchs. Neither class is in the habit of voting at general or local elections; the ethnic minorities are not registered, while the oligarchs are on their yachts and may not even be British citizens anyway. Neither class pays taxes to any great extent, the underclass because they have no income, the oligarchs because they are non-doms. They take no part in local affairs; the underclass because they see no point, the oligarchs because they are too busy travelling between their desirable residences – there is always a helicopter on standby in the paddock.

We find it hard, I think, to take in how odd this state of affairs is, because to some extent this is how we like it. We value self-determination and independence. Life in the old-fashioned town or parish looks to us cramping. The parish magistrates and overseers took an unhealthy interest in the affairs of the poor. The factory owner who lived next to his works exercised an oppressive control over the lives of his workpeople. For us, there were good reasons why paternalism should have become a dirty word. The freedom of the individual ranks top of our list.

Yet disconnectedness can go too far. At the very least we do need to recognize how disconnected the two extremes are now from the middling masses. And if we look at modern Britain in that light, we may come to a subtly different conclusion about what is wrong.

The conventional analysis is now alert to the fact that Britain has become a more unequal society over the past thirty years. The incomes of the top five per cent and the bottom ten per cent have polarized, and there is an ever-growing distance between them. This unpleasant and unexpected development seems to be at the root of social unease and distress. But it may be that the inequality is more a symptom than a cause of the disconnection; in fact, it may be the other way round; the disconnection gives rise, over the years, to the inequality. It is because we have got into the habit of regarding the footloose oligarchs as uncontrollable and the underclass as irredeemable that the inequality has been allowed to grow. Both classes at the extremes seem somehow to exist beyond our reach.

The running argument of this book is that this impression is a false one. The oligarchs can and must be re-connected to the rest of society; so can and must the underclass. I have outlined some of the routes back to social cohesion: the vigorous reform of company law and practice in order to improve transparency, accountability and fairness, the revival of local democracy (not forgetting some sort of mansion tax or new council tax bands at the top end, to remind the oligarchs that they owe a duty to the place where they live); the reform of the welfare state; the revival of technical schools; the spread of the Living Wage. It is entirely possible to apply a modest layer of glue, to both surfaces.

The suggestions tossed out are mostly not original at all. Some of them are already the declared policy of the Coalition or the

Labour Party. Others crop up in the reports of seminars and think tanks, in parliamentary committees, and in inquiries such as the Hutton Review, the High Pay Commission and the Power Commission. My aim rather has been to show how such remedies might fit into a strategy for social coherence; the purpose is to provide a narrative. There was, after all, nothing really new about the component parts of 'Thatcherism'; most of it had been around in free-market and social-conservative circles since 1945. What Margaret Thatcher did was to argue, *ad nauseam*, that, taken together, these parts could transform the situation. They were not only practicable and desirable; they hung together. Thatcher's achievement, like it or loathe it, was to persuade people that old ideas could be made to work. 'Optimism of the will', Lenin would have called it.

In any case, we should not exaggerate the difficulty of the task. Those societies that we are invited to admire, such as Norway and Sweden and Japan, are not *very* equal. They have their billionaires and the people at the bottom who are scratching a living; they too have bums and misfits. But what they do clearly also have is a sense of belonging together, one which is felt at all levels of society and which makes those inequalities more or less tolerable. When a Prime Minister in Scandinavia or Japan says, after some great calamity, that 'We are all in this together', everyone regards it as the statement of an undeniable truth. When George Osborne says it, it sounds like an impudent and rather shaky assertion. Yet it ought not to be, and we can remember times in the not so distant past when this belonging together was taken for granted here too. So it could be again. 'Only connect' is not the only answer, but it is part of the answer.

NOTES

1   20 February 2010, launching Labour's new slogan, 'A Future Fair for All'.
2   *The Times*, 28 October 2011.
3   *Guardian*, 24 November 2011.
4   'Forget class war: blame inequality on globalization', *The Sunday Times*, 23 October 2011.
5   *Daily Telegraph*, 31 May 2003.
6   *Financial World*, June 2005.
7   In Thorstein Veblen, *Absentee Ownership and Business Enterprise in Recent Times* (1923). Another early critic was Walther Rathenau, the visionary foreign minister of the Weimar Republic whose assassination in June 1922 was to trigger hyperinflation and all the other horrors that were to follow in Germany. But like Veblen's work, Rathenau's *Die Neue Wirtschaft* ('The New Economy', 1918) was only a sketchy precursor of Berle and Means.
8   John Maynard Keynes, *General Theory of Employment, Interest and Money* (1936), ch. 24.
9   Niall Ferguson, *The Ascent of Money* (2008), p.133.
10 Adolf Berle and Gardiner Means, *The Modern Corporation and Private Property* (1932), p. 122.
11 Ibid., p. 138.
12 Ibid., p. 188.
13 Ibid., p. 186.
14 Ibid., p. 245.
15 Ibid., p. 276.
16 Ibid., p. 278.
17 Ibid., p. 342.

18 James Burnham, *The Managerial Revolution* (1941), p. 44.
19 Ibid., p. 39.
20 Ibid., p. 40.
21 Ibid., p. 74.
22 Ibid., p. 117.
23 Quoted in Alex Rubner, *The Might of the Multinationals* (1990), p. xv.
24 *Financial Times*, 15 November 2008.
25 *Daily Telegraph*, 31 July 2010.
26 *Guardian*, 8 April 2010.
27 *Guardian,* 16 September 2009.
28 *Missing Out,* Report of the Resolution Foundation, July 2011.
29 *Guardian*, 26 May 2011.
30 *Guardian*, 14 June 2011.
31 *Cheques with Balances: Why Tackling High Pay Is in the National Interest,* Final Report of the High Pay Commission (2011), p. 52.
32 *New Yorker*, 11 October 2010.
33 George Thomas Washington, *Corporate Executives' Compensation: Legal and Business Aspects of Salary and Bonus Plans* (1942), p. 226.
34 *Daily Mail*, 29 October 2011.
35 Katherine M. Savarese, '"Perverting Civilization" or Pursuing Dreams? Economic Arguments about Executive Compensation Practices in the United States, 1890 to 1940' (Harvard, 2010).
36 Emmanuel Saez, 'US Earnings and Wealth Inequality over the Twentieth Century', paper to Harvard Center for History and Economics, November 2009.
37 *Cheques with Balances*, p. 34. See also Thomas Philippon and Ariell Reshef, *Wages and Human Capital in the US Financial Industry, 1909–2006* (2008).
38 July 2004.
39 *Guardian*, 17 June 2011.
40 *Guardian*, 27 January 2010.
41 First published 1948.
42 *Financial Times*, 15 November 2008.
43 *The Sunday Times* and *Sunday Telegraph*, 18 April 2010.
44 John Kay, *Narrow Banking* (2009).
45 Christopher Fildes, 'A new bank from a very old stable', *Spectator*, 9 May 2009.
46 Walter Bagehot, *Lombard Street* (1873), ch. 10.
47 *Sunday Telegraph*, 15 November 2009.
48 Meg Russell, *Building New Labour* (2005), p. 186.
49 Ibid., p. 185.
50 Ibid., p. 208.

51 Ibid., p. 203.
52 Our report was published under the title of *Power to the People* (March 2006).
53 Vernon Bogdanor (ed.), *The British Constitution in the Twentieth Century* (2003) .
54 Anthony Seldon, in Bogdanor, *The British Constitution in the Twentieth Century*, pp. 128–9.
55 Sir Christopher Foster, *The End of Cabinet Government?* (1999), p. 20.
56 Sir Ivor Jennings, *Cabinet Government* (1936), p. 95.
57 *The Sunday Times*, 17 January 2010.
58 *The Times*, 25 October 2011.
59 *The Times*, 7 July 1988.
60 Judgment in *Bulmer v Bollinger*, 1974.
61 *Daily Telegraph*, 2 June 2011.
62 *The Sunday Times*, 19 June 2011.
63 *The Times*, 27 March 2009.
64 *The Times*, 27 March 2009.
65 *Sunday Telegraph*, 26 June 2011.
66 'The Tories and Libdems have become natural allies', *Daily Telegraph*, 25 November 2005.
67 If the election had turned out only a little differently, a couple of percentage points the other way, no doubt there would have been a Lib–Lab Coalition. Say the figures had been Labour 290 MPs, Conservatives 280, Libdems 55, Others 25, Gordon Brown would have been quite entitled to persuade the Libdems to go into Coalition with him. As the figures actually were (Conservatives 306, Labour 258, Libdem 57, Others 29), some sort of Coalition between Conservatives and the Libdems was the legitimate and virtually inevitable outcome.
68 Interim Report, 4.4, pp. 63–4.
69 Ibid., 4.71, p. 85.
70 *Daily Telegraph*, 10 June 2011.
71 Interim Report, 4.64.
72 'The integration of UK retail banking and global wholesale/investment banking within a single legal entity increases the exposure of the UK retail banking system to external shocks' (Interim Report, 4.65–6).
73 Interim Report, 4.65–6, pp. 82–3.
74 And were published in the issue of 26 June 2011.
75 Bournemouth, 6 October 2002.
76 *Guardian*, 3 October 2005.
77 *Guardian*, 28 June 2011.
78 *Daily Mail*, 28 May 2011.

79 Speech to National Policy Forum, 24 June 2011.

80 Published 14 July 2004.

81 30 June 2011.

82 *Daily Telegraph*, 19 August 2011.

83 *The Times*, 31 October 2011.

84 *The Times*, 7 June 2011.

85 16 June 2011.

86 Enoch Powell, *Joseph Chamberlain* (1977), pp. 223–4.

87 The fact that states which were converted to the new faith made little
or no effort to alter their social arrangements to carry this principle into
practice may be deplorable, but it is hardly surprising. The conversion
of large parts of Europe was, after all, largely effected by queens and
princesses who, after being converted themselves, persuaded their hus-
bands, sons and fathers to convert the whole nation. This remarkable
feature enabled Christian values to become the new intellectual and
spiritual orthodoxy without denting the secular power of the king. All
the same, the ideal of equality remained lodged in the mind as a prick
to the conscience and, rather too occasionally, a spur to reform.

88 Like many on the Left before and since, in 1931 R. H. Tawney argued
in his famous essay *Equality* that this isn't necessarily so. In a well-struc-
tured society, he says:

> ... a large measure of equality, so far from being inimical to
> liberty, is essential to it. In conditions which impose co-
> operative, rather than merely individual effort, liberty is, in
> fact, equality in action, in the sense, not that all men perform
> identical functions or wield the same degree of power, but
> that all men are equally protected against the abuse of power,
> and equally entitled to insist that power shall be used, not for
> personal ends but for the general advantage.

Even within that last sentence, the strains of pressing this argument begin to show. 'Co-operative effort' is to be 'imposed'; 'all men'
are 'entitled to insist' that power is used for 'general advantage'. This
is clearly a society in which the State calls the shots. It is this line of
argument, advanced in a dozen different forms down the ages, which
provoked Berlin's famous retort in his footnote to his lecture *Two
Concepts of Liberty* (1958):

> ... nothing is gained by a confusion of terms. To avoid glar-
> ing inequality or widespread misery I am ready to sacrifice
> some, or all, of my freedom: I may do so willingly and freely:

but it is freedom that I am giving up for the sake of justice or
equality or the love of my fellow men. I should be guilt-
stricken, and rightly so, if I were not, in some circumstances,
ready to make this sacrifice. But a sacrifice is not an increase
in what is being sacrificed, namely freedom, however great
the moral need or the compensation for it. Everything is
what it is: liberty is liberty, not equality or fairness or justice
or human happiness or a quiet conscience.

89 By 1916, after eight years in power, the Asquith government, the first
great progressive government of modern times, had scarcely altered the
standard rate of income tax. In 1905/06 it stood at 1/- in the pound.
In 1914, even after Lloyd George's People's Budget of 1909, the rate
was only 1/2d. But it was in that famous Budget that for the first time
an extra tax, known as 'supertax', was levied on higher incomes,
largely to pay for rearming the Navy with dreadnoughts. The result
was that from then on until the Nigel Lawson reforms of the late
1980s, the tax paid at higher levels was not only proportionate but progressive; the more you earned, the higher the percentage rate. After
the declaration of war and the terrible expenditure of blood and
money on the Western front, things moved with great rapidity. By
1917, the income tax rate was 5/- in the pound. A bachelor who
earned £10,000 a year now retained only £6,721 of his pay as
opposed to £9,500 before the war. The figure drifted down to a low
of 4/- in the pound between the wars, although supertax, now
renamed 'surtax', continued to increase as the arms race picked up
again. After the Second World War was declared, income tax took
another giant jump, reaching 10/- in the pound in 1942. This left our
£10,000 a year bachelor with a modest £3,138 a year after income tax
and surtax. That deduction inched down very slowly after the Second
World War. In 1969, the rate was still 8/3d, and it took another
twenty-five years before it came down to the equivalent of 5 shillings
in the pound, although by then shillings were only a faint memory.
90 William Pitt (Tory) devised income tax; William Harcourt (Liberal)
invented death duties; Lloyd George (Liberal) gave us the first supertax on the rich. Even when the Labour Party became a governing
force, it was Selwyn Lloyd (Conservative) who pioneered capital gains
tax and Geoffrey Howe (Conservative) who introduced VAT.
91 In an Epilogue to *Equality* (1931), Tawney rejoiced that 'a somewhat
more equalitarian social order is in progress of emerging'. He felt that
'It is legitimate to feel a modest pride that a course in the right direction has been held by this country against the wind.' But he did not

really acknowledge that this direction had been imposed in the Second World War, as it had been in the First, by a national emergency rather than by an internal political imperative.

92 *Forbes Magazine*, 24 June 2011.
93 *Mind The Gap* (Short Books, 2004).
94 *Guardian*, 19 August 2011.
95 *Guardian*, 19 August 2011.
96 If there is one single bright spot on the horizon, it is Kenneth Baker's initiative to do just that, but it needs to be multiplied tenfold.

FURTHER READING

Aristotle, *Politics*, tr. J. A. Sinclair (Penguin, 1962)

Bagehot, Walter, *Lombard Street* (1873; CUP, 2011)

Berle, Adolf and Gardiner Means, *The Modern Corporation and Private Property* (Harcourt, Brace & World, 1932)

Berlin, Isaiah, *Two Concepts of Liberty* (Clarendon Press, 1958)

Bogdanor, Vernon (ed.), *The British Constitution in the Twentieth Century* (OUP, 2003)

Burnham, James, *The Managerial Revolution* (Van Rees Press, 1941)

Clarke, Kenneth (chair), *Reports of Conservative Party Democracy Task Force: An End to Sofa Politics* (2007); *Power to the People* (2007); *Answering the Question* (2008); *Trust in Politics* (2008)

Dicey, A. V., *The Law of the Constitution*, 8th edn (Macmillan, 1915)

Dorling, Daniel, *Injustice: Why Social Inequality Persists* (Policy Press, 2010)

Ferguson, Niall, *The Ascent of Money* (Allen Lane, 2008)

Galbraith, J. K., *American Capitalism* (Houghton Mifflin, 1952)

The Great Crash of 1929 (Houghton Mifflin, 1954)

The Affluent Society (Houghton Mifflin, 1958)

The New Industrial State (Houghton Mifflin, 1967)

Hargreaves, Deborah (chair), *Cheques with Balances: Why Tackling*

High Pay Is in the National Interest, Final Report of the High Pay Commission (2011)

Hewart, Lord, *The New Despotism* (Ernest Benn,1929)

Hills, John (chair), *An Anatomy of Economic Inequality in the UK: Report of the National Equality Panel* (2010)

Hutton, Will, *Hutton Review of Fair Pay in the Public Sector* (2011)

Jenkins, Simon, *Accountable to None: The Tory Nationalization of Britain* (Penguin,1995)

Jennings, Sir Ivor, *Cabinet Government* (CUP, 1936)

Kay, John, *Narrow Banking* (CSFI, 2009)

Lewis, Michael, *The Big Short: Inside the Doomsday Machine* (Allen Lane, 2010)

McKenzie, Robert, *British Political Parties* (Heinemann, 1955)

Michels, Robert, *Political Parties: A Sociological Study of the Oligarchical Tendencies of Modern Democracy* (Hearst's International Library Co., 1915)

Mount, Ferdinand, *The British Constitution Now* (Heinemann, 1992)

Mind the Gap: The New Class Divide in Britain (Simon & Schuster, 2004)

O'Neill, Onora, *A Question of Trust* (CUP, 2002)

Pareto, Vilfredo, *The Mind and Society* (Harcourt, Brace and Co.,1935)

Resolution Foundation Report, *Missing Out* (2011)

Rubner, Alex, *The Might of the Multinationals* (Praeger, 1990)

Russell, Meg, *Building New Labour* (Macmillan, 2005)

Sampson, Anthony, *The Anatomy of Britain* (Harper & Row, 1962)

Schama, Simon, *The Embarrassment of Riches* (HarperCollins, 1987)

Smith, Adam, *The Theory of Moral Sentiments* (1759; Penguin, 2010)

The Wealth of Nations (1776; Capstone, 2010)

Tawney, R. H., *Equality* (1931; new edition with epilogue, Unwin Books, 1951)

Vickers, John (chair), *The Independent Commission on Banking*:
  Interim Report (April 2011); *Final Report* (September 2011)
Wilkinson, Richard and Kate Pickett, *The Spirit Level* (Allen Lane,
  2009)
Young, Michael, *The Rise of Meritocracy* (Thames & Hudson,
  1958)

BIOGRAPHICAL NOTE

Ferdinand Mount was editor of *The Times Literary Supplement* from 1991 to 2002. He was head of the Prime Minister's Policy Unit from 1982 to 1984 and a director of the Centre for Policy Studies, 1984–91. He was also Vice-Chairman of the Power Commission in 2005–6 and a member of the Conservative Party's Democracy Task Force in 2007–8. He has written regularly for the *Spectator*, the *London Review of Books* and the *Daily Telegraph* and *The Sunday Times*. His memoir, *Cold Cream*, was a bestseller in 2008, and his novel *Of Love and Asthma* won the Hawthornden Prize in 1992. His most recent book for Simon & Schuster was *Full Circle: How the Classical World Came Back to Us.*

ACKNOWLEDGEMENTS

Some of the arguments in this book were first rehearsed in my Orwell Memorial Lecture, 'Orwell and the Oligarchs', given at UCL on 26 November 2010.

An earlier version of the section on inequality was written for my paper, 'Five Types of Inequality', given for the Joseph Rowntree Foundation in Bradford on 10 December 2008.

I am grateful to the Orwell Trust and the Joseph Rowntree Foundation for these opportunities.

INDEX

Note: Subscript numbers appended to page numbers indicate an entry in the Notes section.